# STUDIES IN MEDIEVAL AND RENAISSANCE HISTORY

Volume XI

(Old Series, Volume XXI)

# STUDIES IN
# Medieval and Renaissance History

## Volume XI
## (Old Series, Volume XXI)

EDITORS:

J. A. S. EVANS

R. W. UNGER

**AMS PRESS**
**New York**

AMS PRESS, INC
56 EAST 13th STREET
NEW YORK, NY 10003

ISSN 0081-8224
ISBN 0-404-62850-8 (set)
ISBN 0-404-62861-3 (Vol. XI)

Library of Congress Catalog Card Number 63-22098

Manufactured in the United States of America

# CONTENTS

# INTRODUCTION

*Studies in Medieval and Renaissance History* is a series designed for original major articles in all fields of medieval and renaissance history, from the later Roman Empire to the early modern period. Volumes appear once a year.

*Studies in Medieval and Renaissance History* was formerly published by the University of Nebraska Press, and the impetus for the creation of the series arose from the belief that there was a need for a publication that could accomodate articles that were too long for most of the established scholarly journals. The editors will consider submissions in all areas of history from the late Roman to the Renaissance period. Articles should be sent either to Professor Richard Unger, Head, Department of History, or Professor J. A. S. Evans, Head, Department of Classics, University of British Columbia, Vancouver, B. C., Canada, V6T 1W5. Submissions are sent to outside referees for reading, and every effort is made to see to it that articles which are accepted appear in print promptly. Authors receive twenty:-five free offprints of their articles.

While the series is devoted primarily to the publication of major studies, we welcome occasional bibliographic essays, and brief articles, particularly those dealing with unpublished archival and manuscript resources.

*Studies in Medieval and Renaissance History* is published by AMS Press for the Committee for Medieval Studies at the University of British Columbia, Vancouver, Canada.

# THE MEANING OF
# ALODIS IN THE
# MEROVINGIAN AGE

Theodore John Rivers

# THE MEANING OF *ALODIS* IN THE MEROVINGIAN AGE

Not only has the concept of the allod and the procedure known as allodification attracted the attention of scholars over a considerable period of time, but the term itself, from which these two derivations evolved, has also accumulated a considerable amount of scholarship. The term in question is *alodis,* which is Frankish in origin and made its first appearance in the sixth-century Salic laws. *Alodis* became Latinized as *alodum* in the eighth century, evolved into the version *alodium* in the tenth, and eventually became standardized as *allodium* in the eleventh.[1] Nevertheless, confusion remains over the term, which is caused by more than the ambiguity of the historical sources. In addition to its appearance in the Salic laws (507–511) and its adoption in the Ripuarian (613–634), the historical sources of the seventh and eighth centuries make reference to it as a term already well established among the Franks. Unlike many other Frankish terms evident in the so-called Malberg glosses of the Salic laws, *alodis* had survived, and it exerted an influence subsequently on *formulae,* diplomas, charters, and capitularies. Because of the influence of the Franks on other tribal laws, *alodis* is also found in the laws of the Alamans, Bavarians, and Thuringians.

The earliest derivation of *alodis* was made by Jacob Grimm in his first edition of the *Deutsche Rechtsalterthümer.*[2] *Alodis* is presumed to be composed from two roots: *al,* meaning whole or full, and *ôd,* meaning property or possession.[3] Therefore, *alodis* signifies whole or full property, that is, the legal classification for a fully-owned possession in so far as it is freely held and unencumbered. *Alodis* also means the act or process of inheritance by which property is devolved, and consequently, the actual property (the heritage or ancestral estate) conferred by the law of inheritance. The term also assumed additional

3

meanings as it was perfected by changing economic conditions. Hence, it has come to mean inherited property when distinguished from acquired property, and the freehold (another way of describing *terra propria*) when differentiated from the benefice.

All of these meanings, in one form or another, are set forth in an essay by Otto von Gierke, which laid the foundation for all subsequent research, an essay that is representative of Gierke's scholarship: methodical, careful, and well-documented. Although this essay was originally published in 1908 in a festschrift to the German legal historian Richard Schröder, it was later reprinted with slight modifications in 1914 in the Prussian Academy's multivolume *Deutsche Rechtswörterbuch*.[4] In it, Gierke derives seven meanings for *alodis* and its later variations, with several subdivisions, but for our purposes we are concerned primarily with the first three of these meanings, which indicate that *alodis* underwent evolutionary change. Gierke perceived a term constantly changing due to changing situations, a concept envisioned as falling victim to the economic conditions of its day. Believing these perceptions to be valid, Gierke reasoned that the original meaning of *alodis* was supplanted over time by newly evolving concepts. He says that *alodis* originally meant personal property (meaning no. 1),[5] that it eventually acquired an additional and coexistent meaning of real property (meaning no. 2),[6] and that finally the meaning of personal property gave way entirely and solely to the meaning of real property (meaning no. 3.)[7] Thus, in Gierke's understanding the meaning of the term evolved from movable to immovable property. It is to Gierke's credit that his interpretation is still considered sound today, for not only lexicographers[8] have adopted his view (to say nothing of his nomenclature), but European and American historians as well.[9]

Naturally, Grimm's original etymology has been expanded to other Germanic languagues, notably Gothic, Old English, Old Saxon, Old Norse, and Old High German. Since etymologies are devised for comparative analysis, these comparisons with other languages are made in order to gain access to the possible meanings of words. As a result, *alodis* has been compared to *Goth. alauds, OE aleōd, OS al(l)od, ON alaudr,* and *OGH alōt*.[10] Of course, none of these words except *OHG alode* (not the theoretical *alōt*) is an actual term, but all are mere hypothetical constructions based upon common roots found in these respective languages.[11] They are conceived for purely morphological reasons and are not based upon historical fact. Since there was no actual terms that come anywhere close to *alodis*—again, with the exception of the Old High German—the word must either stand or fall on its own merits. Indeed, we must make a closer analysis of *al* + *ôd* as originally given by Grimm.

As both linquistics and ethnology demonstrate, comparative analysis is devised not to reveal similarities, but to identify differences. Nevertheless, we can accept the claim of current scholarship that *ôd* means personal property because it signifies riches or wealth,[12] and since real property was not included by the early Germans within one's possessions, *ôd* comprises personal property only. But the addition of the prefix *al* to the stem *ôd*, thereby making a new word, should give us cause for hesitation. Surely to describe personal property as whole or full in the sense of complete, makes little sense.[13] Personal property can never be whole or full because it varies from day to day, but the use of this prefix pales in the face of reason. What may be characterized as whole can only be real property because the latter is irreparable. Although it is true that land may be supplemented, seized, or given away, it is always complete no matter what happens to it. And by completeness is meant not the totality of possession, but the plenitude of its essence, that is, not an aggregate, but a fullness. Therefore, we may conclude that *ôd* changed in meaning when *alodis* appeared in the Salic laws. Otherwise, we would have to accept the view that the prefix *al* merely reinforced the distinct meaning of *ôd,* the meaning of personal property. Although a prefix is used primarily to produce a derivative word, whatever *ôd* means, *alodis* means something quite different.

But there are additional arguments that we can bring to bear regarding the difference between the adjectives "whole" and "full." Certainly, the definition rendered by Grimm and adopted by many scholars is somewhat confusing, because to describe *alodis* as full property is not the same as describing it as whole or all property.[14] The latter description means every possible type of property, that is, anything that is part of one's estate, thereby rending it complete. It is more to the point to describe *alodis* as full property, because what is held in full ownership may not be the totality of one's estate.[15] Property is full only in the sense that it is not dependent upon someone else, that its possession is grounded solely in the possessor and could be willed without any lien. If *alodis* means full ownership in property, such property must refer to land because only land would warrant such a conspicuous and obtrusive statement; only land would need to be so well defined, since the property that mattered most in the Middle Ages was land. Indeed, when the Franks settled in Gaul, they imitated the Gallo-Romans by becoming landlords. They desired to own land, to farm it, to profit by it, and to will it to their heirs. Like all new settlers, they were a land-hungry people, a people whose livelihood was derived by working the land.[16]

## I.

As already noted above, *alodis* made its first appearance in the sixth-century Salic laws, and specifically in *Pact. leg. Sal.* 59. The latter is one of the most famous of all the Salic laws, for not only does it lend itself to controversy—which has attracted the attention of numerous legal historians—but it is also the law that forbade any woman from inheriting land. Because of the fragmentary nature of *Pact. leg. Sal.* 59 and its importance within the Germanic law of inheritance, the entire law is given here:

[Title] 59: De alodis.
    1. Si quis mortuus fuerit et filios non dimiserit, si pater, si mater sua superfuerit, ipsa in hereditatem succedat.
    2. Si pater aut mater non fuerit et fratrem aut sororem dimiserit, ipsi in hereditatem succedant.
    3. Si isti non fuerint, tunc soror matris in hereditatem succedat.
    4. Si vero sorores matris non fuerint, sic sorores patris in hereditatem succedant.
    5. Et inde si patris soror non fuerit, sic de illis genera-tionibus, quicumque proximior fuerit, ille in hereditatem succe-dat, qui ex paterno genere veniunt.
    6. De terra vero Salica nulla in muliere portio aut her-editas est, sed ad virilem sexum, qui fratres fuerint, tota terra pertineat.
    Ubi vero alodis ad nepotes post longum tempus evenit, ut ipsum dividant non per stirpem sed per capita.[17]

As the text indicates, *Pact. leg. Sal.* 59 concerns the law of inheritance, but it is a law that is both incomplete and ambiguous. It merely describes the law for those who die without children and who are related to the maternal side of descent. The paternal relatives are not included, nor is the mother's brother.[18] Nevertheless, the law does delineate the distribution of property to both lineal and collateral heirs, but only to those descended matrilaterally. But up to the time that the Salic laws were promulgated in the early sixth century and shortly thereafter, it is logical to conclude that anyone who bequeathed an *alodis* died intestate because the will, which is a Roman and not a German declaration, had not yet made an impact on Merovingian society.[19] Thus, the Salic law of inheritance assured the distribution of one's estate but, much like the will, was incapable of determining it.

Because *alodis* can defensibly be derived from *ôd,* many scholars have surmised that it describes personal or movable property only. This also is the conclusion of Gierke (meaning no. 1). Nevertheless, the fact that some scholars who have studied the law in question disagree with this conclusion calls for reexamination of the evidence.[20] Although the law offers no evidence that personal property is discussed, there is evidence that *alodis* is coterminous with inheritance *(in hereditatem succedat* or *succedant)* and that it denotes all property subject to the law of inheritance, that is, everything that a parent leaves to his children at his death. This term does not exclude any particular type of property that would normally fall within its sphere of influence, although the magnitude of the latter remains to be defined. Since *alodis* is also a technical term, its technicality acquires an exclusive meaning, an exclusivity restricted to real property only. For not only was land valuable as the principal source of wealth in the Middle Ages, but so was its heritability. Certainly, the heritability of land was presumed to be implicit in its possession.[21] *Alodis* was always a distinct and well-defined concept, meaning both the land itself and the right of inheritance to this land descendible from one's ancestor. Thus, land and the hereditary estate are coterminous.

Nevertheless, there was slight differences between the meanings of heritance and the hereditary estate, and their differences are obvious. Inheritance means both the act or process of possession and the property that is inherited. The act of inheritance concerns the succession of property, whereby the title of ownership is conferred. On the other hand, the hereditary estate simply means whatever property (the heritage) passes to the heir(s) on the death of the ancestor. Thus, inheritance and the hereditary estate are not two descriptions for the same thing, that is, they are not coterminous concepts. Of the two, inheritance is more inclusive because it incorporates whatever the hereditary estate contains. The reverse is not true. In addition, inheritance also signifies the legal means to take possession of the hereditary estate, that is, the right of succession or devolution of property. Clearly, inheritance, is a legal term, and an apparent one. To utilize inheritance as the act or fact of possession always encompasses whatever the possession is. And the possession is the ancestral or hereditary estate. Thus, the latter is simply a description for real property obtainable by means of inheritance.[22] And inheritance is distinguished from other types of real property, as that obtainable either by purchase (*conparatum*) or acquired by some other means (*attractum* or *contractum*). Real estate obtained by means other than inheritance is an acquest, representing nonancestral property,[23] but acquests eventually become part of the hereditary estate when the latter descends to the heir(s). Hence, for property to be regarded as hereditary or ancestral, it must be descendible from an ancestor, with the blood relationship as its only relevant factor. Once again, we find that inheritance, that is, *alodis*, is a term of limitation, restricted only to real property descendible from one's ancestor and limited solely to those who could attain to it.

Of course, it was rarely the intention of Germanic law to impart to personal property an ancestral character because personal property is highly variable. An ancestral quality could be given only to that property that was fixed and permanent, to that which symbolized the inviolability of ownership. Conditioned by the facticity of land itself, the latter was sacred because it could be passed down from generation to generation without corruption. And these observations are applicable in addition to the utility of the land. Therefore, to speak of *alodis* as the hereditary or ancestral estate is to speak of land. However, only in modern times has the description "hereditary or ancestral estate" come to mean the totality of all property, both real and personal.

This confusion over the totality of property descendible at one's death has led to yet another perception of *Pact. leg. Sal.* 59, which assumes that personal property is discussed under sections 1–5 (where *hereditas* is used) and that real property is discussed under section 6 (where *terra salica* is used).[24] It has been inferred that since maternal relatives are the only relatives enumerated in sections 1–5, these sections must deal with personal property because Germanic law, with the exception of the *Leges Visigothorum*, was consistent in the exclusion of daughters when the inheritance of real property was conferred upon sons.[25] Despite these assumptions, there is no evidence to substantiate the view that personal property is discussed in sections 1–5. Nor can we accept the view that since the procedure for the paternal relatives is presumed already known and therefore is excluded from *Pact. leg. Sal.* 59, what is provided for in sections 1–5 can only be the procedure for maternal relatives, and their share of the accumulated property of the deceased is movables only. In fact, if sections 1–5 concern personal property and section 6 concerns real property, the rubric should represent all property, both real and personal. Nevertheless, meaning no. 1 does not interpret *Pact. leg. Sal.* 59 from this perspective, since it assumes that *alodis* in this law signifies personal property solely. As is apparent from the text itself, *Pact. leg. Sal.* 59 is the source of much ambiguity.

We need to remind ourselves, however, that the Germanic peoples perceived property as either real or personal, that is, either fixed and inviolable (land) or subject to relocation and change (chattels). But unlike Roman law, which made no distinction between real and personal property as far as the laws of inheritance were concerned, Germanic law did distinguish between them. Hence, Germanic law not only perceived that there is a natural and self-evident difference between real and personal property, but it also devised inheritance laws that corresponded to this bifurcation.[26] Consequently, there were two categories among the Germans that dealt with inheritance—one for real property and another for personal property, although the laws that have survived for these categories are both incomplete and fragmentary. *Pact. leg. Sal.* 59 concerns the law of inheritance of real property for those relatives who were related matrilaterally to the deceased, although there probably were laws that concerned the descent of real property for those related patrilaterally. And, of course, *Pact. leg. Sal.* 59 pertained only to those who died without children surviving them. The reciprocal law of inheritance that concerns personal property also has not come down to us. The only distinction in *Pact. leg. Sal.* 59 is not between real and personal property but between land in general (sections 1–5) and a particular type of land called *terra salica* (section 6). Therefore, title 59 does not divide property between movables and immovables, but between *terra (in universum)* and *terra salica.*[27]

This equivalancy between *terra* and *alodis* is emphasized also by the evolution of the manuscript tradition, which unfortunately is problematical. The earliest version of the *Pactus legis Salicae*, that is, the A text, has *de terra vero*. The later C, D, and E texts, which are Carolingian versions, add *salica* to *terra;* thus, these later texts have *de terra vero salica*. Much effort has been devoted to an elucidation of these manuscripts. But regardless of the introduction of *salica*, which has been variously interpreted as Salic as well as *sala* (hall or demesne), our primary concern is with *terra*. In fact, yet another text, the H text or so-called *Lex Salica Heroldina*, gives *de alode terrae* for *Pact. leg. Sal.* 59,6, thereby equating *terra* with *alodis* to the exclusion of *salica*.[28] *De alode terrae* is simply a general description for the inheritance of land without the influence of the qualifier *salica*, which may demonstrate, despite considerations to the contrary, the subordinate role *salica* assumed with reference to *terra*.

## II

Gierke's second meaning of *alodis*, which concerns both real and personal property is subdivided into several categories: the totality of property, the heritage or ancestral estate, the bequest of the dead, and inherited property differentiated from acquired property. For these four distinctions, he uses numerous sources comprising laws, decrees, *formulae,* charters and capitularies to demonstrate the point. But these sources need to be analyzed carefully because one can easily equate the heritage or hereditary estate with the entire property obtainable by the heir(s), thereby confusing what this property is when one considers the bifurcated procedure of inheritance. As we have already indicated, the law of inheritance was not in the least arbitrary. And these four subdivisions of Gierke's meaning no. 2 are dependent upon the general meaning, which is a designation for entire property (*ganze Vermögen*).[29] In support of his argument, reference is made to Ripuarian, Alamannic, Bavarian, and Thuringian laws, two decrees of a synod held under the Bavarian duke Tassilo, and ten references to various *formulae* (*Marculfus, Turonenses, Andecavenses, Arvernenses,* and the *Cartae Senonicae*). An analysis of these sources follows.

The Ripuarian laws, promulgated during the first third of the seventh century, exemplify strong influence from the Salian Franks because 75 of their 231 laws have direct parallels to the *Pactus legis Salicae*. *L. Rib.* 57 (56 in Sohm's edition) is one of these laws. Its parallel is *Pact. leg. Sal.* 59. *L. Rib.* 57 deals with the law of inheritance in the following manner:

[Title] 57: De alodibus.

1. Si quis absque liberis defunctus fuerit, si pater si mater superstites fuerint, in hereditatem succedant.

2. Si pater materque non fuerint, frater et soror succedant.

3. Si autem nec eos habuerit, tunc soror matris patrisque succedant. Et deinceps usque quinto genuculo qui proximus fuerit, in hereditate succedat.

4. Sed dum virilis sexus exteterit, femina in hereditate aviatica non succedat.[30]

Since *L. Rib.* 57 is based upon *Pact. leg. Sal.* 59, whatever is the judgment of the latter will also be the judgment of the former. Much like *Pact. leg. Sal.* 59, *L. Rib.* 57 is a law that deals with that aspect of inheritance when an individual dies without issue. Although less inclusive in its description for those who would inherit if one died childless, nevertheless, the law uses *hereditas* in the general sense, meaning real property only. In addition, the fourth clause of the law refers to *hereditas aviatica,* which is universally understood by historians to be a reference to land and is the Ripuarian equivalent to the Salic *terra salica,* the patrimonial (landed) estate.[31] Here, too, *L. Rib.* 57 deals with two types of land, *terra (in universum)* and the patrimonial estate *(hereditas aviatica).*

Instances of *alodis* (or derivations thereof) in the *Lex Alamannorum,* which is believed to have been promulgated between 717 and 719, are minor as well as obscure, and are merely two in number. Manuscript Al to *L. Alam.* 54,1 has *alodo,* for which all other manuscripts have *ad dandum,* that is, in so far that these manuscripts have not compounded the problem by containing other scribal errors (such as *ad reddendum* and *addum*). Although *alodo* appears to fit the context of law 54,1, *ad dandum* fits it beyond question: "Dotis enim legitima 400 solidis constat aut in auro aut in argento aut mancipia aut qualecumque habet ad dandum."[32] Thus, we may conclude that there is no reference to *alodis* in this law, but there is a misspelling *(alodo)* that does not fit the context and makes no sense. The second and last reference in the *Lex Alamannorum* is found in an addition to manuscript B18 to law 44 (law 43 to text A): "Si ante ducem hoc iudicium renuerit et iniustum iudicium ipse proposuerit et sequentes idoneos non habuerit et contradixerit, . . . Insuper regi vel duci MDCCC denarios conponat, et illi, qui recte iudicavit et hoc recusavit, LX solidos conponat, vel dimidiam partem allodii sui perdat, quod in ducis sit potestate."[33] As the law says, one was held liable to pay sixty solidi for refusing to adhere to a lawful judgment, but in lieu of this payment, one would suffer the loss of one half of his *allodium*. Although land was rarely confiscated for the payment of a debt, the likelihood of confiscation intensified if either the king or duke was involved, which is the case here. Furthermore, the spelling of *allodium* in place of *alodis* indicates the likelihood that the allod under discussion is the freehold, the *terra propria* distinguished from the benefice. But the spelling of *allodium* also indicates the age of the manuscript *(Codex bibliothecae caes. Vindobonensis* 601), which is believed to be from the twelfth century. All of these conclusions indicate that *alodis* means land only.

Likewise, there are four references to *alodis* in the *Lex Baiuvariorum* (744–748), and all of them, unlike the Alamannic laws, are of principal concern. The dictionary entry by Gierke cites only two of these four references, and he defines *alodis* differently for the two he does cite. He defines *alodis* in *L. Baiu.* 2,1 as entire property (hence, its inclusion in the discussion here) and *alodis* in *L. Baiu.* 17,3 (Merkel's edition, *textus legis tertius),* now 16,17 (Schwind's and Beyerle's edition) as real property only. *L. Baiu.* 16,17 is referred to in meaning no. 3, but we will discuss it here. The remaining two Bavarian laws are 1,1 and 12,8. The laws are:

> 1,1 (rubric): Ut si quis liber Baiuuarius vel quiscumque alodem suam ad ecclesiam vel quamcumque rem donare voluerit, liberam habeat potestatem.
>
> 2,1: . . . Ut nullus [liber (Beyerle)] Baiuuarius alodem aut vitam sine capitale crimine perdat. . . .
>
> 12,8: Quotiens de conmarcanis contentio nascitur, ubi evidentia signa non apparent, in arboribus aut in montibus nec in fluminibus, et iste dicit: "hucusque antecessores mei tenuerunt et in alodem mihi reliquerunt" et ostendit secundum propriam arbitrium locum; . . .
>
> 16,17: De his qui propriam alodem vendunt vel quascumque res et ab emptore alter abstrahere voluerit et sibi sociare in patrimonium. . . . Iste vero dicit: "Non ita sed mei antecessores tenuerunt et mihi in alodem reliquerunt, et vestita est illius manu, cui tradidi, et firmare volo cum lege." . . . [34]

In none of these laws does *alodis* signify anything other than real property. In laws 1,1 and 16,17, it is used to represent land, and all other types of property are clearly described as *quascumque res.* Furthermore, *L. Baiu.* 16,17 is often cited by historians as proof that *alodis* means real property only.[35] Since the Bavarian laws use *alodis* for real property in law 16,17, it would be inconsistent if the term was used to designate both real and personal property in law 2,1. Due to the fact that *alodis* is a common noun, we cannot accept the assumption that this term represented both real and personal property within one Bavarian law while simultaneously signifying only real property in another. In law 2,1, *alodis* must be interpreted as inheritance, designating the hereditary estate, because confiscation of property meant land only. Although confiscation was regarded to be an equivalent to the loss of life when one was found guilty of a capital offense, the severity of this punishment would be somewhat attenuated if one lost movables only. But it would be rare that this punishment included both real and personal property. Lastly, law 12,8 refers to *alodis* as inheritance when the latter means the hereditary estate, since the characterization of real property is made manifest in the form of trees, mountains, and rivers, all of which, naturally, designate land.

*Alodis* is also found in the Thuringian laws of inheritance, which are believed to have been promulgated by Charlemagne in 802–803. Because these laws were promulgated in the Carolingian age, their sole reference to *alodis* should already contain that meaning which it carried throughout the Middle Ages, the meaning of real property only. The laws, which are drawn from only one title and which are five in number, are involved, but not convoluted.

[Title] 2: De alodibus.

26. Hereditatem defuncti filius non filia suscipiat.

27. Si filium non habuit qui defunctus est, ad filiam pecunia et mancipia. Terra vero ad proximum paternae generationis consanguineum pertineat. Si autem nec filiam non habuit, soror eius pecuniam et mancipia. Terram proximus paternae generationis accipiat. Si autem nec filium nec filiam neque sororem habuit, sed matrem tantum superstitem reliquit, quod filia vel soror debuerunt, mater suscipiat, id est pecuniam et mancipia. Quodsi nec filium nec filiam nec sororem aut matrem dimisit superstites, proximus qui fuerit paternae generationis, heres ex toto succedat,

tam in pecunia atque in mancipiis quam in terra. Ad quemcumque hereditas terrae pervenerit ad illum vestis bellica, id est lorica, et ultio proximi et solutio leudis debet pertinere.

28. Mater moriens filio terram, mancipia, pecuniam dimittat, filiae vero spolia colli id est murenulas, nuscas, monilia, inaures, vestes, armillas, vel quicquid ornamenti proprii videbatur habuisse.

29. Si nec filium nec filiam habuerit, sororem vero habuerit, sorori pecuniam et mancipia, proximo vero paterni generis terram relinquat.

30. Usque ad quintam generationem paterna generatio succedat. Post quintam autem filia ex toto, sive de patris sive de matris parte in hereditatem succedat; et tunc demum hereditas ad fusum a lancea transeat.[36]

These laws may have used *Pact. leg. Sal.* 59 as a model, but they go far beyond what the Salic laws contain. Obviously, *alodis* here signifies inheritance, comprising both paternal and maternal estates. But although land and movables are included in these laws, a closer look at them dissuades one from this view.

No matter what the paternal estate comprised under the Thuringian laws, land always went to sons, and movables along with slaves went to daughters. The maternal estate was similarly divided, with the sons taking the land, and the daughters, movables.[37] In these laws, *hereditas* means land that the sons inherit. The simplicity of this condition was complicated if there were no son surviving the father. If this happened, land that would normally have gone to the son went instead to the closest relative of the deceased, while movables and slaves went to the daughter. In order to prevent land from passing out of the jurisdiction of the father's lineage, law 27 provided that the closest relative of the paternal kindred would become the heir of everything *(heres ex toto succedat)*, that is, movables, slaves, and land, if no son, daughter, sister, or mother survived the deceased. Apparently, when *totus* is added to *hereditas*, the totality of a person's possessions is implied, since *totus* is an emphatic adjective that leaves no doubt that both real and personal property are meant. By itself *hereditas*, as the Thuringian laws indicate, invariably signifies real property, and it is all that is needed to convey this meaning. *Totus hereditas* or *heres ex toto* is the exception to the norm, that is, the exception to the normal bifurcation of property between land (sons) and movables (daughters). Only when there were no descendants from the father's kin beyond the fifth generation would land pass to a daughter, and here she inherited everything (*ex toto*).[38] Thus, these laws indicate that *alodis* means inheritance in the general sense of the term, that inheritance implies the hereditary (landed) estate, and that in order to devolve all the property that an individual possessed at the time of his death required the addition of a qualification (*ex toto*) that annulled the regular bifurcation of property. *Alodis* and *hereditas* each mean land, and *totus hereditas* or *heres ex toto* means land plus movables. Of course, these laws were anachronistic when they were promulgated by Charlemagne in the early ninth century because they denied inheritance of land to women, except when certain conditions were met.

The above are all the laws that are referred to as evidence in Gierke's meaning no. 2, evidence for the alleged totality of property. As already indicated, we have added one Bavarian law (16,17) which Gierke discusses under meaning no. 3, and two other Bavarian laws (1,1 and 12,8) that he does not discuss.[39] Except for one canon (no. 14) promulgated at the synod of Neuching by the Bavarian duke Tassilo in 772, which makes reference to *alodis*, all the remaining evidence for meaning no. 2 relates to ten references from five formulary compilations. Although we could increase the documentation, we will limit ourselves for the present to those that Gierke relies upon.

The majority of the references to *alodis* in the *formulae* are taken from that of Marculf, a compilation that remains controversial. Originally dated from the late sixth to the early seventh century and based, in part, upon the Salic laws, it is now more traditionally dated from the mid-seventh to the early eighth century, and is attributed to the monastery of Saint-Denis.[40] It consists of some 92 letters, charters, and mandates divided into two books, 40 in book 1 and 52 in book 2. Meaning no. 2 makes only five references to this formulary, which is supplemented by references to others *formulae*, namely *Turonenses, Andecavenses, Arvernenses,* and the *Cartae Senonicae,* all of which are enumerated below. Much like the Germanic laws cited in this section, references to *alodis* in the Merovingian *formulae*—documents that were intended to be used as models for various legal transactions—are often presumed to mean both real and personal property.[41]

The first reference in the *Formulae Marculfi* cited for the alleged totality of property is 2,10, and much like the addition of *totus* to *hereditas* as discussed above, *omnis* here is added:

> . . . ego vero pensans consanguinitatis causa, dum et per lege cum
> ceteris filiis meis, abuncolis vestris, in alode mea accedere minime
> potueratis: ideo per hanc epistolam vos, dulcissime nepotis mei,
> volo, ut in omni alode mea post meum discessum, si mihi su-
> prestetis fueretis, hoc est tam in terris, domibus, accolabus, man-
> cipiis, viniis, silvis, campis, pratis, pascuis, acquis aquaerumvae
> decursibus, movilibus et inmovilibus, peculium utriusquae sexus,
> maiorae vel minore, . . . [42]

And *omnis* applies not only to the lands, buildings, tenants, slaves,
vineyards, forests, fields, meadows, pastures, and water and waterways, but also to cattle, both bulls and cows, large and small. *Omnis*
like *totus* is an emphatic adjective, which is introduced into the text
to delineate and define a commonplace situation. We expect, therefore, to find all types of property included, but *omnis* removes the
emphasis from *alodis* and acquires it itself.[43] Additionally, the qualifier
*movilibus et inmovilibus* is often added to so many documents that it
has become commonplace, and we expect to find it whenever we
encounter charters. Indeed, it seems to have been utilized frequently,
almost habitually. *Movilibus et inmovilibus* modifies and clarifies *in omni
alode mea* just as *omnis* modifies *alodis*. The text goes on to include all
household utensils that the mother, that is, the donor's daughter, had
received from the father's estate:

> . . . omnique suppellectile domus, in quocumque dici potest, quic-
> quid suprascribta genetrix vestra, si mihi suprestis fuisset, de alode
> mea recipere potuerat, vos contra abunculos vestros, filius meus,
> prefato portione recipere faciatis. Et dum ipsius filiae meae, ge-
> netricae vestrae, quando eam nuptum tradedi, in aliquid de rebus
> meis movilibus drappos et fabricaturas vel aliqua mancipia in so-
> ledos tantos tradedi, vos hoc in partae vestra supputare contra
> filiis meis faciatis; et si amplius vobis insuper de presidio nostro
> obvenerit, tunc cum filiis meis, abunculis vestris, porcionem vobis
> ex hoc debita recipeatis;. . . [44]

The household utensils are derived not from the paternal *alodis* but,
as the text indicates, from the movable goods of the maternal inheritance. The addition of cloth, jewelry, and slaves derived from the
father's movable property should not be confused with the personal
property discussed above, because this property was given to the

father's daughter when she married as her dowry (*eam nuptum tradedi*) and has nothing whatsoever to do with inheritance.

Thus, the question of what type of property *alodis* comprised revolves around *movilibus et inmovilibus*. Of course, the question over agricultural and indentured servants, be they free or slave, is whether or not they have a holding. Those with a holding are themselves considered to be immovable property, whereas those without a holding are movable.[45] We can be quite sure that the *accolas* in *Form. Marc.* 2,10 have their own land to till and therefore are immovable, but we also know that the fate of *mancipia* is to be incumbent upon an estate. Thus, *movilibus et inmovilibus* should not be interpreted literally, unless we refer to *peculia*. But even agricultural servants are appurtenances to land, since they are utilized on an estate and are merely extensions of it. The basis of *alodis* therefore remains unchanged even with this formulary, a term that describes land and landed possessions subject to the law of inheritance. We should also keep in mind, of course, that the *Formulae Marculfi* was compiled at approximately the same time as the Alamannic and Bavarian laws, but before the Thuringian, and there is no question that *alodis* in the former refers to real property only. Certainly, whatever *alodis* means in one of these documents, it most likely should mean in all the others.

Similarly, another document containing reference to *alodis* is *Form. Marc.* 2,14, which concerns an agreement between two parents for the equal distribution of their property to their two sons, and naturally the basis of their property is land:

> Quicquid enim inter propinquos de alode parentum, . . . Ideoque dum inter illo de germano suo illo de alode genetoribus eorum illis bonae pacis placuit adque convenit, ut eam inter se, manente caritate, dividere vel exequari deberint; quod ita et fecerunt. Accepit itaque illi villas nuncupantes illas, sitas ibi, cum mancipia tanta illas. Similiter et illi accepit econtra in compensatione alias villas nuncupantes illas, sitas ibi, cum mancipia tanta illas. . . . [46]

As is apparent in *Form. Marc.* 2,14, the parents' intention is to devolve their property to their two sons in equal proportion. The fact that the parents have agreed to do this is apparent from the contract, but we should note that there is no mention of daughters, presumably, because they had none or none survived. Since we know that when there are daughters, the latter inherit movables while sons inherit land,[47] it follows that sons would inherit all property, whether real or personal in the absence of daughters. Thus, when this contract goes on to enumerate personal property, that is, cloth, jewelry, and utensils, we should find their inclusion to be no cause for alarm:

> . . . De presidio vero, drappus seu fabricaturas vel omne subpellectile domus, quicquid dici aut nominare potest, aequa lentia inter se visi sunt divisisse vel exequasse, . . . [48]

Like *Form. Marc.* 2,10, these movables are not derived from the father's possessions, but from the mother's. And although movables are encompassed by the general category of inheritance, they are not part of *alodis* proper, since the latter specifically is applicable to land and landed possessions. Thus, some confusion may be derived with the use of *alodis,* since it means inheritance generally without specific reference to the type of property encompassed and means land explicitly when the latter is clearly and definitively enumerated. Hypothetically, if there were a daughter, she would inherit the movables, and her husband, if she married, would inherit the *alodis* from his father. The movables in this contract are merely a supplement, and are added simply to indicate that all property from the parents was intended to be equally distributed between their two sons. It is true that the movables in question are derived from the mother's estate, which could also include land, but since *alodis* is a term of limitation, it is applicable to real property only.

Furthermore, the father and the property that devolves from him are given further emphasis in *Form. Marc.* 2,14 because in addition to the reference to the paternal inheritance (*alode parentum*) at the beginning of the contract, there is reference to the father's inheritance solely (*alode genetore):* "de ipsa alode genetore eorum amplius requirendi pontefitium habere non dibiat [*sic*]."[49] And reference to the father's inheritance reassures that its essence is land. Of course, any ambiguity caused by rhetoric simply aggravates the difficulty.[50]

But there is no difficulty with the interpretation of *alodis* in *Form. Marc.* 2,7, which concerns the reciprocal donations of a husband's property to his wife if he predeceases her and of the wife's property to her husband if she predeceases him because they are childless. And the bequest includes all types of property, that is, land, estates, houses with all their movables, tenants, slaves, vineyards, forests, fields, meadows, water and waterways, gold, silver, clothing, bulls and cows:

> . . . Proinde dono tibi dulcissima coniux mea, si mihi in hunc seculum suprestis fueris, omni corpore facultatis meae, tam de alode aut de conparatum vel de qualibet adtractu, ubicumquae habere videor, et quod pariter in coniugium positi laboravimus, tam terris, villabus, domibus cum omni presidio, accolabus, mancipiis, vineis, silvis, campis, pratis, acquis aquerumve decursibus, aurum, argentum, vestimenta, peculium utriusque sexus, maiore vel minore; ita ut, dum advixeris, usufructuario ordine valeas possidere vel dominare, . . . [51]

But all of this property is noted to have come into their mutual possession by various means during the course of their marriage, only one means is by inheritance, since the bequest says that property was also obtained by purchases and acquisitions (*conparatum vel de qualibet adtractu*). Unless the origin of property is clearly defined, it is impossible to differentiate purchases and acquisitions from inheritance. Of course, property acquired by an ancestor was included in the inheritance of a descendant. Nevertheless, *Form. Marc.* 2,7 does not prove that *alodis* incorporates both real and personal property. It cannot be used to substantiate this assertion.

Similarly, the use of *Formulae Turonenses* 14 and *Formulae Andecavenses* 41 (the former of the eighth, and the latter of the seventh century) following Gierke's reference to *Form. Marc.* 2,7 does not substantiate his assertion that *alodis* comprises all types of property when the latter are included in a mutual bequest. *Form. Turon.* 14 is closely parallel to *Form. Marc.* 2,7, and, much like *Form. Marc.* 2,10, it has the addition of *mobilibus et inmobilibus,* but for the same reason given above for *Form. Marc.* 2,10, the qualifier "movables and immovables" describes only predial property, and neither cloth, household goods, nor utensils. The *accolas, mancipia,* and *liberti,* even if indentured to an estate, cannot move from it, for the people as well as the soil were in bondage. Thus:

> . . . Ergo dono tibi donatumque esse volo locello, re proprietatis meae, nuncupante illo, situm in pago illo, cum terris, aedificiis, accolabus, mancipiis, libertis, vineis, silvis, pratis, pascuis, aquis aquarumve decursibus, mobilibus et inmobilibus, cum omni su-

praposito suisque adiecentiis, tam de alode quam et de conparato seu de qualibet adtracto, . . . [52]

Furthermore, the property enumerated in *Form. Marc.* 14 has been derived from more than inheritance because acquisitions and other property procured are included *(conparato seu de qualibet adtracto)*. But apart from this reason, it is apparent that real property is the basis of this *formula* because it says so: *dono . . . re proprietatis meae, nuncupante illo.*

Another formulary, *Form Andecav.* 41, has been cited to illustrate that personal property is included along with real property when reference is made to *alodis,* whereas the text shows the opposite, and for the same three reasons given for *Form. Marc.* 14: *alodis* signifies that real property is obtainable by inheritance, that real property incorporates appurtenances, and that real property may be described as what is known as a domain. In sum, *Form. Andecav.* 41 says:

> . . . in pago illo et illo ex allote [*sic*] parentum meorum habire vidior, . . . tam in domibus, edificies, mancipiis, viniis, sillvis [*sic*], agris cultis et incultis, pratis, acolabus, . . . tam quod mea proprietas esse videtur, . . . [53]

Because agricultural servants, regardless if they are free, freed, or slave, are merely appurtenances to an allodial domain, references to this fact should reinforce the nature of *alodis,* such as is evident in yet another eighth-century formulary, the *Formulae Arvernenses.* Here, documents nos. 3 and 4 indicate that slaves are included in the *alodis,* bu in all likelihood they are bound to an estate. This fact is evident in *Form. Arvern.* 3, which refers to its *ancilla* as a *mancipia:* "ancilla mea nomen illa una cum infantes suos illus et illus, quem de alode visi sumus habere, . . . de eorum mancipia."[54] However, *Form. Arvern.* 4 remains exceptional because it does not qualify its *servus* as a *manicipium,* that is, as an agricultural worker indentured to an estate.[55] So we find an exception in *Form. Arvern.* 4, but how can we accept this formulary when so much evidence conflicts with it? Either the use of *alodis* in *Form. Arvern.* 4 is correct or all the other uses of *alodis* already cited are incorrect. Most likely, the *servus* is a *mancipium,* but the document does not say so.[56]

We have already encountered the use of *omnis* in *Form. Marc.* 2,10. It appears again in *Form. Marc.* 2,9, which is another charter referred to for meaning no. 2.[57] And here the qualifier *omnis* is also used:

> . . . Sed dum et ipsa, peccatis meis fatientibus, ab hac luce discessit, et vos omni alode ipsius genetrice vestrae illa, iuxta quod et ratio prestetit, mecum exinde in presentia bonorum hominum, aut reges, altercantes, per ipsam epistolam, quam in eam feceramus, contra nos evindicastis, et in vestra potestate omne alode ipsius recipistis; sed dum mea adfuit petitio, et vos, ut condecet bonis filiis, voluntatem meam obtemperantes, ipsas villas vel res, qui fuerunt genetrice vestrae, quas ego eidem condonaveram, . . . [58]

The conjunction *vel* gives the option that either real property or other property (*villas vel res*) is manifested in this charter, but *et* should be substituted—although *vel* may infrequently be read as "and." Nevertheless, the text continues to qualify *alodis* when it says that the son (the recipient of this charter) had previously received property from his mother's inheritance (*alodis*) in addition to having received other landed estates: "tam quod vestrum antea de parte genetrice vestrae fuit alodae, quam et villas alias nuncupantes sic."[59] Hence, the meaning of *alodis* is qualified and delineated by *villas alias nuncupantes,* and a *villa* was, of course, a settlement or landed estate. Indeed, many other *formulae* in Marculf's compilation also attest to this fact, such as 1,12, 2,4, 2,6, 2,9, and 2,14, all of which infer that the meaning of *alodis* and the designation of *villa* are synonymous.

The fact that *alodis* signifies land and landed estates is undoubtedly made manifest in yet another formulary from Marculf's compilation. This *formula* is 2,12, and its Latin is so evidently clear that there is no question that *alodis* is distinguished from movable property.[60] It is evident that *Form. Marc.* 2,12 is written in the form of a criticism of the existing inheritance laws because the latter in large part denied the devolution of land to women when there were also sons. The author of this charter protests the customary bifurcation of property:

> Carta, ut filia cum fratres in paterna succedat alode [rubric]. . . . Diuturna, sed impia inter nos consuetudo tenetur, ut de terra paterna sorores cum fratribus porcionem non habeant; . . . [61] Ideoque per hanc epistolam te, dulcissima filia mea, contra germanos tuos, filios meos illos, in omni hereditate mea

> aequalem et legitimam esse constituo heredem, ut tam de alode
> paterna quam de conparatum vel mancipia aut presidium nos-
> trum, vel quodcumque morientes relinquaeremus, . . . [62]

Apart from the use of *omnis* in this charter, which signifies all property
as already discussed above, the meaning of *alodis* is evident more than
once in the text, for not only does it say that the purpose of this
charter is to include the daughter as a beneficiary to the paternal
landed estate *(terra paterna)*, it also differentiates *alodis* as land from
movable property *(de alode paterna . . . aut presidium nostrum)*. Thus,
*alodis* is a predial term because it relates to land or accessories attached
to it.

    *Cartae Senonicae* 45, which is another eighth-century *formula,*
also makes reference to *alodis. Cart. Senon.* 45 is closely similar to *Form.
Marc.* 2,12, but makes no mention of personal property. Rather, it
refers to *omnes res meas.* The relevant parts of this document are:

> . . . de res meas, quod mihi ex alode parentum meorum obvenit,
> apud germanos tuos, filios meos, minime in hereditate succidere
> potebas [*sic*]. . . . in omnes res meas, tam ex alode parentum meo-
> rum quam ex meum contractum mihi obvenit, in pago illo, in loco
> que dicitur ille, in quascumque pagis aut terretoriis, ubicumque
> habere videor, . . . [63]

Apart from *omnis,* it is obvious that real property is the basis of this
*formula,* but acquisitions *(contractum)* have also been added. The basis
of real property is evident because the document identifies *alodis* and
its additions *(contractum)* as territorially fixed, that is, as immovable
property.[64]

    Gierke's second meaning also refers to two canons from the
Neuching synod, which was convened by duke Tassilo of Bavaria in
772, despite the fact that only one of these canons contains reference
to *alodis.* And this canon (no. 14) refers to the legal claim that one
could make for a thief's *alodis* if he were killed while stealing another's
property: "De his, qui supradictis homicidiis debita morte in furto
reperti sunt, ut si quis huius interfecti parentele eum, qui in suo
scelere captus est, vindicare temptaverit, a propria alode alienus ef-
ficiatur."[65] Although one can make the implication—as one can for
*L. Baiu.* 2,1—that the totality of the thief's estate is meant, the sources
support the view that when property was confiscated, it is generally

understood to mean land only.[66] We may infer that *alodis* here means inheritance, and the latter signified the hereditary estate of one's ancestor. Although canon 17 of the Neuching synod is incorrectly cited for meaning no. 2 as yet another reference for *alodis* nevertheless its language confirms that *alodis* in all likelihood in canon 14 means *hereditas*, that is, the ancestral landed estate, since the *propria alode alienus* of canon 14 is clearly the *proprio alienatur patrimonio* of canon 17.[67]

We indicated above that there are a number of subdivisions that may be assigned to meaning no. 2, and these subdivisions, which are really alternate meanings of *alodis*, depend upon the general meaning of the totality of all property, both real and personal. Since no conclusive evidence that *alodis* signifies the totality of all property is forthcoming from meaning no. 2, it is our belief that these alternate meanings pertain to real property solely, and they include the heritage or hereditary estate, the bequest of the dead, and property obtained by inheritance when distinguished from property obtained by means other than inheritance, namely, by acquisition. Some of the sources utilized for these alternate meanings are the same sources used for the general meaning, particularly, *L. Rib.* 57, *L. Thur.* 26–33 (Eckhardt's edition, 26–30), *Form. Marc.* 2,7, 2,9, 2,10, 2,11, and 2,14, *Form. Andecav.* 41, *Form. Arvern.* 4, *Form. Turon.* 14, and *Cart Senon.* 45. Furthermore, other sources are used, notably, additional *epistolae* from these formulary compilations, Merovingian and Carolingian diplomas, charters of the monasteries of St. Gall and Freising, and other *formulae* hitherto not utilized (principally, *Salicae Merkelianae, Salicae Bignonianae, Bituricenses,* and *Lindenbrogianae*). Since we also accept that *alodis* means the hereditary estate as an additional meaning to its general meaning as well as inherited property when distinguished from acquisitions, we also accept these additional meanings as further modifications and subdivisions to the general meaning.[68] But our interpretation of all of these additional sources is real property exclusively. Of course, it is the implication of meaning no. 2 that the hereditary estate, the bequest of the dead, and inherited property all pertain to the totality of property, but none of these additional sources can be cited as evidence that *alodis* signifies real and personal property. Although we will not have to delve into these additional sources as deeply as we were compelled to do regarding the sources cited for the general meaning, it will be necessary to discuss only one of them, which demonstrates beyond a doubt that at all times *alodis* signifies real property only.

The source that needs elucidation is *Form Marc.* 1,12. It is a conclusive and unmistakable document. Its language and rhetoric leave no doubt that *alodis*, once again, is a totally predial term. *Form. Marc.* 1,12 concerns a mutual donation of a husband and wife, and is somewhat parallel to *Form. Marc.* 2,7. In *Form. Marc.* 1,12, all property within the possession of this childless couple is delineated within two distinct categories: real and personal. Real property is described first, followed by a description of personal property. And real property is subdivided into three types: donations, inheritance, and acquisitions:

> . . . Dedit igitur predictus vir ille per manu nostra iam dictae coniuge sua illa villas noncupantes [*sic*] illas, sitas in pago illo, quas aut munere regio aut de alode parentum vel undecunque ad presens tenere videtur, cum terris, domibus et citera [*sic*]. Similiter in conpensatione rerum dedit predicta faemina antedicto iogale suo illo villas nuncupantes illas, sitas in pago illo, cum terris et cetera, . . . [69]

Because the language is very clear, we are left with a distinct understanding of the nature of this couple's real property. We are informed that not only did the husband acquire property by his own means (*undecunque*), but he also was the recipient of a royal donation (*munere regio*). In addition, he had also received an inheritance from his parents (*de alode parentum*). His wife, on the other hand, also had real property, but whose origins are not specified. Even if one were to make a most cursory reading of *Form. Marc.* 1,12, it would reveal unmistakably that *alodis* is characterized as a type of real property and falls within the real property category. Hence, the text indicates that *alodis* is not to be confused in any way with personal property, whose description immediately follows the enumeration of real property. And personal property contains the typical movables evident in so many other documents discussed so far, namely, gold and silver, jewelry, cloth, clothing, and utensils: "seu presidiae domus eorum, aurum et argentum, fabricaturas, drappus, vestimenta vel omne subpellectile eorum, pars parte per manu nostra visi sunt condonasse."[70] Hence, the application of *alodis* in *Form. Marc.* 1,12 indicates a twofold meaning, the act or process of inheritance as well as the actual property devolved.

## III.

The third meaning of *alodis* that we wish to consider is that of real property solely, which, of course, is also our contended definition. Since Gierke's interpretation and our own agree in this case, there is no need to expound his sources, which are basically the same as the others discussed so far: *formulae*, charters, and capitularies, plus the reference to *L. Baiu.* 17,3 (now 16,17). Because *alodis* evolved into the freehold or the *terra propria* of the formative eighth and ninth centuries, it was juxtaposed to the fief, and many of the sources cited for meaning no. 3 indicate this relationship.[71]

Since property obtained through inheritance was intended to be completely controlled by the heir, it was property possessed in full ownership, free from all obligations. Wherever it survived in subsequent centuries, the allod retained intact is innate quality of free ownership. In a sense, the allod was equivalent to *peculiare*, a term in Carolingian usage that meant private property which could not legally be appropriated. But the basic characteristic of the allod was challenged in an age that found it to be anachronistic, since the concept of free and unencumbered property was incongruous with feudalism, whose beginnings have been attributed to the Merovingian age.[72]

Because land was the principal source of wealth in the early Middle Ages, it became the means by which many men derived a living. But the early Middle Ages was a time of violence and uncertainty, so much so that free landholders were quite incapable of protecting their own property without seeking protection from powerful men. These landholders would surrender their land to a lord and would receive it back as his tenants. Thus, land was leased to dependent tenants, who in turn did some service for their lord. Since the free landholders of allods were continually under attack by economic persuasion and political pressure to surrender their allods to some lord and to receive them back as fiefs, the unconverted allod had a greater chance of survival only wherever feudalism was weak. Thus, the allod became more common in Germany than in France, with the exception of Languedoc. In a feudal age, the allod was uncommon because it did not conform to the typical manner of land ownership in its day. It did not conform with the fundamental concept of feudalism: *nulle terre sans seigneur.* The allod signified an exclusive and unconditional ownership of land. The fief, on the other hand, signified only partial ownership, conditioned upon the right of some-one else. The fief was a dependent tenure, perpetually heritable. It truly was *une terre avec seigneur.* Thus, the allod and the fief were opposites.[73]

IV

The documentary evidence indicates that *alodis* included, but was not limited to *hereditas.* It represented real property, but also signified the heritability of this property. Hence, *alodis* leads to the study of *hereditas.* In large part, the bone of contention is *Pact. leg. Sal.* 59, but since a bifurcated law of inheritance was universal among all the Germans regardless of their national origin, with the exception of the Visigoths, the law of the Salian Franks should be substantially the same as the law of inheritance in other Germanic laws. If we possessed no charters, *formulae,* or capitularies that refer to *alodis,* we should still be able to conclude that *alodis* signified real property, and real property only. Admittedly, *Pact. leg. Sal.* 59 makes reference to both *hereditas* and *terra* within its text and only *alodis* in its rubric, with the exception of *Lex Salica Heroldina,* but the affinity of these three terms implies that they are all associated with each other. But there have been many inconsistencies in the interpretation of *Pact. leg. Sal.* 59 because al-though it has been presumed by some scholars such as Sohm and Amira to encompass all property (personal property in sections 1–5, and real property in section 6),[74] the dictionary entries of Niermeyer and Schneider (in Prinz) define it as personal property only.[75] Pre-sumably, *Pact. leg. Sal.* 59 will remain forever a matter of controversy. But even if one misunderstands *alodis* in *Pact. leg. Sal.* 59, one should have no difficulty interpreting subsequent sources that make refer-ence to it. Surely, the bifurcated law of inheritance would give us some guidance, but these subsequent sources themselves render un-mitigated proof of its meaning.

We are now, therefore, in a position to understand that *alodis* signifies the fullness of property, not its totality. And fullness means that it is not wanting in any quality, that it possesses both thoroughness and inviolability. Such a perception could only be applicable to land. The sources discussed in this essay indicate that *alodis* is a type of real property (*Form. Marc.* 1,12: *munere regio aut de alode parentum vel un-*

*decunque*), clearly delineated from movables (*Form. Marc.* 2,12: *de alode paterna aut presidium nostrum*) and differentiated from purchases and acquisitions (*Form. Marc.* 2,7: *de alode aut de conparatum vel de qualibet adtractu; Form. Turon.* 14: *de alode quam et de conparato seu de qualibet adtracto*). Other qualifications apply to the possibility of its confiscation when its owner is guilty of a serious crime (*L. Alam.* 43 [text A], *L. Baiu.* 2,1, Neuching canon 14). Furthermore, there is overwhelming evidence to demonstrate beyond a doubt that *alodis* as an indication of the heritage or hereditary estate, when described in general as inheritance (*Pact. leg. Sal.* 59, *L. Rib.* 57, *L. Thur.* 26–30), is territorially fixed (*L. Baiu.* 12,8: *in arboribus aut in montibus nec in fluminibus, . . . tenuerunt et in alodem*) within an identifiable county (*Form. Andecav.* 41: *in pago illo et illo ex allote* [*sic*] *parentum; Cart. Senon.* 45: *ex alode parentum . . . in pago illo*) as a domain or landed estate (*Form. Marc.* 2,9: *alodae, quam et villas alias nuncupantes*). Indeed, the sources demonstrate that *alodis* did not evolve from movable to immovable property. Rather, these sources show that *alodis* was a consistent term throughout the Merovingian period, that it never lost its exclusive meaning of real property, and that it never acquired the meaning of personal property.

## Notes

This essay is dedicated to the memory of my uncle Clement De Munck (1896–1988): "Ecce dedi vobis omnem herbam adferentem semen super terram."
1. *Allodium* is the basis for the English allod (or alod) and the French *alleu*. German acquired the Latin form *allodium* only in the nineteenth century. Prior to this time, German expressed the idea of full property with *eigen*, which was a Germanization of *alodis* made in the tenth century. The Italian and Spanish terms have been left essentially unchanged from the medieval Latin.

For a recent etymology of *alodis*, *v* Friedrich Kluge, *Etymologisches Wörterbuch der deutschen Sprache*, 21st ed., ed. Walther Mitzka (Berlin, 1975), s.v. *allod*. *V* also the dictionary entries of Otto von Gierke, "Allod," in *Beiträge zum Wörterbuch der deutschen Rechtssprache: Richard Schröder zum siebenzigsten Geburtstag* (Weimar, 1908), cols. 103–138; reprinted with slight modifications in the *Deutsches Rechtswörterbuch (Wörterbuch der älteren deutschen Rechtssprache)*, ed. Preussischen Akademie der Wissenschaften, 5 vols. (Weimar, 1914–1932), 1, cols. 486–502. Cf. J.F. Niermeyer (ed.), *Mediae latinitatis lexicon minus* (Leiden, 1954–1976), s.v. *alodis*, and Johannes Schneider, "Alodis," in *Mittellateinisches Wörterbuch bis zum ausgehenden 13. Jahrhundert*, ed. Otto Prinz (Munich, 1967), 1, cols. 494–498. *V* also Joseph Balon, *Grand dictionnaire de droit du Moyen Age* (Namur, 1973), fasc. 3, s.v. *alodis*, which contains a bibliography.
2. (Göttingen, 1828), pp. 492–493. This derivation was repeated and expanded in

Grimm's second, third, and fourth editions. Reference to the fourth and last edition is *Deutsche Rechtsalterthümer,* eds. Andreas Heusler and Rudolf Hübner, 2 vols. (Berlin, 1899; r.p. 1956), 2, pp. 3–4.

3. Ibid., 2, p. 4: "Zusammensetzung von al (totus, integer) und ôd (bonum), soviel wie al-eigen, mere proprium." It is highly unlikely that *alodis* is anything other than Frankish, certainly anything other than Germanic. Nevertheless, the Germanic provenance of the term has been doubted, particularly by Karl Müllenhoff, "Die deutschen Wörter der Lex Salica," in Georg Waitz, *Das alte Recht der salischen Franken* (Kiel, 1846), p. 278, and by Friedrich Diez, *Etymologisches Wörterbuch der romanischen Sprachen,* 4th ed. (Bonn, 1878) s.v. *allodio.* Cf. Numa D. Fustel de Coulanges, *Histoire des institutions politiques de l'ancienne France,* 6 vols. (Paris 1888–1892; r.p. 1964), 4, pp. 161–162. Otto Behaghel, "Odal," *Sitzungsberichte der bayerischen Akademie der Wissenschaften,* philos.-hist. Klasse, 1935, Heft 8, p. 4, believes *alodis* to be derived from ON *odal,* since the latter was the heritable farm, the family estate.

4. *V* n. 1 above for full citation.

5. "Bei seiner Entstehung kann es nur das fahrende Gut im Gegensatz zum liegenden Gut bezeichnet haben. . . . Es ist aus inneren Gründen wahrscheinlich, dass bei der Abfassung der L. Sal. das Wort *alodis* noch lediglich auf die Fahrnis bezogen wurde." *Deutsches Rechtswörterbuch,* I, col. 487. Likewise, Karl Lamprecht, "Zur Sozialgeschichte der deutschen Urzeit," in *Festgabe für Georg Hanssen zum 31. Mai 1889* (Tübingen, 1889), p. 69.

6. "Die *alodis* umfasst daher nunmehr liegendes und fahrendes Gut." *Deutsche Rechtswörterbuch,* I, col. 488.

7. "In der späteren frk. [fränkischen] Zeit setzt ein neuer Sprachgebrauch ein, der unter Allod zuerst vorzugsweise und dann ausschliesslich liegendes Gut versteht entsprechend der gleichzeitigen Begriffsverengung von *eigen* und *erbe*." Ibid., col. 491.

8. Notably, Niermeyer and Schneider (in Prinz), cited in n. 1.

9. Such as Heinrich Tiefenbach, *Studien zu Wörtern volkssprachiger Herkunft in karolingischen Königsurkunden: Ein Beitrag zum Wortschatz der Diplome Lothars I und Lothars II,* Münstersche Mittelalter-Schriften, 15 (Munich, 1973), pp. 97–98, and Michael J. Hodder, "Allod" in the *Dictionary of the Middle Ages,* ed. Joseph R. Strayer (New York, 1982), 1, p. 190.

10. *V* e.g., Kluge, *Etymologisches Wörterbuch,* 21st ed., s.v. *allod.* The equivalents to the Frankish *al* are Goth. *alls,* OE *eal,* OS *all,* ON *al,* and OHG *al.* Equivalents to *ôd* are Goth. *auda,* OE *eád,* OS *ôd,* ON *audr,* and OHG *ôt.*

11. Reference to OHG *alode* is derived from one manuscript (Trier, Stadtbibliothek, OHG and MGH fragment no. 4) reprinted in its entirety in J.H. Hessels, ed., *Lex Salica: The Ten Texts with the Glosses, and the Lex Emendata* (London, 1880), p. xliv. The edition in the MGH does not print this fragment in one place, but integrates its individual sections internally. Hence, the reference to "[title] LXII. *fon alode,*" which is one of ten titles to the OHG fragment, is found in MGH LL 4/1: 12.

12. In addition to Kluge (n. 10 above), *v* also Ferdinand Holthausen, *Gotisches Etymologisches Wörterbuch* (Heidelberg, 1934), s.v. *auda;* Joseph Bosworth and T. Northcote Toller, *An Anglo-Saxon Dictionary* (Oxford, 1898; repr. 1972), s.v. *eád;* Ferdinand Holthausen, *Altsächsisches Wörterbuch,* 2nd ed. (Cologne, 1967), s.v. *ôd;* Ferdinand Holthausen, *Wörterbuch des Altwestnordischen* (Göttingen, 1948), s.v. *audr;*

and Rudolf Schützeichel, *Althochdeutsches Wörterbuch,* 3rd ed. (Tübingen, 1981), s.v. *ōt.*

13. Both whole and full, of course, are derived from Grimm's description of *al* as *totus* and *integer.* Nonetheless, it is attributed more to subsequent scholars than to Grimm that "full" has replaced "complete" for *integer.* In addition to Kluge, Gierke, and Niermeyer, cited n. 1 above, *v* also Werner Goez, "Allod," in *Handwörterbuch zur deutschen Rechtsgeschichte,* ed. Adalbert Erler and Ekkehard Kaufmann (Berlin, 1971), 1, cols. 120–121, and Karl Heinz Burmeister, "Allod," in *Lexikon des Mittelalters,* ed. Robert Auty et al. (Munich, 1977), 1, cols. 440–441.

14. Wilhelm Kaspers, "Wort- und Namenstudien zur Lex Salica," *Zeitschrift für deutsches Altertum und deutsche Literatur,* 82 (1948/50), 325, makes no distinction between *voll* and *ganz.* Wolfgang Jungandreas, "Vom Merowingischen zum Französischen. Die Sprache der Franken Chlodwigs," *Leuvense Bijdragen,* 44 (1954), 129, prefers *ganz,* but his addition of free *(frei)* as yet another meaning of *al(l)* is premature and merely anticipates the freehold *(allodium)* of later centuries.

15. Cf. Claudius Frhr. von Schwerin, "Allod," in *Reallexikon der germanischen Altertumskunde,* ed. Johannes Hoops (Strasbourg, 1911), 1, p. 65. It seems that Eberhard G. Graff, *Althochdeutscher Sprachschatz oder Wörterbuch der althochdeutschen Sprache,* 6 vols. (Berlin, 1834–1842), 1, s.v. *alod,* disagrees.

16. These arguments apply whether or not the Germanic invaders seized land from the Gallo-Roman population when they invaded Gaul or were compensated by the latter in lieu of land with subsidies from the collection of taxes. Sooner or later, the invaders became landlords. Moreover, the expansion by the Franks into southern Gaul had accelerated in the last quarter of the sixth century as Chilperic's laws, promulgated in 575, indicate. Particularly noteworthy is Chilperic's first law in his eleven law edict, the *Edictus domni Chilperici regis pro tenore pacis,* which constitutes law 106 (Eckhardt's edition) of the *Pactus legis Salicae.* Here, the establishment of the law of succession in the south of Gaul is given equal status with that in the north. *V* my article entitled "An Analysis of the Place-Name *Turrovaninsis* in 'Edictus Chilperici' (Cap. 1) and Its Relationship to Inheritance Rights South of the Garonne River (ca. A.D. 575)," *Francia,* 12 (1984), 632–634.

17. MGH LL 4/1: 222–224. Translated into English in my *Laws of the Salian and Ripuarian Franks* (New York, 1986), pp. 106–107. Cf. the later Carolingian redaction, *Lex Salica (Recensio Pippina),* 93; MGH LL 4/2: 162, 164 (D text). *Alodis* also appears in *Pact. leg. Sal.* 66: *De rebus in alode patris;* MGH LL 4/1: 238.

18. The classic interpretation of this law is Heinrich Brunner, "Kritische Bemerkungen zur Geschichte des germanischen Weibererbrechts," *ZRG, GA,* 21 (1900), 1–19; repr. in his *Abhandlungen zur Rechtsgeschichte: Gesammelte Aufsätze,* ed. Karl Rauch, 2 vols. (Weimar, 1931), II, pp. 198–217, esp. pp. 209–215. *V* also Karl Kroeschell, "Söhne und Töchter im germanischen Erbrecht," in *Studien zu den germanischen Volksrechten: Gedächtnisschrift für Wilhelm Ebel,* ed. Götz Landwehr, Rechtshistorische Reihe, 1 (Frankfurt, 1982), pp. 95–96. One should also consult Alexander Callander Murray, *Germanic Kinship Structure: Studies in Law and Society in Antiquity and the Early Middle Ages,* Toronto University Studies and Texts, 65 (Toronto, 1983), pp. 201–215.

19. For Merowingian wills, *v* Ulrich Nonn, "Merowingische Testamente. Studien zum Fortleben einer römischen Urkundenform im Frankenreich, "*Archiv für Diplomatik,* 18 (1972), 1–129, esp. 25–35. The earliest Merovingian will is that of Regimius of

Reims (533); however, its authenticity, like the authenticity of other sixth-century wills, has been questioned. It should also be noted that none of the sixth-century nor seventh-century Merovingian wills makes reference to *alodis*. The same is also true for Gregory of Tours' *Decem libri historiarum (Historia Francorum)*.

20. A case in point is Burmeister, *Lexikon des Mittelalters*, I, col. 440: "Die Ansicht von Sohm und Gierke, dass allod ursprünglich nur die Fahrnis bezeichnet habe, hat sich freilich nicht durchgesetzt." Cf. Heinrich Geffcken, ed., *Lex Salica zum akademischen Gebrauche* (Leipzig, 1898), p. 223. Apparently, it needs to be reiterated that *eigen*, the German translation of *alodis*, means real, not personal, property. Jacob and Wilhelm Grimm, *Deutsches Wörterbuch* (Leipzig, 1862), III, col. 96.

21. This condition is true for all property owners. It was also true, contrary to theoretical feudalism, for fief holders who struggled to ensure that their lands would pass to their heirs and not revert to their lords. *Capit. miss. Niumagae dat.*, c. 6. MGH Capit 1: 131.

22. Karl August Eckhardt, who is well known for his editions and translations of medieval documents, has translated *alodis* differently at different times. In his 1935 translation of the Salic laws, he translates *alodis* as inheritance *(Erbschaft)*, but in the second edition of this translation, he renders it as hereditary estate *(Erbgut)*. V his *Die gesetze des Merowingerreiches, 481–714* Germanenrechte, Texte und Übersetzungen, 1 (Weimar, 1935), p. 87, and his 2nd ed. (Göttingen, 1955), p. 171. This change in translation also conforms with Eckhardt's edition (and translation) in his *Pactus legis Salicae, 65-Titel-Text*, Germanenrechte Neue Folge, Westgermanisches Recht, 2/1 (Göttingen, 1955), p. 339.

23. This distinction of differentiating immovables into heritables and acquests was unknown in Roman law. It owes its origin to the Franks. Emile Chénon, *Histoire generale du droit français public et privé*, 2 vols. (Paris, 1926–1929), II, p. 230.

24. For these views, v Rudolf Sohm, *Die Fränkische Reichs- und Gerichtsverfassung* (Weimar, 1871), p. 118 and n. 57; Karl von Amira, *Erbenfolge und Verwandtschafts-Glierderung nach den alt-niederdeutschen Rechten* (Munich, 1874), p. 2; and Paul Vinogradoff, *Custom and Right*, Instituttet for Sammenlignende Kulturforskning, Serie A: Forelesninger (Oslo, 1925), p. 44, among others. More recently, also v Alexander Bergengruen, *Adel und Grundherrschaft im Merowingerreich*, Vierteljahrschrift für Sozial- und Wirtschaftsgeschichte, Beiheft 41 (1958), 51–52. The latter's suggestion that *Pact. leg. Sal.* 59 is based upon *Lex Rom. Burg.* 28 (*De luctuosis hereditatibus*) has not been sufficiently analysed nor challenged.

25. Notably, *L. Visig.* 4,2,1 and 4,2,9; MGH LL 1: 174 and 177.

26. In addition to *Pact. leg. Sal.* 59 and 108 and *L. Rib.* 57 (56), the bifurcated law of inheritance is contained for the most part in *L. Burg.* 14, 42, 51, and 78, *L. Alam.* 55, *L. Thur.* 26–30, *L. Fran. Cham.* 42, and *L. Sax.* 41 and 44. V the studies of Émile Glasson, "Le droit de succession dans les lois barbares," *Revue historique de droit français et étranger*, nouvelle revue, 9 (1885), 585–593; Rudolf Huebner, *A History of Germanic Private Law*, trans. Francis S. Philbrick (Boston, 1918; r.p. New York, 1968), pp. 164–169, 698, which is a translation of Huebner's *Grundzüge des deutschen Privatrechts* (Leipzig, 1908); Chénon, *Histoire generale du droit français*, I, pp. 419–420, 444–452; and Geoffrey MacCormack, "Inheritance and Wergild in Early Germanic Law," *The Irish Jurist*, n.s. 8 (1973), 143–163 and 9 (1974), 166–183.

Furthermore, Roman law empowered one to disinherit one's children, with the exception of one-quarter of the paternal estate as established by the Falcidian law (*Lex Falcidia* 35,1), but the Franks had no such power. Intestacy among the Franks appeared to have had greater assurances of succession than did testacy among the Romans because the former could not disinherit their heirs. Moreover, not only were the Franks prevented from disinheriting anyone, with the exception that they could disinherit themselves (*Pact. leg. Sal.* 60), but they also could not forestall the inheritance of real property. Because personal property was less valuable, it was subject to a different procedure, but the law of succession was never arbitrary. (A point well taken by Hermann Conrad, *Deutsche Rechtsgeschichte*, 2nd rev. ed., 2 vols. [Karlsruhe, 1962–1966], I, p. 161.) Indeed, all property was inherited in accordance with a formula prescribing that land would be the last possession surrendered in order to satisfy a debt. The Franks also had the option of designating an heir where none existed by legally adopting one in the public ceremony known as *affatomie*. *V Pact. leg. Sal.* 46; MGH LL 4/1: 176–181. Similarly, *L. Rib.* 50 (48 and 49); MGH LL 3/2: 101. Although the alienation of real property was unknown in the early Merovingian period, it made its appearance by the eighth century, when the church created a need for it.

27. The equivalency of *terra* and *alodis* has long been noticed by scholars, and notably by Du Cange, *Glossarium mediae et infimae latinitatis*, s.v. *alodis*. More recently, this conclusion has also been reached by Joseph Balon, but he has gone one step beyond this and has equated *alodis* with *terra salica*. Nonetheless, the latter relationship alters the equation considerably because *terra salica* is merely a particular type of land, believed to be the patrimonial estate, i.e., the ancestral household and the land directly attached to it. *V* his *Les fondements du régime foncier au Moyen Age depuis la chute de l'empire romain en occident*, Anciens pays et assemblées d'états, 7 (Louvain, 1954), pp. 56–59. Also expanded in his *Traité de droit salique: Etude d'exégèse et de sociologie juridiques*, 4 vols., Ius Medii Aevi, 3 (Namur, 1965), II, pp. 562–568. But Balon's explanation is somewhat contrived. He uses circumventing and irrelevant evidence, such as his references to Frankish titles in the Salic laws or references to Frankish geography, to explain why *alodis* and *terra salica* are coterminous concepts, although he is correct in equating *alodis* with some type of *terra*.

28. The *Lex Salica Heroldina* is a name attributed to the edition of the Salic laws by Johannes Herold (Basel, 1557) and not to the manuscript (containing an 80-title text) upon which it is based. Because this manuscript is now lost, Herold's edition has become the source for the 80-title redaction. For *Pact. leg. Sal.* 59,6 (*Heroldina*), see MGH LL 4/1: 223 and 225.

29. Described as *gesamte Vermögen* in Gierke's original 1908 essay. *V Beiträge zum Wörterbuch der deutschen Rechtssprache*, col. 108.

30. MGM LL 3/2: 105. Translated into English in my *Laws of the Salian and Ripuarian Franks*, p. 192.

31. The equivalency of *terra salica* with *hereditas aviatica* is also evident in several other sources. For example, see a charter from the monastery of Weissenburg (a.d. 742): "Haec omnia sicut iam diximus, tam de aviatico quam de paterno sive de materno sive de comparatu vel de quacumquelibet adtractu." Anton Doll, ed., *Traditiones Wizenburgenses: Die Urkunden des Klosters Weissenburg, 661–864.* (Darmstadt, 1979), n. 52 (p. 241). *V* also a charter from the abbey of Gorze (a.d. 788), which enumerates "*donamus . . . mansos, casas, campos, prata, silvas, vineas, pomifera, aquas aquarumve decursus, quicquid de paterno, materno, vel de aviatico, seu de comparato, aut de qualicumque*

*adtractu ad nos legibus pervenit."* Armand d'Herbomez, ed., *Cartulaire de l'abbaye de Gorze* (Paris, 1898–1901), no. 28 (p. 58).

33. MGH LL 5/1: 112. Translated into English in my *Laws of the Alamans and Bavarians* (Philadelphia, 1977), p. 84. Andreas Heusler, *Institutionen des deutschen Privatrechts,* 2 vols. (Leipzig, 1885–1886), II, p. 326, does not question the Latin, but merely raises the possibility that real property could comprise part of the dowry.

33. MGH LL 5/1: 104. This addition is not incorporated into my translation.

34. MGH LL 5/2: 268, 292, 402, and 442 respectively. Konrad Beyerle's edition of the Bavarian laws in his *Lex Baiuvariorum: Lichtdruck Wiedergabe der Ingolstädter Handschrift des bayerischen Volksrechts* (Munich, 1926) has a different title to law 1,1 without mention of *alodis* and therefore has only three references to it. The respective pages to laws, 2,1, 12,8 and 16,17 in Beyerle's edition are 50, 128–130, and 160–162. Since my translation of the Bavarian laws is based upon Beyerle's edition of the Ingolstadt manuscript (the oldest extent manuscript), there is no reference to *alodis* in the translation to law 1,1. V my *Laws of the Alamans and Bavarians,* pp. 124, 152, and 163–164 respectively for the remaining laws.

35. Gierke, *Deutsches Rechtswörterbuch,* 1, col. 492. Similarly, both Niermeyer and Schneider (in Prinz), n. 1 above, also equate *alodis* in *L. Baiu.* 16,17 with real property.

36. Karl August Eckhardt, ed. and trans., *Die Gesetze des Karolingerreiches, 714–911,* Germanenrechte, Texte und Übersetzungen, 2/3 (Weimar, 1934), pp. 38–40. The older edition of Karl Friedrich von Richthofen has nine laws (26–34), whereas Eckhardt has five (26–30). Richthofen's edition also places these laws under title seven, not title two. V MGH LL (Folio) 5: 123–129.

37. Cf. *Lex Francorum Chamavorum* 42: "Si quis Francus homo habuerit filios, hereditatem suam de sylva et de terra eis dimittat et de mancipiis et de peculio. De materna hereditate similiter in filiam veniat." Ibid., 275.

38. Law 44 of the *Lex Saxonum,* promulgated at the same time as the Thuringian laws, has a similar provision when no sons survived the death of a father: "Qui defunctus non filios sed filias reliquerit, ad eas omnis hereditas pertineat; . . ." Ibid., 72.

39. Of the modern lexicons, only Schneider (in Prinz) makes a reference to *L. Baiu.* 1,1, and here he interprets *alodis* as entire property (*bona omnia, gesamte Vermögen*).

40. Alf Uddholm, *Formulae Marculfi: Études sur la langue e le style* (Uppsala, 1954), p. 22. Heinz Zatschek, "Die Benutzung der Formulae Marculfi und anderer Formularsammlungen in den Privaturkunden des 8. bis 10. Jahrhunderts," *MIÖG,* 42 (1927), 265–266, dates this collection between 700 and 720.

41. Notably, Gierke makes this presumption, but adds that some *formulae* concern real property only: "In einigen Formeln kann bereits überhaupt nur das Grundeigentum gemeint sein. So in *Form. Marc.* 2,12." *Deutsches Rechtswörterbuch,* 1, col. 489. So immediately, we have a qualification to a generalization, whereby the latter does not apply in every case.

42. MGH, Form: 82. This formulary and all formularies in Marculf's compilation have been rendered into French in Alf Uddholm, *Marculfi Formularum: Libri Duo* (Uppsala, 1962).

43. Likewise, *omnis* may modify appurtenances, e.g., "cum sylvas vel omnia adjacentis ad se pertinentes, cum domibus et mancipiis, sicut jam in tuam ditionem tradidi, cum mobilibus et immobilibus, in integrum volo esse donatam, . . ." L.G.O. Brequigny and J.M. Pardessus, eds., *Diplomata, chartae, epistolae, leges alique instrumenta ad res Gallo-Francicas spectantia,* 2 vols. (Paris, 1843–1849; r.p. 1969), I, p. 204 (the

will of Bertram of Le Mans, a.d. 616). *V* also *Form. Marc.* 1,33 for *omnes res suas;* MGH Form: 64.

44. Ibid., p. 82.
45. *V Divisio regnorum* (a.d. 806), c. 11: ". . . rerum immobilium, hoc est terrarum, vinearum atque silvarum servorumque qui iam casati sunt sive ceterarum rerum quae hereditatis nomine consentur, excepto auro, argento et gemmis, armis ac vestibus necnon et mancipiis non casatis et his speciebus quae proprie ad negotiatores pertinere noscuntur. . . . " MGH Capit 1: 129.
46. MGH Form: 84.
47. For example, *v L. Thur.* 26–30 above. Cf. the discussion below for *Form. Marc.* 2,12.
48. MGH Form: 84.
49. Ibid.
50. On this note, *v* the view of Fustel de Coulanges, *Histoire des institutions politiques,* IV, p. 152, who, I believe, was led astray by ambiguous rhetoric. Likewise, *v* his reference (ibid., p. 153, n. 1) to *Cartae Senonicae* 29 (MGH Form: 198) that *alodis* incorporates gold, silver, cloth, utensils, and cattle. Of course, the document says no such thing. What *Cart. Senon* 29 does say is that the *alodis* will be divided between two brothers, and that it is made up of real property. Although the text goes on to enumerate additional (movable) property, it is not part of the *alodis* and it is clear from the Latin that this additional property, albeit specifically named, relates to nonpredial property, hence, not part of the paternal inheritance. *Cart. Senon.* 29 is really quite straightforward. In fact, this document indicates that its author did not need to go into such specific detail in order to convey its meaning. The relevant parts of *Cart. Senon.* 29 are: ". . . . placuit atque convenit inter illo et germano suo illo de allote [sic], qui fuit genitore illo, ut inter se aequalentia dividere . . . Accepit ille de parte sua manso in pago illo, . . . Aecontra ad vicem accepit ille de parte sua manso in pago illo, . . . Etiam aurum, argentum, drapalia, aeramen, peculium, presidium utriusque sexus, mobile et inmobilibus, inter se aequalentia visi fuerunt dividissent, . . . Ibid., pp. 197–198.
51. Ibid., p. 79.
52. Ibid., pp. 142–143.
53. Ibid., pp. 18–19.
54. Ibid., p. 30.
55. Fustel de Coulanges, *Histoire des institutions politiques,* IV, p. 156, n. 1, also interprets slaves as movable property in *Form. Arvern.* 4. For the text, *v* MGH Form: 30.
56. The strict difference between *servus* and *mancipium* is not always maintained in medieval sources, nor should we expect such a critical differentiation to be evident simply to facilitate our scholarly research, and for this reason, there seems to be a conflict between the description of slave in *Form. Arvern.* 4 and the Thuringian laws cited above. Since we have already seen that the Thuringian laws confer slaves upon a daughter when there is a son who is capable of inheriting land and these slaves are described as *mancipia,* the Thuringian laws appear to confer part of what we describe as predial property upon daughters who are assumed not to be entitled to receive them. Nevertheless, the basis of real property, that is, land, continues to be conferred upon sons. Consequently, the Thuringian laws confer land upon sons, while conferring what is another type of predial property (*mancipia*) upon daughters, who presumably would bring them to their husbands' estates, when daughters married, to work their husbands' *alodis.*

57. But Gierke says of this document the opposite of what he says for *Form. Marc.* 2,10, that is, *alodis* means real property only: "Manchmal werden nur Grundstücke hervorgehoben." *Deutsches Rechtswörterbuch*, 1, col. 489.
58. MGH Form: 81.
59. Ibid. Niermeyer, *Mediae latinitatis lexicon minus*, s.v. *alodis*, meaning no. 3, refers to *Form. Marc.* 2,9 as evidence of inheritance consisting of both personal and real property.
60. *V* n. 41 above.
61. Most likely, a reference to *Pact. leg. Sal.* 59,5.
62. MGH Form: 83.
63. Ibid., p. 205.
64. All additional references to *alodis* in Marculf's *formulae* relate to land, since they signify either inheritance (1,12, 2,4, 2,6, and 2,11) or the hereditary estate (1,20). None of these additional references are discussed by Gierke.
65. MGH Conc 2/1: 102–103.
66. There are many examples of this tendency in Gregory of Tours, *Decem libri historiarum (Historia Francorum)*, notably 3,18, 5,6, 9,35, and 9,39. Confiscation (sometimes deliberate theft) of property varied, depending upon the wealth of the victim, although all of one's possessions could be seized (7,22 and 29). There are no good examples in either Fredegar's *Chronica* or the *Liber historiae Francorum*. Likewise, the Salic *chrenecruda* ceremony pertained to real property only. *V Pact. leg. Sal.* 58; MGH LL 4/1: 218–221. A parallel to the Carolingian capitularies is the *Capitulare Haristallense* (a.d. 779), c. 9: "Ut latrones . . . beneficium et honorem perdat." MGH Capit 1: 48.
67. MGH Conc 2/1: 103, c. 17: "Ut si quis in virtute coniunctus a propria coniuge adulterina separatus fuerit, eiusque ex cognatione coniugis propter eandem dimissionem qui eum persequere temptaverit, a proprio alienatur patrimonio."
68. As a further modification to meaning no. 2, Gierke says that when *alodis* stands alone without *parentum* appended, it represents both inherited and acquired property. But his reference to *Form. Marc.* 1,33, his principal source presented as proof of this fact, ignores the relationship between *reliqua alode*, which he quotes, with *de alodo* [*sic*] *parentum*, which he does not quote. There is no difference in the meaning as far as *alodis* is concerned. Furthermore, the historical sources disprove Gierke's assumption because of the use of the comparative phrase *de alode quam et de conparato vel de qualibet adtracto,* or approximate variations thereof. And this comparative phrase occurs in hundreds of documents. The reference to Gierke noted here is *Deutsches Rechtswörterbuch*, I, col. 490. Apparently, Gierke's rendering in all likelihood is where Niermeyer, *Mediae latinitatis lexicon minus*, s.v. *alodis*, meaning no. 5, is derived. Similarly, the Freising charters, among others, have also given us other terms for both acquisitions (*lucrationes*) and purchases (*emptiones*), which are merely alternate words for property obtained in addition to the hereditary estate. *V* Theodor Bitterauf, ed., *Die Traditionen des Hochstifts Freising*, Quellen und Erörterungen zur bayerischen und deutschen Geschichte, neue Folge, 4 (Munich, 1905; r.p. Aalen, 1967), no. 32 (p. 60) and 43 (pp. 70–71) respectively. (*V* also no. 56, 92, 95, 112, 136, 262 etc.) Therefore, *alodis* always signified landed possessions obtained by the law of inheritance, and excluded all other types of property. As already indicated, whatever acquisitions an ancestor possessed were subsequently incorporated into the hereditary estate that was conferred upon the heir(s) at the

time of the ancestor's death. *V* Jean Brissaud, *Manuel d'histoire du droit privé* (part 3 of his *Manuel d'histoire du droit français*) (Paris, 1908), p. 207, n. 2. For the latter work, I have avoided the English translation of Rapelje Howell, *A History of French Private Law* (Boston, 1912; r.p. New York, 1968) because of his erroneous rendering of *propres* (that is, immovables) as personal possessions. *V* also the introductory discussion of *propres* in Ralph E. Giesey, "Rules of Inheritance and Strategies of Mobility in Prerevolutionary France," *American Historical Review*, 82 (1977), 272.

69. MGH Form: 50.

70. Ibid.

71. Notably, *Capit. miss. spec.*, c. 10: ". . . nostra beneficia habent distructa et alodes eorum restauratas." *Capit. miss. Niumagae dat.*, c. 18: ". . . in beneficio aut in alode." *Capit. de causis div.*, c. 4: ". . . ipsi alodi aut illud beneficium." *Capit. miss. Aquis. prim.*, c. 14: "De beneficiis destructis et alodis restauratis." *Concil. et capit. de cler. percus.*, c. 6: ". . . in nostro regno beneficium non habeat et alodis eius in bannum mittatur;. . . " *Capit. Hloth. de exped. contra Sarrac.*, c. 8: ". . . sine beneficiis sunt et alodos atque peccunias [*sic*] habent, . . . " *Edict. Pistense*, c. 22: ". . . in uno tantum comitatu alodem vel beneficia habent . . . " *Capit. Karol. Vernense*, c. 6: ". . . infra parrochiam beneficia et alodum non habent . . . " MGH Capit 1: 100, 132, 136, 153, 362; 2: 66, 319, 373 respectively.

72. François-Louis Ganshof, *Qu'est-ce que la feodalité?*, 5th ed. (Paris, 1982), p. 19.

73. On many of these thoughts, "v" Marc Bloch, *Feudal Society*, trans. L.A. Manyon, 2 vols. (Chicago, 1964), 1, pp. 171–173, and Jean-Français Lemarignier, *La France médiévale: Institutions et société* (Paris, 1970), pp. 169–170.

74. *V* n. 24 above.

75. *V* n. 1 above for full citation.

# THE MATERIAL SITUATION OF THE WORKING POPULATION IN THE TOWNS OF WEST POMERANIA IN THE ERA OF THE "PRICE REVOLUTION": 1500–1627

Rudolf Biederstedt
Greifswald

# The Material Situation of the Working Population in the Towns of West Pomerania in the Era of the "Price Revolution": 1500–1627

The sixteenth century was full of fundamental changes in the economic and political structure of the Baltic area. Developments which had started in the previous century revealed themselves more clearly and led to clearly visible consequences. In international trade, the Hanseatic League had fallen to second place, behind the Netherlands, despite an increase in the absolute volume of trade.[1] The treatment of these competitors and of English merchants varied greatly, always determined by their respective usefulness. The competition was the reason for many internal Hanseatic quarrels. The increasing transfer of maritime exports, especially grain, to Dutch ships, damaged seafaring, shipbuilding, and trade in the Hanseatic towns. The towns were deprived of further profit by decreases in storage rights (*Stapelrecht*), demanded both by the landed gentry and by princes who were also large landowners. The charge was to overcome a decrease in the real value of their ground rents. It allowed them to sell agricultural produce directly to West European bulk purchasers and thus avoid some Hanseatic intermediary.

The inability to abandon the old Hanseatic ways of trading for the emerging free competition in world trade, caused the Hanseatic economy to fail further behind. While the town council oligarchies tried to keep things as they had been, their power base in the individual towns increasingly slipped away from them. At the beginning of the seventeenth century it could no longer be denied that the Hanseatic League, despite increases in maritime trade, was dying. Merchant shippers in Greifswald pronounced in a down-to-earth

39

manner "dass sie nit einen Fliegenfuss von der Hanse hätten" ("that they didn't have a fleabite from the Hansa").[2]

The inevitable consequences of the weakening of the economic position of the Hanseatic League was a decline in its political influence. In the "Feud of the Counts" ("*Grafenfehde*") of 1534/35 it once again attempted to win back its position by military means, but in vain. After this, its power decreased steadily. The rising monarchies of Scandinavia and Russia endeavored to throw off the pressure of Hanseatic privileges and monopoly.[3] By repelling foreign economic influence these states also increasingly gained political freedom of action. The closure of the branch offices in Novgorod (1494) and London (1598) were clear signs of the shrinking of Hanseatic power.

The internal political structures of the Hanseatic towns were shaken by social and political conflict between the middle and lesser bourgeoisie on the one hand and the self-centered and corrupt ruling council families on the other. The former struggled to gain rights to participate in government. The first wave of quarrels was often interwoven with the radical religious changes in the third and fourth decades of the sixteenth century. The second wave at the beginning of the seventeenth century created in a substantial number of towns political structures, such as institutions for citizens to be represented, which lasted for centuries.[4]

The start of the Thirty Years' War, in which the rulers fighting for supremacy in Europe attempted to make good through war their claim to power—often combined with religious reasons—allowed the battle for supremacy of the Baltic, the *Dominium maris Baltici*, to break out again. The Hanseatic League was already too weak to take an active part in this war. For the majority of the towns in the League there remained no other option to them but to attach themselves to a powerful partner, whether their territorial overlord or some foreign power. And it was these very helpers who took from the town the last trace of their former independence.

The ducal house of Pomerania produced only a very few descendants who rose above the mediocrity of the hunting, feasting, and revelling country squires of the time. But even the most significant of these, Bogislaw X (d. 1523), did not succeed in freeing himself from the shackles of estate supervision, despite all his attempts to consolidate central power. The pitiful financial situation of his successors, caused by uneconomic management of the princely estate, the *Domanium*, by the falling real value of their fixed revenue, mostly a property tax,[5] and by the expenses of a sophisticated and lavish court forced them again and again to buy the agreement of the Estates to special financial allowances by offering concessions and abandoning planned reforms. Within the Estates the self-interest of individual groups, especially the economic conflict between the towns and the nobility, prevented the effectiveness of this body as a factor for developing the state or the economy. They were only united in their endeavors to prevent the growth of ducal power. Each stood up for his own privileges, defended himself doggedly against all competitors and rejected innovations.[6]

Despite this resistance the dukes succeeded in extending their influence in this period. The confiscation of the rural monasteries and their lands (1534) in the course of the introduction of Lutheranism into the duchy strengthened ducal power. Through skilful political manoeuvers in moments of weakness of the Pomeranian Hanseatic towns[7]—especially during the conflicts among the towns at the beginning of the seventeenth century—the dukes were able to reduce further the independence of these towns and to weaken their ties with the Hanseatic League.

There was no change in the unsatisfactory and stagnating conditions which had prevailed in the previous century when, on divisionn of the inheritance in 1532, the West Pomeranian[8] area became largely independent. Not until 1625 did an admittedly sickly and weak ruler again unite all parts of the duchy. He died in 1637 as the last of his line. His policies—neutralist, hesitant and hampered by the estates—could not prevent his duchy being occupied by Wallenstein's troops in autumn 1627 under the pretence of a contractual agreement. From then on Pomerania, which earlier had played a mostly insignificant role in politics, was just a toy of the wrangling powers.

Pomerania was also a backward country in economic terms. Production and trading methods had hardly changed in centuries. The attempt of the dukes to create a center for textile manufacturing by founding the town of Franzburg near the former monastery of Neuencamp in 1587 failed as a result of the unfavourable preconditions of the enterprise. Other foresighted plans for the development of the economy remained only partly executed, or not at all.

The population of the land, both peasants and nobles, fought the trade monopoly of the towns and tried to avoid it where they could. The hawking trade of the Scots and so-called pedlar-grocers increased, despite all protests of the towns.[9] The easiest monopoly of the towns for the landed gentry to avoid was in the brewing of beer, as they owned brewing rights. They were also able to avoid the *Stapelrecht* of the towns by selling grain directly to mostly West European buyers.[10] Here the dukes as large landowners were ahead of the landed gentry offering tempting examples, and also granting trading licences to rural artisans. Thus, despite all the backward traits in the 125 years treated here, the economy took on more extensive dimensions and began to overcome its purely local character.[11]

The condition of the peasants at least had deteriorated as a result of the secularization of the ecclesiastical possessions since the new landlords made them work more than the old ones. However various peasant regulations and other contemporary sources point to a degree of prosperity.[12] This changed when, at the end of the century the Duke of Wolgast began to expropriate peasants and to have the land of their farms managed as *Ackerwerke* (estates). Other landowners, including the towns, followed this example. On the one hand, the falling real value of their ground rent, fixed and paid in cash, and on the other the rising price of grain, forced them to take into their own hands both agricultural production and sale.

A further deterioration in the condition of the peasants came after 1611 when an attempt was made to lease or mortgage numerous ducal estates to private individuals, who could demand unlimited work from peasants owing services. The squandering in the *Domanium* went so far that Duke Philipp Julius of Wolgast, fond of travelling, wasteful and therefore in constant financial difficulties, attempted in 1623 to mortgage the whole island of Rügen to Denmark.[13]

In the towns there were several obstacles to a further development of the economy. From the middle of the sixteenth century the herring with increasing frequency had failed to appear off the southern Swedish coast[14] and had deprived the towns in the Wendish area of a significant source of income. Goods listed as still being exported were beer, grain, wax, and honey,[15] although the last two cannot have played an important role because of their small quantity. The decline of earlier markets and of trading links could not even be made good by expanding the Spanish trade during the Spanish-Dutch conflict (1566–1609)[16], since, although such journeys promised great profit, they involved an equally great risk.

Under these conditions the artisans, who were becoming more and more limited to local and rural markets, also suffered indirectly. Likewise, the work for the native fleet also suffered. The increasing pressure for competition did not led the artisans in the direction of manufacturing production but to greater regimentation and ossification to prevent free competition. Guildsmen like merchants were still attached to such old views that they saw their salvation only in the traditional ways of trading and producing goods in guilds and towns.[17] The guilds occasionally gave vent to their ill-feeling by active participation in struggles against the town councils. By inviting the princes into the town at the beginning of the seventeenth century as supposed helpers, they improved the lot of the princes, but not of themselves.[18]

The European famine crisis of 1571 evidently did not make itself felt strongly in Pomerania.[19] It is not clear whether it was more the losses caused by the northern Seven Years War which brought about the collapse of the leading Pomeranian business house of Loitze in Stettin (1572)[20], or the results of the famine or the bankruptcy of a whole range of important Dutch firms.[21] The bankruptcy of the house of Loitze resulted in a whole chain of economic collapses, among others among in the nobility of the area of Stettin. The business links of the firm with West Pomerania were evidently fewer.

As our investigations will show, the 1570s and 1580s were a period of relative stability,[22] followed, admittedly, in the second half of the 1590s by a sharp price increase. How much of an effect the crisis of the "Coin Cutters" (*Kipper und Wipper*) (1621–23) had on West Pomerania, and how this crisis affected the cost-of-living index will first be examined with reference to the original material used here. In any case, the Pomeranian mints in the service of rulers and towns, did not abstain from producing low-quality coins. The land was also inundated from outside, from all quarters, with such coinage.[23] However, the *"Heck"* coins did not become so widespread in Pomerania as in other parts of Germany.

The statistical material which forms the basis of the following explanations is taken from the author's collection *Wages and Prices in West Pomerania 1500–1627 (Löhne und Preise in Vorpommern 1500–1627)* the development, primary sources, extent, and limits of which has already been reported elsewhere.[24] Here only a few series of wages or prices will be used, series which are statistically extensive enough and which in the case of the prices, concern the typical goods considered critical to the study of social history. It is in the nature of the sources that the original material comes predominantly from the towns. There are few sources for this period from rural areas.

By West Pomerania, as the area is still referred to today, we understand the former Duchy of Pomerania-Wolgast, that existed from 1532 to 1625. Its borders were roughly the Baltic coastline, the river Oder and a line running through Stettin (Szczecin) - Pasewalk - Altentreptow - Demmin - Damgarten.[25] This then is an attempt to cover at least a part of the area which is still *terra incognita* to investigations of wages and prices.[26] This gap is also conspicuous in the overall picture.[27]

Figures 1–10 show, unless otherwise indicated, the arithmetical mean (symbol $\bar{X}$) for every five or fifteen years in relation to the initial value of 100, which has mainly been obtained from the period 1500–1524. The values shown are unweighted, each coming from one five-year period or from three five-year periods. They are based on the coins and measures of the time. It is impossible to use bullion equivalents, because details about the weight and content of the Stralsund shilling are of little use.[28] These details would have no influence on the decisive issue, that of the relationship between income and prices, because for some time both wages and prices were paid in the same currency. Naturally it is less possible to compare the tables of pure wages and prices with those of other authors, who use the precious metal equivalent.

In the interest of statistical reliability only those details from the original material have been used which compleely rule out any mistakes or misinterpretations.[29] This has resulted in the exclusion of a high percentage of the details from the original material.[30]

If two or more values are missing between two available values, then the graph is interrupted, but if only one is missing, it is continued.

The sources allow the representation only of those wages which were paid directly by the employer to the employee. These are mainly trained building workers and day laborers, who did not sell their labor to a master craftsman but to a client. In the case of skilled manual workers who sold the product of their work or who, as journeymen, delivered it to their master, it cannot be established how much of the wage is hidden in the final price of the product. On top of everything it is not possible to ascertain how great a percentage if any of the wages came from the master, the journeyman, or the apprentice. Here, then, only the prices of goods from independent master craftsmen would be usable. But it cannot be established with certainty who the independent masters were.

Even if the wages of a journeyman or an apprentice are known here and there from the area of small-scale production, they are still not usable since the unknown items of board and lodging in his master's house would have to be added to the total. Available prices for the work carried out by the repair craftsman in the service sector are also only usable if they can be unambiguously classified according to specific individuals and to production time. Wages, and their function as a price fixing factor, are therefore only exactly ascertainable in a few areas.

The seasonal fluctuations in wages cannot be determined with statistical accuracy, since the sources give no dates but merely he financial year—generally from Michaelmas to Michaelmas. For this reason our graphs lump together summer and winter wages indiscriminately. According to the assessments of the author, the often lower winter wages of trained building workers, as well as their shorter working hours, rest on the fact that the wage earner was unable to carry out adequate work on the building site because of the weather, and instead had to keep his head above water by taking general work which was therefore less well-paid.[31] Hence it could happen that a master bricklayer received a payment for clearing rubble in the winter which was the same as the summer wage of his odd-job-man. Conversely, the journeyman who carried out the work of a master (*"Meisterknecht"*, "master labourer",[32] or among the builders *"Kellenknecht"*, "trowel labourer") was paid like a master.[33] Dangerous work brought in supplements of up to 50 percent.

When calculating the yearly wages of trained building workers, the indisputable fact that they were sometimes without work, depending on the weather in winter, cannot be dealt with hee. Full employment is therefore assumed, but one must also assume a certain reduction in income during the winter.[34]

Comparisons with those with steady incomes—servants in the towns, parsons, sextons, and similar employees—have not been made, since their income is rarely exactly ascertainable, and hence provides no statistically acceptable basis for comparison.[35]

Among the skilled building workers the bricklayers were the most important, the " 'basic wager earners' of historical wage statistics."[36] The development of their wages shows a remarkable differentiation up to 1627 (Figure 1). The highest rate of increase is shown in the wages of the journeymen (428%), and the lowest in those of the masters (341%). The handymen fell in between with 470%. It is surprising that, relatively, the wages of the masters increased the least. There is not sufficient original material to examine this issue in every other trade. In the case of carpenters (Figure 2) ther was a similar relationship between the wages of masters and those of journeymen as in the case of the bricklayers.

The increase in wages among unskilled workers was, at any rate, not without exception smaller than that of the skilled workers: the increase varied from 356% for chaff cutters to 457% for male day labourers (Figure 3). In four unskilled trades the average increase for the years 1600/27, compared with 1520/24, is 382%; for three master trades (builder, carpenter, and roofer) it is 346%. There is therefore no way in which it can be claimed that the wage increase for unskilled workers was less than it was for skilled workers[37] (see also Figure 10).

The significance of this phenomenon is probably to be found in the fact that the master was a house-owner and normally also an arable farmer. In order to become a master he had to prove his own household management which at that time was generally identical with owning one's own house. In most of the towns of West Pomerania, however,a certain area of arable land belonged to each holding, which was part of the public parish land of the town.[38] As a farmer, albeit on a small scale, the master was better safeguarded against increases in the prices of food grains than was the unlanded and therefore more mobile journeymen or unskilled worker. The employer had to make good at least in part the increase in price of the basic foodstuff by raising the wages of these workers, if he was unwilling to run the risk of their moving away. The danger of migration was especially acute in times of war and among the unmarried, but it was less so in the case of the masters. Yet, since the grain price increases were considerably greater than the wage increases for unskilled workers, they were hit much harder by the rise in prices than were the masters.[39]

A comprehensive graph of the wages of eight different building workers (Figure 8) reveals an increase in wages for the period 1615/27 of 375% compared with 1520/24.[40]

Findings in the original material about the payment of working women are few. The wages of the female day workers started at only a little, or not at all, less than the men. The increase up to the end of the sixteenth century is the same. First the wages of the men rose significantly, and those of the women to a lesser degree, so that in the 1620s there existed a cnsiderable difference: X̄ for women in the years 1615/27 was 332%, but for men 450%. It follows from other scattered information on the work of unskilled female workes that they generally received the same wage for the same work as the unskilled men.[41] In agriculture this principle seems to have been usual to a large extent.[42]

The key position in the food economy before the production of potatoes was occupied by grains. Wheat was used to an insignificant extent; the bread of the typical consumer in Northern Germany was rye bread.[43] The price of rye in West Pomerania shows a steady upward movement, and from about 1610 it soars steeply. In Stralsund this tendency does not stop after the period of the coin cutters but continues to increase, whereas the general development in the coastal areas of the North and Baltic Seas, and in the West Pomeranian hinterland shows a clear decrease in the price of rye from 1624 onwards.[44] Such a high rate of increase for this period like that in Stralsund has not yet been found for any other area of Germany.[45] As the prices in the agricultural hinterland did not participate in this increase, the cause cannot be put down to a crop failure but only to increased export.[46]

In remarkable contrast to the development of the price of rye is that of rye flour. One would suppose that both would run parallel to each other. But Figure 4 shows, for instance, during the famine of 1545/46 a peak for flour but not for grain. And while the price for grain rose astronomically towards the end of the period under investigation (1620/27: 1769%) the price of rye flour stayed at 550%. One possible explanation would be this: in the case of the prices for rye it is possible that in part it was Stralsund prices that forced the graph upwards.[47] Bread grain for milling in local mills was from time to time given away at a reduced price from the stores of the communal administration[48] and that act may perhaps have been enough to keep the price increase of flour moderate. But this interpretation is not certain.

The price of the final product—bread—cannot be given, as the variations in the price of bread grain were offset not by changes in price, but through changes in the weight of the bread.[49] These are, however, not known.

Except for the differences mentioned, the graph for the price of rye shows an increase which corresponds to the trend of the general development in Northern Europe.[50] Over the short term occasional differences are shown. Thus the European famine of 1570/71 does not stand out. The peak in the second half of the 1590s is detectable in other areas too.[51] The slump in prices shortly afterwards was general in Europe. The reason that the price of a product which was both so sought after and, as is shown by investigations of other towns[52], sensitive to general economic conditions, did not in West Pomerania closely follow the pattern in neighboring districts presumably lies in the fact that West Pomerania was somewhat out of the way, not deeply involved in international commerce and so not often affected by short-term fluctuations elsewhee.

The other variations of grain did not undergo as dramatic a price development. The fact that barley rose sharply (to 80% in 1620/26) is explicable as it was the basic ingredient of beer, at that time one of the few exports of this area. Moreover, light beer was important as a popular drink. Here too the graph for the price of barley (1620/27: 808%) differs clearly from its derivative barley groats (638%). Oats, at 598%, rose less. Wheat played a subsidiary role and is not indicated on the graph for the periods 1500/25 and 1620/30 because of the lack of data.[53]

The increase in the price of beer is only moderate throughout the sixteenth century and does not being to accelerate until about 1620. It cannot be forgotten that beer was one of the few products the price of which was officially regulated by the authorities (beer tax). The maintenance of the price was enforced. Therefore, since these are not real market prices, the increase (1620/27: 516%) is not shown.

In the sector of the supply of protein, fish naturally played an important part of this coastal area. The price of salted herring rose from what had until then been the main fishing grounds off the south Swedish coast[54], which began in the 1550s, is not significant. The price increase also remains moderate, although it is more than the German average.[55] The increases in the case of green (fresh) herring and the Norwegian dried, salted cod are conspicuous. The large price increase for fresh herring, occurring fairly regularly every twenty-five years, suggests a certain periodicity to their disappearance from the Pomeranian coast. Astonishingly, Norwegian dried fish hardly rose at all in price (1620/27: 139%). On the whole, the price increases for fish came nowhere near those for grain.

Meat, a further component of the supply of protein, shows a similar development. Here too the increases remain moderate, at the most 523% in the case of lamb, 506% for geese.[56] The price of chicken even fell towards the end of the period. Meat prices had already proved more stable than those for grain in the price decrease of the late Middle Ages.[57] There are no records available for beans. The increase for another source of protein, peas, was however 641%, which was more than for meat. Perhaps this was caused by great demand because peas, alongside beans, were otherwise the cheapest source of protein.

In the case of fats too, butter and bacon fat were limited in their increase, at the most 759% in the case of butter and 480% for bacon fat.[58] In all, it can be said that agricultural vegetable products rose considerably more in price than animal products. Here West Pomerania is within the general trend of Europe.[59]

Foodstuffs which were imported over a long distance, exotic groceries and spices, occupy a special position. They show a remarkably small price increase. The price of saffron also rose significantly only during the last decade of the period under examination, from 184% up to that time and then rose to 460%. Up to this point the price graph is the same as the general European development.[60] Salt, which played an important part both as foodstuff and as preservative, is treated below with manufacturing production.

Forest and garden produce, with a higher wage component, yield, with one exception, a relatively moderate pice increase of between 550% and 700%. In contrast, natural produce show very different price developments. While birch greenery and straw[61] rose sharply, other products, such as loam, wax and onions stayed within the region of 300% to 500%. It is difficult to find a reason for these differences.

As an example of manufactured products with a high wage component, the price graphs of shoes are given. Because these concern almost without exception deliveries to town servants and hospital inmates[62], one can be fairly sure that the quality of the shoes was, at the most, mediocre. The graphs show throughout a medium increase between 390% and 670%. Other goods with a similar production pattern behaved in various ways. While writing paper showed a conspicuously small increase (1620–27: 229%), fabric (800%)[63] and canvas (510%) rose considerably more. The price of candles rose 490%.

Here mention can be made of salt. Separating the different types of salt (Lüneburg, Kolberg, Scottish etc.) is not always possible.[64] The primary sources refer to only two clear groups: salt without any further description and Bay salt (from the French Atlantic coast). Here it is shown that Bay salt (368%) rose less than salt generally (479%). Bay salt, as an import article shows a graph that is more similar to the Middle European phenomenon: a rise—with delay in comparison to other areas—in the second half of the 1570s, an ensuing price drop, in the second half of the 1590s a new peak, then a strong fall until 1610, and finally a further rise.

The prices for bricks and tiles are significant for the building trade and along with this, indirectly, for buildings and rents. They rise moderately: bricks to 440%, tiles to 368%, and lime to 380% (all figures for 1620/27).

Building rents are hard to present exactly. First, there are not enough details from the same type of building, and second, the expression *Haus* (house), *Bude* (hut, room) and *Keller* (cellar) are used all too arbitrarily. They are even, in all probability, only technical taxation terms which say little about the actual quality of the building.[65] We can only say from the sources that the rent increase for so-called cellars was about 300%, for *Buden* (eaveshouses) about 400% and for gabled houses about 300%. Because these buildings were often owned by the Church and were rented cheaply to widows of Church employees, school teaches, and others, no sociological conclusions can be drawn from these price increases.

The West Pomeranian towns were still to a large extent involved with the agriculture of their immediate surroundings.[66] The small towns, such as Jarmen, Altentreptow, Damgarten, or Gützkow, were purely towns whose citizens farmed smallholdings.[67] Therefore the cost of ground rent played a considerable role in fixing prices as a price fixing factor. The increase in lease prices took place gradually, since the lease sums were each fixed by contract for several years. Therefore they are only to be valed as real market prices in the year in which the agreement was drawn up, and after that as stipulated prices. The moderate increase, in one case 423% from 1545/49 to 1610/20, in another about 380% from 1500/19 to 1615/24, concerns only those areas of land which belonged to an institution (towns and their institutions, churches). Private landowners were, according to our experience, less moderate, but we have no figures. This increase is on the one hand a sign of the growing burdens on the leaseholders, and on the other of the growing profits from leasing land. A comparison between the price graphs of agricultural vegetable production and the lease prices shows that the income from the lands rose only slightly more than the income from the leases, viz. the grain price 4 ¼–fold from 1550 to 1620, and the leases for instance of St. Mary's Church in Stralsund a good three-fold. The difference between the two figures should be identical with the profit of the middlemen, since grain prices are usually to be understood as final consumer prices. If one takes the local rye price in Stralsund, the lease increase (305%) coincides almost exactly with the rye price increase (308%).

Wage and price figures are of value for social history only when the relationship between the two is shown. One presentation, which shows the "rye wage" according to the older Schmoller school (Figure 8), shows that the reduction in buying power of builders' wages does not begin with the rapid price increases from 1615 on. The decrease had started as early as the second third of the fifteenth century.[68] The reduction in purchasing power in the following decades was then less. Even during the time of the worst price increase, from 1615 on, the real value is not less than it had been in the second half of the 1590s.[69] The enormous price increase had therefore been to some extent cushioned by wage increases (cf. also the food graphs in Figures 9 and 10).

Furthermore, the "rye wage" shows that the clear wage difference between the three groups in the bricklaying trade that had prevailed at the beginning of the sixteenth century had decreased. The wages of masters, journeymen, and handymen were related ($\bar{X}$ 1500/19) roughly in the ratio 4 : 3 : 1.8, but in 1620/27 the relationship was about 4 : 3.6 : 2.4. There is a similar development in the case of carpenters. The purchasing power of builders' wages expressed in rye had decreased in this time to an average of 21.7%.

The situation was not very different in the building trades in general. The average worker in the trades shown in Figure 8 was able to buy in 1615/30 only 24% of the rye which he would have been able to buy in 1500/19. Here too is the tendency of rye flour to deviate from rye shows up: the purchasing power of wages for rye flour only fell to 64%.

The same calculation for larger groups of products is shown in Figures 9 and 10. It follows that the disappearance of purchasing power was at its most marked in manufactured goods with a small wage component, namely at 40%. The decrease was smallest in the case of manufactured products with a high wage component, at about 84%. Here the role of those wages, which had risen relatively, in fixing prices shows up clearly. The graph for the real value of these products is actually above 100% for the period from about 1570 to 1610. Food-stuffs, at about 68%, move between the two mentioned extremes. One should not overlook the fact that the graph for this group of products falls sharply in the first half of the 16th century,[70] almost returns to 100% in 1570/80, in 1600/15 falls again to its value in 1540/55, and towards the end of the period under investigation shows a slight recovery.[71] The purchasing power of the wages of unskilled workers behaves in the same way (Figure 10), but these were somewhat better off than the building handymen.

Therefore, the greatest decrease in purchasing power was for those goods which did not play a decisive role in everyday life. But at the same time changes in consumptuous habits have been deliberately not taken into account.[72]

In conclusion we can summarize from the results collected that the changes in material conditions of the urban working population can be described as follows:

1. The decline in the purchasing power of wages in the area of foodstuffs began as early as the second third of the sixteenth century and continued from then on, moderately but steadily. The gap between prices and wages[73] therefore gradually became increasingly wide. The masters were less affected by this than were the dependent or unskilled workers, since the masters usually had a farm (albeit sometimes very small) in addition to their job, and therefore profited from the price increase for farm products or, could, being partly self-sufficient, be cushioned against the effects of this.[74]

2. The inflationary development of prices from about 1615 on was absorbed only partially by intensified wage increases. The sweeping statement that the difference between wage and price increases had been "evened out in the first decades of the 17th century"[75] cannot be endorsed. Only in the area of foodstuffs was there a slight improvement in the second and third decades. However, even in the case of food, there can be no talk of a recovery of the purchasing power of wages as had existed at the beginning of the sixteenth century and again in the 1570s and 1580s.

3. There is evidence of the tendency for wages of journeymen but more especially of unskilled workers to rise more than those of masters. This was caused by the lesser mobility of the masters.

4. The price of grain rose more than prices of all other products, except straw.

5. The price of grain rose more than prices of their derivatives, flour, groats, and malt.

6. The price of food rose roughly at the same price as the prices of manufactured goods. But the price of those manufactured goods with a high wage component increased relatively little, despite higher wages.

Thus West Pomerania's development lay within the general European development[76], although it differed in occasional details. This proves on the one hand how important it is to conduct quantitative investigations in those areas as yet not examined (Brandenburg, Mecklenburg, etc.). On the other hand, it shows that results from wage and price investigations in inidividual rural or economic areas cannot simply be extrapolated to other regions or the economy in general.[77]

The decline in purchasing power in the period of the inflationary development from 1615 on was not more acute than the population had already been experiencing since the second third of the previous century. This explains not only the incredible absence of hunger revolts, despite the crisis and the still seething political conflicts of the time, but also the fact that even complaints about the impoverishment of the masses were expressed only rarely and then not as matters of priority.[78] Typically enough, the loudest complaint about the high prices and the misery "of the dear poor" came from the ducal court.[79] This was understandable, since those receiving fixed incomes—in this case from taxes, customs, duty, rent and the like—were relatively those most affected by the currency depreciation.

## NOTES

The author is indebted to Professor Dr. Diedrich Saalfeld of Göttingen for his critical and friendly comments, and sincere thanks go to him, as well as to Gareth Evans of Greifswald for the translation of the manuscript.
Published through the courtesy of the editors of the *Jahrbuch für Regionalgeschichte, Leipzig* (GDR).

1. Johannes Schildhauer, Konrad Fritze and Walter Stark, *Die Hanse,* 2nd edition, Berlin 1975, p. 253. This title has been used in various ways to provide an overall view. Likewise Philippe Dollinger, *La Hanse* (Paris 1964) ed. 3. For general tendencies of the Hanseatic trade *v* Karl-Friedrich Olechnowitz, *Handel und Schiffahrt der späten Hanse* (Weimar 1965), especially pp. 182–183, and Herbert Langer, *Stralsund 1600–1630* (Weimar 1970), Ch. 2 and 3. pp. 126–160.

2. Rudolf Biederstedt, *Untersuchungen zur Entstehungsgeschichte der ersten ständigen Bürgerparlamente in Greifswald und anderen vorpommerschen Städten 1600–1625* (Greifswald 1967), I, p. 25 (MS. Stadtarchiv Greifswald).

3. Schildhauer et al., loc. cit., (v n. 1), pp. 232, 239.

4. cf. Biederstedt, *Bürgerparlamente* (v n. 2).

5. Martin Spahn, *Verfassungs- und Wirtschaftsgeschichte des Herzogtums Pommern von 1478 bis 1625* (Leipzig 1896), p. 178.

6. cf. Martin Wehrmann, *Geschichte von Pommern*, 2nd ed. (Gotha 1919–1921), II, p. 56.

7. After all thirteen towns in the whole duchy belonged to the Hanseatic League.

8. The term West Pomeranian corresponds here to the German *Vorpommern*, the part of Pomerania west of the Oder, and should not be confused with the Polish use of the term.

9. Cf. Ilse von Wechmar and Rudolf Biederstedt, "Die schottische Einwanderung in Vorpommern in 16. und frühen 17. Jahrhundert." In: *Greifswald-Stalsunder Jahrbuch* (henceforth *GSJ*), V, (Rostock, 1965), pp. 7–28. Cf. also Spahn, loc. cit., (v n. 5), p. 164

10. For methods used v Langer loc. cit., (v n. 1), p. 31, and Biederstedt, *Bürgerparlamente* (v n. 2), p. 23 and n. 40.

11. Spahn, loc. cit., (v n. 5), p. 174.

12. The financial situation of the peasants was good as long as they sold their agricultural produce directly to the purchaser in the town without landowners acting as middlemen. That way peasants could enjoy a share of the agrarian prosperity. Langer, loc. cit., (v n. 1), p. 31.

13. Wehrman, loc. cit., (v n. 6), p. 117.

14. Ibid., p. 97. Wehrmann dates the absence of herring "towards the end of the century", Spahn, loc. cit., (v n. 5), p. 172, as the middle of the century.

15. Langer, loc. cit., (v n. 1), pp. 130, 264. Wehrmann, loc. cit., (v n. 6), p. 9.

16. cf. Schildhauer et. al., loc. cit., (v n. 1), p. 244.

17. Ibid., p. 258. Spahn, loc. cit., (v n. 5), pp. 169, 171.

18. 1604 in Greifswald, 1612–16 in Stralsund.

19. cf. Figures 4 and 8.

20. cf. Martin Wehrmann, *Geschichte der Stadt Stettin* (Stettin 1911), pp. 215–17.

21. Wilhelm Abel, *Massenarmut und Hungerkrisen im vorindustriellen Europa* (Hamburg/Berlin, 1974), p. 80.

22. It can be judged to be a sign of prosperity that in 1583 in the small town of Greifswald there were eleven working goldsmiths. In 1600 there were only eight. Stadtarchiv Greifswald, Rep- 14 F Goldschmiede No. 2, fol. 2–3. Also Fritz Adler, "Die Greifswalder Goldschmiede und ihr Amt." In: *Pommersche Jahrbücher*, 34, Greifswald, 1940, p. 80. Similarly in Wismar, cf. Friedrich Techen, *Geschichte der Seestadt Wismar* (Wismar, 1929), pp. 150, 159.

23. Although the Pomeranian dukes boasted that they allowed no poor-quality coinage to be minted (Johann Carl Dähnert, *Sammlung . . . Pommerscher und Rügischer Landesurkunden*, III, Stralsund 1769, p. 664) and although Spahn, loc. cit. (v n. 5) p. 166, is in agreement, this is not in fact true. On many occasions from 1612 onwards they had been warned by the Saxon Diet to cease the minting of low-quality coins. Cf. Bernd Kluge, *Der Münzfund von Krien. Zur Münz- und Geldgeschichte Pommerns und des Sechslings im 16. und frühen 17. Jahrhundert*. Ph.D. Thesis. Berlin 1982, p. 109.

24. Rudolf Biederstdt, "Löhne und Preise in Vorpommern 1500–1627", In: *GSJ* XII, Weimar 1979, S 13–17.

25. In twenty years of collecting material, no data has been found from Pasewalk.

26. Cf. Biederstedt, "Löhne" (*v* n. 24), p. 14 and n. 4. Only Rostock has been (unsatisfactorily) covered, cf. Ursula Hauschild, *Studien zu Löhnen und Preisen in Rostock im Spätmittelalter,* Köln/Graz 1973 (Quellen und Darstellungen zur hansischen Geschichte, N.F. Vol. XIX).

27. E.g., in Abel, loc. cit. (*v* Ref. 21) and in the *Handbuch der deutschen Wirtschafts- und Sozialgeschichte,* ed. Hermann Aubin and Wolfgang Zorn, I, Stuttgart 1971.

28. Neither the numismatic collection of the state museums in Berlin nor the Cultural History Museum in Stralsund were able to give exact dates about the equivalent precious metal prices of the Stralsund shilling. But such a calculation of the equivalent would be of little use to the matter here. Since Stralsund did not adhere to the decisions of the Diet of Saxony, but instead continued to mint coins at full value (cf. Kluge, loc. cit. (*v* n. 23) pp. 109; 121–122), the older, better shillings continued to circulate in the land, so a value cannot be established for the equivalent precious metal price of the current coinage which, moreover, did not consist only of shillings.

29. Included here are all cases where a suspicion still remains that, apart from the wages, alone additional payments were made (free meals, tips, tax reductions, etc.) Careful attention should also be paid to the fact that the wages were quoted or calculated for one person. Cf. on the other hand E. Schollier, *Loonarbeid en honger. De Levensstandaard in de XVI eeuw te Antwerpen,* Antwerpen 1960, p. 65, who deals with the data from his source "Jan en Peter en noog meer andere" simply as applying to three persons. His transference of the cost of living of the eighteenth century into the sixteenth also seems unreliable (Ibid., p. 158 ff.)

30. Concerning the difficulty of obtaining exact figures, cf. F.P. Braudel and F. Spooner, "Prices in Europe from 1450 to 1750." In: *The Cambridge Economic History of Europe,* IV, Cambridge 1967, p. 426, and Hauschild (*v* n. 26), pp. 3 and 22 n. 98.

31. Cf. Biederstedt, "Löhne", (*v* n. 24), p. 16.

32. *v* also Eberhard Schmieder, *Geschichte des Arbeitsrechts im deutschen Mittelalter,* I, (Leipzig 1939), pp. 127–128.

33. Ibid., p. 128.

34. Biederstedt, "Löhne" (*v* n. 24), p. 16.

35. These "salaries" are comprised of a multitude of often unascertainable cash payments, of unascertainable work in kind (payment in kind, service, tax remission, free lodgings, etc.) and finally of totally unascertainable incomes from official duties (fees). For difficulties even with simple wages see Schmieder loc. cit. (*v* n. 32), pp. 36–38.

36. Abel, loc. cit. (*v* n. 21), p. 14.

37. It was similar in other areas of Germany. Cf. George Philippi, "Preise, Löhne und Produktivität in Deutschland von 1500 his zur Gegenwart." In: *Konjunkturpolitik,* XII (Berlin 1966), p. 323 and Pictures 19 and 20. Similar is Dietrich Saalfeld, "Die Wandlungen der Lohn- und Preisstruktur während des 16. Jahrhunderts in Deutschland" In: *Beiträge zu Wirtschaftswachstum und Wirtschaftssstruktur im 16. und 19. Jh.,* ed. Wolfram Fischer, (Berlin 1971): Schriften des Vereins für Socialpolitik N.F. Vol. 63), p. 12 and Illustration 2.

38. Rudolf Biederstedt, "Häuserbuch der Alstadt Greifswald." In: *GSJ* 11, (Weimar 1977), p. 128. Before that: Carl Gesterding, *Beitrag zur Geschichte der Stadt Greifswald,*

*Greifswald 1827* p. 7, No. 4, n. 2. For various other North German towns see Friedrich Techen, "Bürgerrecht und Lottacker in Wismar." In: *Hansische Geschichtsblätter*, 24 (1918), p. 169. At the request of the Council of Wolgast for an equal division of the parish land of the town "as in the other towns," Duke Philipp Julius issued an edict on 29 September 1623 that each existing plot of land in the town was to be granted a certain quota of the parish land, corresponding to its tax category, as "a peculiar heritable pertinence to the end of time". STA Greifswald, Rep. 10, No. 1349. Absent in J.C. Dähnert, *Sammlung Pommerscher . . . Landesurkunden*, Stralsund, 1765–1802.

39. Cf. also Fig. 4.

40. The values are not equal because there are four series of masters' wages but only two each for journeymen and handymen. This selection is unavoidable because there is no sufficiently detailed series of wages available for the other members of the building trades.

41. The relationship does not change until the beginning of the seventeenth century.

42. Biederstedt, "Löhne", (*v* n. 24), p. 16, according to the record STA Greifswald, Rep. 5, Tit, 81, No. 2 (lfd. No. 365), Visitation of the Clempenow Domain in 1625, which contains numerous but not yet evaluated agricultural wage figures.

43. In the Duchy of Pomerania-Stettin the percentage of wheat cultivation is given as 0.9%, that of rye 37%, that of barley 24% and that of oats 33.8%, by Bogdan Wachowiak, *Gospodarcze polozenie chlopow w domenach Ksiestwa Szczecinskiego w XVI wieku*, Szczecin 1967, *p. 216, Tab. 13. Cf. also Hauschild loc. cit. (v* n. 26), p. 82.

44. Cf. Abel loc. cit. (*v.* n. 21), p. 148.

45. Ibid., p. 19, Figure 1, and p. 119, Figure 23. For further information, see Pierre Jeannin, "Preis-, Kosten- und Gewinnunterschiede im Handel mit Ostseegetreide (1550–1650)", "In: *Wirtschaftliche und soziale Strukturen im säkularen Wandel. Festschrift für Wilhelm Abel* Schriftenreihe für ländliche Sozialfragen, H. 70), Hannover 1974, p. 500; *v* also *Handbuch der deutschen Wirtschaftsund Sozialgeschichte (v* n. 27), p. 299.

46. For the hypothesis of price correspondence between two trading areas cf. Walter Achilles, "Getreidepreise und Getreidehandelsbeziehungen europäischer Räume im 16. und 17 Jahrhundert." In: *Zeitschrift für Agrargeschichte und Agrarsoziologie*, 7, Frankfurt am Main 1959, pp. 32–53.

47. A good example of the connection between export and price is given in Abel, loc. cit. (*v.* n. 21), p. 110, Fig. 18.

48. Cf. Rudolf Biederstedt, "Zum Problem der Löhne und Preise im Spätmittelalter." In: *GSJ* 9, (Weimar 1970), p. 75; 78 n. 20.

49. Cf. Tax- und Victualienordnung des Herzogs Philipp Julius von 1622, edited in Dähnert loc. cit. (*v* n. 23), pp. 758–9. Cf. also Ernst Kelter, *Geschichte der obrigkeitlichen Preisregulierung in der Zeit der mittelalterlichen Stadtwirtschaft* (Bonner staatswissenschaftliche Untersuchungen 21), Jena 1935, pp. 15–16; 50–51.

50. Cf. Abel loc cit. (*v* n. 21), p. 104 Fig. 17 and for similar relationships in Stockholm Eli F. Heckscher, *Sveriges economiska historia från Gustaf Wasa*, Stockholm 1935–36, Appendix Fig. 4.

51. Cf. note 44 and Abel loc. cit. (*v* n. 21), pp. 99–110 as well as *Handbuch* etc. (*v* n. 27), p. 406.

52. Cf. Abel loc cit. (*v* n. 21), p. 61 Fig. 8.

53. Cf. n. 43. Between 1525–29 and 1615–19 wheat rose by 410%, and rye by 391%.

54. Cf. here p. 42 and n. 14.
55. Saalfeld loc. cit. (*v* n. 37), p. 10, records for Germany as a whole an increase of only 200%. But here it should be borne in mind (*v* above p. 44) that he, like other authors, refers to "Germany", but that the whole of the northeast, with the exception of Danzig and Königsberg, is missing from this source material.
56. Here the conclusion of Philippi loc. cit. (*v* n. 37), pp. 308 and 321, Fig. 16, do not apply for West Pomerania.
57. Cf. Diedrich Saalfeld, "Die landwirtschaftlichen Faktoren in der Entwicklung der hoch- und spätmittelalterlichen Kulturlandschaft in Südniedersachsen", In: *Beiträge zur niedersächsischen Landesgeschichte. Zum 65. Geburtstag von Hans Patze*, ed. Dieter Brosius and Martin Last (Hildesheim 1984), p. 253.
58. In contrast to the graph for butter per pound, the graph for butter per *Verndeel* (there has been as yet no success in relating the two units of measure) shows a comparable but smaller increase. Possibly this can be traced to several unusually high values for $\bar{X}$ for 1520/24 which reflect deliveries to the ducal court.
59. Cf. also Abel loc. cit. (*v* n. 21), p. 21.
60. Ibid., p. 20 with Fig. 2 traces this small increase to the decrease in transfer costs and the price pressue from the newly emerging spice trade of Lisbon to Venice.
61. Birch greenery was regularly bought by the Church for Whitsun decorations.
62. But not all hospital inmates should be regarded as poor, as often happens. Even if the hospitals of coastal towns took in impoverished burghers or their widows or orphans into their "Poor Houses", most of the *Prövener (praebendarii)* had bought their way in by paying a considerable sum, sometimes singly, sometimes twice, in two payments (*Pröven*) and enjoyed lifelong free lodgings, heating, etc.
63. Fabrics have a sketchy price series. If it is permissible to imply the intensity of trade of a product from the number of records in the sources, then it cannot be established that the West Pomeranian market was flooded by English textile production (Spahn, loc. cit. (*v* n. 5), p. 173.
64. The local salt production (Greifswald, Richtenberg) had long before 1500 come to a standstill. Cf. Heinrich Berghaus, *Landlbuch von Neu-Vorpommern und der Insel Rügen*, I, Anklam/Berlin 1868, p. 158 and *Deutsches Städtebuch*, Stuttgart/Berln 1939, p. 221.
65. Cf. Biederstedt, "Häuserbuch" (*v* n. 38), p. 131, n. 10.
66. Cf. Konrad Fritze, *Bürger und Bauern zur Hansezeit* (Abhandll. z. Handels- u. Sozialgesch. XVI), Weimar, 1976.
67. Spahn loc. cit. (*v* n. 5), p. 168 says that this was common. Among the towns, except for Stralsund, there were however considerable differences, e.g. between Greifswald and Richtenberg.
68. Similar for Southern Germany in Christian Heimpell, *Die Entwicklung der Einnahmen und Ausgaben des Heiliggeisthospitals zu Biberach an der Riss von 1550–1630* (Quellen u. Forschungen z. Agrargeschichte XV), Stuttgart 1966, p. 76.
69. Maria Bogucka asserts the same facts, when she comments (Handel zagranyczny Gdanska w pierwszej polowie XVII wieku, Wroclaw/Warszawa/Kraków 1970, p. 136 with Fig. F and p. 107) that the grain prices, expressed in their silver equivalent, had not risen after 1595, but had instead fallen. But it seems that 1595, which was a year of extreme price increases, cannot be used alone for the basis of comparison.
70. A parallel case comes from Antwerp, described by Schollier loc. cit. (*v* n. 29), pp. 126–130, as the "period of insufficient wage adjustment."

71. Cf. Abel loc. cit. (v n. 21), p. 27 Fig. 4.

72. This area, which is based very unsatisfactorily on exact sources, (cf. Saalfeld loc. cit. (v n. 37), pp. 17; 20) should be examined as part of an investigation into the living standard. The material is available.

73. For the causes of the price revolution and the wage-price gap cf. Hans Mottek, *Wirtschaftsgeschichte Deutschlands,* I, Berlin 1964, pp. 334–335.

74. Of course, the average master had a larger family to feed.

75. Langer loc. cit. (v n. 1), p. 84 with reference to Hoszowski.

76. Cf. Abel loc. cit. (v n. 21), p. 21 and Philippi loc. cit. (v n. 37), p. 323

77. To give just one example, the increase in the price of herring on the coast of West Pomerania is double that given by Saalfeld for Germany. Saalfeld loc. cit. (v n. 37), p. 10.

78. v n. 48.

79. The Porters' Revolt in Stettin, 1616, was a revolt about beer prices, and not a hunger revolt. Wehrmann, *Stettin* (v n. 20), pp. 252–256. Techen loc. cit. (v n. 22), pp. 170–188 does not waste any words on the crisis years, despite broad coverage. Langer loc. cit. (v n. 1), pp. 69–70; 75ff.; 87 and especially 214 gives no complaints from the years of the highest price rises. Likewise Biederstedt, *Bürgerparlamente* (v n. 2) finds among all the townspeople's complaints none about the rapid increase in the cost of living (ibid., p. 24). Also, recently, Johannes Schildhauer and Herbert Langer give only complaints about the price of wood, in: *Geschichte der Stadt Stralsund,* Weimar 1984, Ch. 2 and 3, p. 142.

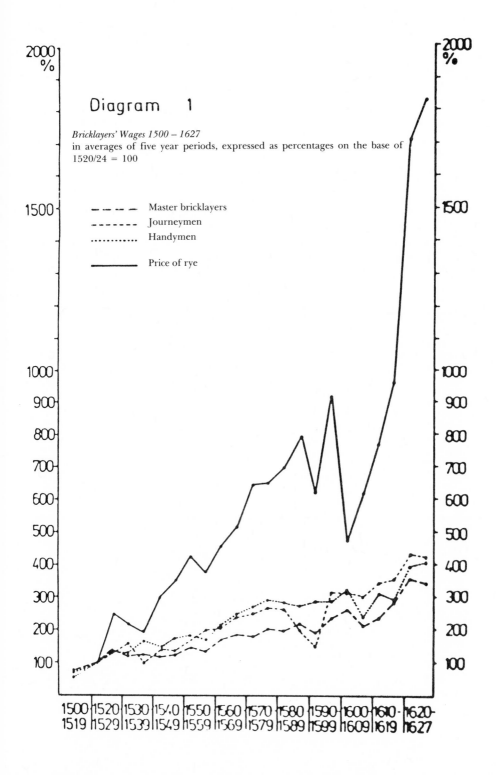

Diagram 1

*Bricklayers' Wages 1500 – 1627*
in averages of five year periods, expressed as percentages on the base of
1520/24 = 100

– – – – Master bricklayers
-------- Journeymen
.............. Handymen

——— Price of rye

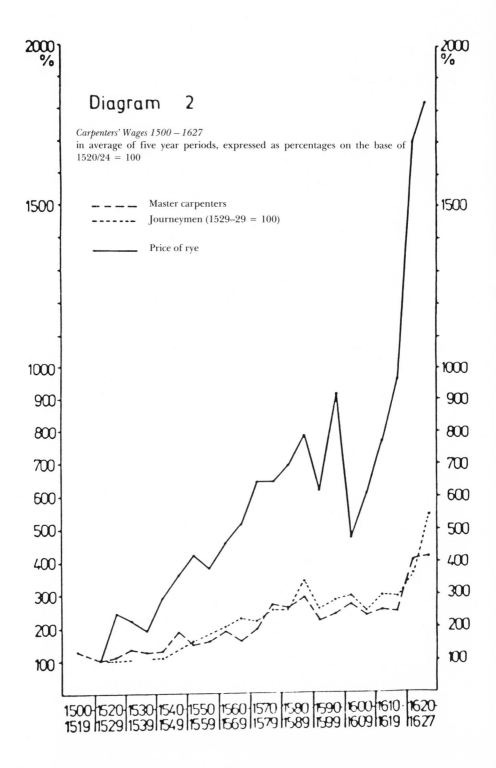

Diagram 2

*Carpenters' Wages 1500 – 1627*
in average of five year periods, expressed as percentages on the base of
1520/24 = 100

‒ ‒ ‒ ‒  Master carpenters
·········  Journeymen (1529–29 = 100)

————  Price of rye

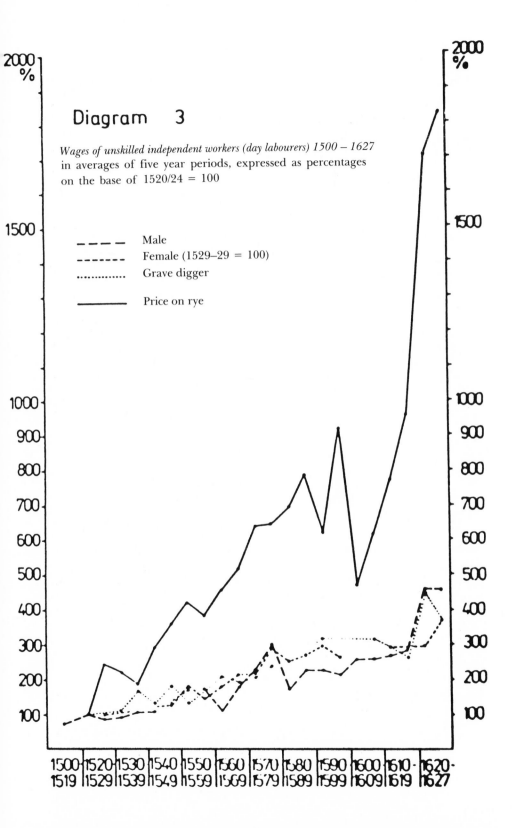

## Diagram 3

*Wages of unskilled independent workers (day labourers) 1500 – 1627* in averages of five year periods, expressed as percentages on the base of 1520/24 = 100

– – – – Male

------- Female (1529–29 = 100)

.............. Grave digger

——— Price on rye

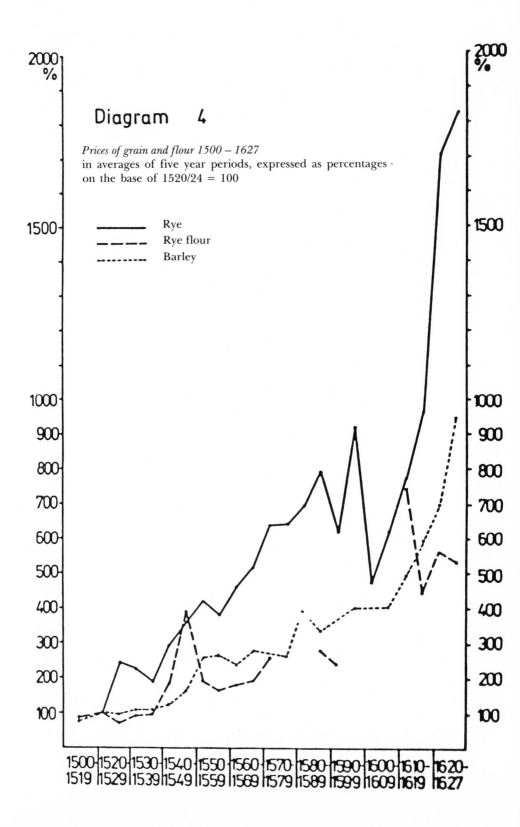

Diagram 4

*Prices of grain and flour 1500 – 1627*
in averages of five year periods, expressed as percentages
on the base of 1520/24 = 100

——————  Rye
– – – – –  Rye flour
··········  Barley

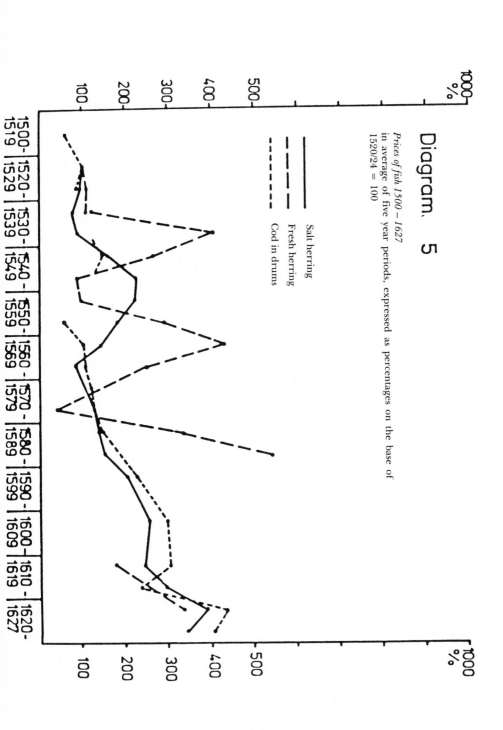

Diagram. 5

*Prices of fish 1500 – 1627*
in average of five year periods, expressed as percentages on the base of
1520/24 = 100

———— Salt herring
– – – – Fresh herring
- - - - - Cod in drums

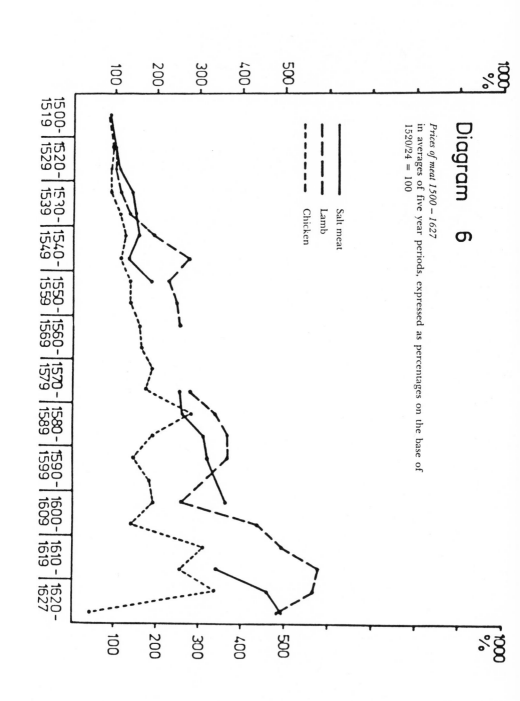

# Diagram 6

*Prices of meat 1500 – 1627*
in averages of five year periods, expressed as percentages on the base of
1520/24 = 100

Salt meat

Lamb

Chicken

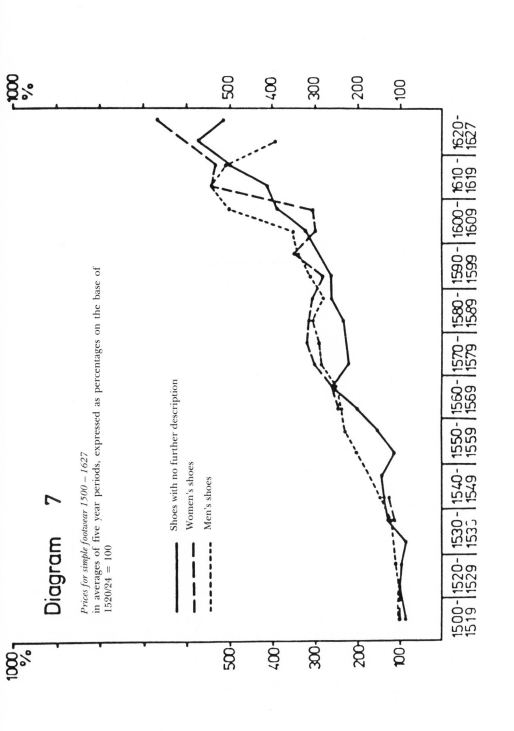

# Diagram 7

*Prices for simple footwear 1500 – 1627*
in averages of five year periods, expressed as percentages on the base of 1520/24 = 100

Shoes with no further description

Women's shoes

Men's shoes

| 1500- | 1520- | 1530- | 1540- | 1550- | 1560- | 1570- | 1580- | 1590- | 1600- | 1610- | 1620- |
| 1519 | 1529 | 1535 | 1549 | 1559 | 1569 | 1579 | 1589 | 1599 | 1609 | 1619 | 1627 |

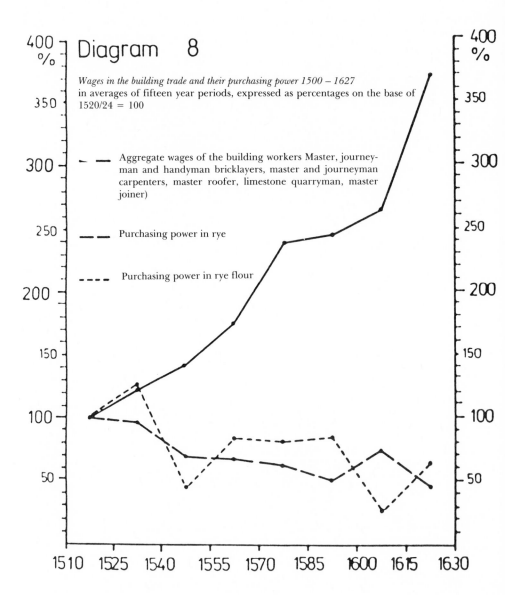

Diagram 8

*Wages in the building trade and their purchasing power 1500 – 1627*
in averages of fifteen year periods, expressed as percentages on the base of
1520/24 = 100

— — Aggregate wages of the building workers Master, journeyman and handyman bricklayers, master and journeyman
carpenters, master roofer, limestone quarryman, master
joiner)

— — Purchasing power in rye

- - - - Purchasing power in rye flour

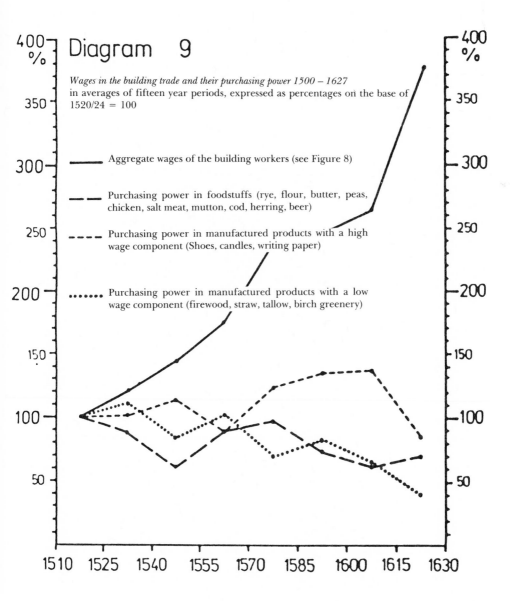

# Diagram 9

*Wages in the building trade and their purchasing power 1500 – 1627*
in averages of fifteen year periods, expressed as percentages on the base of
1520/24 = 100

———————— Aggregate wages of the building workers (see Figure 8)

— — — Purchasing power in foodstuffs (rye, flour, butter, peas, chicken, salt meat, mutton, cod, herring, beer)

- - - - Purchasing power in manufactured products with a high wage component (Shoes, candles, writing paper)

•••••• Purchasing power in manufactured products with a low wage component (firewood, straw, tallow, birch greenery)

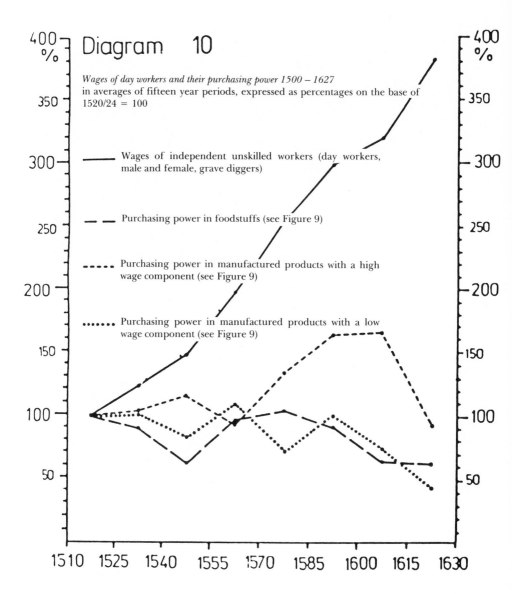

Diagram 10

*Wages of day workers and their purchasing power 1500 – 1627*
in averages of fifteen year periods, expressed as percentages on the base of
1520/24 = 100

———— Wages of independent unskilled workers (day workers, male and female, grave diggers)

— — Purchasing power in foodstuffs (see Figure 9)

----- Purchasing power in manufactured products with a high wage component (see Figure 9)

······ Purchasing power in manufactured products with a low wage component (see Figure 9)

# THE KNOWLEDGE OF GREEK IN WESTERN EUROPE IN THE FOURTEENTH CENTURY

Gunar Freibergs
Los Angeles Valley College

# THE KNOWLEDGE OF GREEK IN WESTERN EUROPE IN THE FOURTEENTH CENTURY

After the Byzantine grammarian Manuel Chrysoloras had come to Florence in 1397 as teacher of Greek, Leonardo Bruni lauded the event as the triumphant return of Greek letters to Italy after an absence of 700 years.[1] The historian Kenneth M. Setton, of course, has characterized this utterance as nothing more than a demonstration of "what little regard rhetoric has for the facts,"[2] for it is now well established that knowledge of classical Greek was present in Italy as well as in other parts of Western Europe for most of the Middle Ages.[3] So well, in fact, is this documented, that another Renaissance scholar, Robert Weiss, has not hesitated to label the supposed disappearance of the knowledge of Greek by the fourteenth century as simply a myth.[4] Yet myths do lead charmed lives, for not only did John Aldington Symonds, more than a century ago, lament "how utterly Greek had been lost"[5], but now the most recent edition of a Western Civilization text by Mortimer Chambers and associates quotes Bruni's sweeping eloquence verbatim as if it were the most credible of truths.[6] Happily, a similar text by Crane Brinton et al. correctly points out that formal instruction in Greek was revived in Florence some thirty-five years before the event celebrated by Bruni.[7] But then, alas, it proceeds to perpetuate a further error by proclaiming that Boccaccio actually "succeeded in learning Greek,"[8] even though almost a century earlier Georg Voigt had pointed out that he learned surprisingly little and could never read a Greek author.[9] To the myth about the knowledge of Greek having been lost is thus added another about how it was recovered. From these examples it appears that much of the factual material brought forth by painstaking research over the last one hundred years has not yet managed to filter its way down to the authors who compose today's texts. A review of the scholarly discoveries about the knowledge of Greek in Western Europe in the century preceding Chrysoloras' resumption of its systematic instruction is, therefore, in order.

The distorted views regarding the status of Hellenic studies in the *Trecento* appear to owe much of their origin and persistence to the fact that for a considerable time after the sweeping rhetoric of humanists such as Bruni had declared that the knowledge of Greek letters had been lost, scholars appear to have taken almost a delight in rallying to their support with convenient proof texts. Thus the phrase "Graecum est nec potest legi" became virtually a cliché, in spite of the fact that the Florentine jurist Accursius (d. 1260), who knew Greek, had uttered it only because it was politically inconvenient to be taken for a Byzantine sympathizer.[10] Similarly Roger Bacon has been quoted as complaining that in his time (1267) there were in all Europe not four men who knew Hebrew, Greek, or Arabic, when in fact he was referring to those who knew the grammar; in the next sentence Bacon goes on to explain that there were many who could speak these languages, but few who had mastered the grammar and could teach them.[11] Also the complaint of Humbert about Romans, that at the Second Council of Lyon (1274) the Roman curia had hardly anybody who could handle Greek correspondence, has been used to bolster the misconception, even though William of Moerbecke, the great translator of the works of Aristotle, was present at the occasion, and with him a Franciscan from Constantinople.[12] Even Petrarch is cited as lamenting that at around the year 1360 there were in Italy only nine men knowledgeable in Greek, when in fact the poet had only been talking about "friends of Homer" and had gone on to specify by name those who could teach Greek.[13] When these misinterpretations are exposed, the state of Hellenic studies in the Latin West takes on a much more positive appearance.

In several parts of Western Europe familiarity with Greek language, institutions and practices did survive into the Fourteenth Century. This was especially the case with the south of Italy, the *Magna Graecia* of antiquity, which had contributed much to the revival of knowledge during the Norman period and would continue to do so under its Angevin kings.[14]

The translating of medical treatises had begun here in the reign of Charles II of Naples. Under the patronage of his son Robert

I (1309–1343) this reached a scope and intensity unequalled anywhere else in Europe at the time.[15] The Greek manuscripts in his library were augmented in the 1330s by the gift of a work of Galen from the Byzantine Emperor Andronikos III.[16] King Robert did not know Greek himself, but he employed as translators Greek-speaking natives of Southern Italy. Leone de Solis of Altamura and Raimondo di San Germano concentrated on medical treatises. Shemaiah ben Elijah, a Jew, rendered some philosophical works from Greek into Hebrew.[17] Azzolino da Roma, a judge from Otranto, may have been the one who translated a legal book as well as some treatises on astronomy, physics and theology. But the most prolific of them all was Niccolò da Reggio, who translated fifty-six works of Galen, four texts from the *Corpus Hippocraticum*, a medical treatise by Nicholas Mirepsos, and a religious work by Sophronius, Patriarch of Jerusalem, during an active career which lasted from 1308 till about 1350.[18]

These Neapolitan translators were the last representatives of a scientific tradition which was typical of the Middle Ages. The Greek writings of interest to them belonged entirely to subjects connected with an established faculty of learning, such as theology, philosophy, medicine, or the natural sciences. They occupied themselves with supplementing, correcting, and reconciling the works of their predecessors. The translations they produced were painfully literal versions in which every word had to stand, *de verbo ad verbum*, for its Greek equivalent, with emphasis on accuracy, not polite letters.

Also at Robert's court were at least five early Italian humanists. Yet there is no evidence of any contacts between the two groups. They shared the same patron and the same library, but the interests were different. The translators cared little for poetry and belles lettres, while the humanists had no more than a passing interest in Greek medicine. They moved in different worlds, one of which was drawing to a close with the death of King Robert and Niccolò and the dismemberment of the Angevin Library, the other just beginning to appear.[19]

Elsewhere in Italy, too, Greek had not been entirely lost. In Salerno it was still known at the medical school.[20] At Grottaferrata, only fifty miles south of Rome, mass was celebrated according to the Byzantine rite, and at least in the early part of the century Greek-speaking monks still copied Greek manuscripts.[21] From time to time, also, individuals with a knowledge of Greek tended to appear in Padua, a city in close proximity to Venice, which in turn had strong ties to the Byzantine world. In Padua someone was observed arguing a legal case by reading in Greek from Homer's *Iliad*.[22] Leontius Pilatus, a Greek, obtained a copy of Homer there in 1359.[23]

Outside of Italy, some Greek institutions also lingered on in Paris. The oldest of these was the Abbey of St. Denis, where, as at Grottaferrata, Greek manuscripts were still being copied, Greek was used in the liturgy, and the monks still spoke a little Greek.[24] The city also housed the College of Constantinople, a missionary school for oriental youths which in 1285 had boasted six masters and twenty students.[25] Greek appears to have been taught at the University of Paris in 1325–26.[26] But none of these institutions were effective disseminators of the Greek language during the fourteenth century. By 1362 the College of Constantinople had dwindled to one student and was abandoned. Greek disappeared from the university after 1326, and plans to revive its teaching in 1349 and again in 1384 never came to fruition.[27]

Of more significance were Greek-speaking individuals who resided in the city at the beginning of the century. The Italian doctor and astrologer Peter of Abano (ca. 1250–1316), having learned Greek in Constantinople, spent ten years in Paris (1295–1305)[28] at the medical school, where he began the series of translations which eventually grew to comprise fourteen of Galen's medical works, the completion of Galen's *Therapeutic Method* begun by Burgundio of Pisa, the *Problems* of Aristotle, and the *Problems* of Alexander of Aphrodisias.[29] Whether Peter did any teaching of Greek at Paris, or at Padua, to which he moved in 1305, is not known. He was certainly qualified, and may have done so.

There was also Theoctistus, Byzantine Archbishop of Adrianople, an advocate of church reunion who spent a quarter of a century in the West.[30] After a twenty year residence in Rome, details of which are not known, he came to Paris late in 1309 in an attempt to persuade Charles of Valois to actualize the union of the churches through a military conquest of Constantinople. As with Peter, it is not known whether Theoctistus offered any instruction in Greek during his residence in Rome or the twenty-five week stay in Paris. In these years he did, however, compose two works in Greek: a letter to a disciple dealing with Trinitarian theology, and an apology on John of Damascus, of which only a fragment survives. Both these examples show the presence of competent Hellenists in Italy and Paris early in the Fourteenth Century.

In England the situation was a little better. Greek studies had reached their peak here with Robert Grosseteste and continued under Roger Bacon, who compiled a Greek grammar.[31] He may also be the author of a Graeco-Latin lexicon of 16,000 words which survives in a manuscript dating from around 1300.[32]

It was possibly with the assistance of such study aids that Richard of Bury (1287–1345), Bishop of Durham, acquired what his contemporaries regarded as a "good knowledge of Greek."[33] He also advocated the provision of Greek and Hebrew grammars for the use of students. John Erghom, Augustinian friar at York around 1370, could read a Greek psalter.[34] Around 1360 Peter Philargus (ca. 1340–1410), a native of Crete, entered the Franciscan convent at Norwich. From there he proceeded to Oxford as lecturer on the *Sentences*, and 1378 found him doing the same at Paris. He retained his command of Greek throughout his life, and may have taught it informally at Oxford and Paris, and perhaps even Norwich.[35] A possible pupil of his in England may have been the Benedictine Cardinal Adam Easton (ca. 1330–1397). Known as a Hebraist, Easton had also somehow acquired a working knowledge of Greek, which enabled him to translate the treatise *De veritate catholica* into Greek, as well as render Aristotle's *Meteora* into Latin,[36] the only works translated by an Englishman during the century.

It is possible that Greek was taught at Oxford between 1320 and 1325, but on the whole there appears to have been no more interest in languages here than at the University of Paris.[37]

The only formal school at which Greek enjoyed a protracted existence was the one maintained by the curia in Avignon, where the coming and going of diplomats from the East created a need as well as a means for regular instruction. In 1317 Pope John XXII appointed Conrad de Cammin, a Franciscan, as "magister linguarum . . . in diversis scientis et linguis peritus," which included Greek.[38] The next year he was succeeded by Bonifatius, who held the post till 1328.[39] In 1342 it passed briefly to the Greek Barlaam,[40] and Simon Atumanus taught Greek there privately in 1366. By 1389, however, the position of "magister linguarum" had been abandoned.[41]

It was also because of missionary and diplomatic contacts with the East that knowledge of Greek had been acquired by not a few members of the missionary orders. The Dominican William Bernardi de Gaillac spent the years 1299-1301 in Constantinople, where he quickly mastered the language and translated some works of St.

Thomas into Greek.[42] After returning to the West he lectured on the Bible and theology in Domincan houses throughout Provence until his death in 1333.[43] Though the sources say nothing about his teaching Greek, it is unlikely that this man, regarded by modern scholars as a superior Hellenist,[44] would have lectured on theology for a third of a century without making use of his linguistic skill. Another Dominican with a knowledge of Greek, Jordan da Rivalto (d. 1311) of Florence, was lector at the *stadium generale* of the order.[45] In 1326 Andreas Dato, a Dominican from Crete who was fluent in Greek, presented Pope John XXII in Avignon with a Greek translation of the *Thesaurus veritatis fidei* of Bonacursius of Bologna.[46]

An outstanding example of Hellenic studies is found in the experiences of Angelo Clareno da Cingolo (d. 1337), leader of the Italian Fraticelli. Exiled to Greece in 1295 with a group of his sympathizers, he quickly became fluent in speaking and reading Greek.[47] Returning to Italy in 1305, he spent some years in Perugia, Rome, and Avignon, finally taking refuge in Calabria.[48] During that time he translated the *Rule* of St. Basil, the *Dialogues* of St. Macarius, an unspecified treatise of St. John Chrysostom, and the *Scala paradisi, Liber ad pastorem, Vita Daniele monaco* and *Litterae abbatis Raithuni* of John Climacus.[49] These translations, as well as his extensive knowledge of the Greek Fathers, set him apart as one of the important medieval translators of patristic writings.[50] His interest in the Greek language he retained till the end, for sometime during the last three years of his life a visitor found him mending a Greek codex.[51] In addition to these, there were about a dozen other mendicants about whose Greek studies nothing is known apart from the fact that they either acquired knowledge of the language in the West, or brought it back with them from Byzantium.[52]

It was also through contacts with envoys from Constantinople that knowledge of Greek began to spread among the early humanists. Petrarch took Greek lessons from Barlaam of Seminara (ca. 1290–1348) at Avignon in 1342 and again in 1346–47. What is not very often publicized is that, contrary to his own reports that he had to cut the studies short because of the death of his teacher, Petrarch himself was responsible for the premature termination of his venture into Hellenism. As Francesco Lo Parco long ago showed, Petrarch broke off the studies and departed from Avignon some months before Barlaam's demise, apparently bored with the tedious devotion that the study of a foreign language requires.[53] He appears to have had an interest in the contents of Greek literature, but not the patience to master more than the most basic rudiments of the language.[54] The meager knowledge thus gained he tried to augment with solo sessions from the *Triglossos* of Gerard of Huy,[55] a work containing the alphabet, numerals, some vocabulary and a little phonology in Greek, Latin, and Hebrew. He also employed a now lost *Pentaglossos*, which had the additional languages of Arabic and Syriac.[56] In 1348 he met in Verona the Byzantine ambassador Nicholas Sigeros, who later sent him a manuscript of Homer's *Iliad* and *Odyssey*.[57]

Some years later, at Padua, Petrarch encountered Leontius Pilatus (d. 1366), a Greek from Calabria and former pupil of Barlaam, who translated for him Homer's works and also Euripides' *Hecuba*, autographs of which survive in Florence and Venice.[58] The marginal glosses and notations in the latter show that Leontius was not interested in merely turning out a translation, but concentrated also on linguistic and exegetical studies, as well as on textual criticism. He is now perceived as an honest Hellenist who knew the Greek and Latin classics and was heir to a great Byzantine classical tradition.[59] His translations, however, suffered from an insufficient knowledge of Latin,[60] and this may have been the reason, combined with some objectionable personal mannerisms, that caused Boccaccio to describe him as uncouth and ignorant.[61] Through Petrarch, Boccaccio was able to engage Leontius to lecture on Greek at the studio in Florence for the years 1360–62.[62] In spite of the fact that he attended the lectures and kept Leontius as a permanent guest in his home, Boccaccio never progressed much beyond the knowledge of the Greek alphabet, a fact that should not necessarily be attributed to any fault of his teacher.[63] Leontius was a competent Hellenist, the first to occupy a university chair in Greek, and first since antiquity to translate the Greek poets.

There was also his contemporary, Simon Atumanus (d. ca. 1383), a Greek expatriate who had come with Barlaam to Avignon, succeeded him as Bishop of Gerace in Calabria (1348–66), then became Bishop of Thebes (1366-N79) and ended his days in Rome around 1383.[64]

Simon had an avid interest in the Greek classics and contributed much to Greek studies in Italy. To Avignon he brought with him a manuscript, now in Florence, containing works by Sophocles, Hesiod, Euripides, and Aeschylus, and which contains notes, arguments and scholia added by Simon in 1348.[65] He is also known to have owned at least eight other Greek manuscripts, mostly classics.[66] In 1366, while at Avignon, he taught Greek to the Apostolic Secretary,

Francesco Bruni of Florence.[67] In 1373, while on another visit to Avignon, he translated Plutarch's *De cohibenda ira* for Cardinal Peter Corsini.[68] Twenty years later Coluccio Salutati brought this work under fire as a "half Greek" product in an "uncultivated style," made by someone who "did not possess the slightest literary skill in Latin." The problem appears to have been that Simon used the old *de verbo ad verbum* style, which grated on the humanist's ear.[69] Simon's greatest contribution was a monumental *Biblia Triglotta*, produced during his years in Thebes. This was a translation of the Old and New Testaments in parallel Hebrew, Greek and Latin columns, a sample page of which he presented to Pope Urban VI in Rome in 1381.[70] While in Rome, too, he taught Greek privately to Raoul de Rivo, the future Dean of Tongres, who paid Simon a deserving tribute by comparing him to Jerome in his command of Latin, Greek, and Hebrew.[71]

A Greek-speaking native of Southern Italy, too, was Paul, papal diplomat in negotiations with Byzantium, and finally Latin Patriarch of Constantinople. In 1369 Paul was one of six high officials meeting in Rome, three Latin and three Byzantine, who, as bilingual witnesses, were to ratify the documents of Emperor John Paleologus' acceptance of the Latin faith. These were, on the Greek side: Demetrios Kydones, Michael Strongilo and Philip Kykandyles. On the Latin side there were: Paul of Constantinople, Nicholas "Arenopolitanus," a Catalan bishop from Rhodes, and Antonio Ballester, a Franciscan.[72]

Demetrios Kydones (1324–98) had learned Latin as a diplomat in Milan, which soon led to his translating Aquinas' *Summa contra gentiles* into Greek.[73] His friend and fellow Latinist, John Lascaris Kalopheros, visited Venice and France in 1387–88.[74]

It is to Demetrios that Italy owes the introduction of Manuel Chrysoloras to Florence. The former had been planning for a long time to return to Italy, and finally managed a visit to Venice in 1390–91. In 1395 he returned with Chrysoloras, and was met in Venice by two young Florentines anxious to learn Greek.[75] One of them, Jacopo Angeli da Scarperia, returned with them to Constantinople, where he became Chrysoloras' student and soon produced a Latin version of five of Plutarch's *Lives*. Meanwhile Salutati wrote to Chrysoloras, inviting him back with the words: "It is God who summoned you to Italy." The response came soon, and with it the inauguration of a new chapter in the history of humanism.[76]

No discussion of Fourteenth Century translations from the Greek would be complete without reference to the contributions of Juan Fernández de Heredia, Grand Master of the Hospitallers at Rhodes. When Heredia returned from Greece to Avignon in 1382, he brought with him a number of Greek books and an Aragonese translation of thirty-nine of Plutarch's *Lives.* These had been first rendered from classical into demotic Greek by a Dimitri Kalodiki, and from there by Nicholas of "Drenopolis"[77] into Aragonese. Heredia, who may have known no more than a smattering of Greek himself, must also have brought a number of Greek translators with him to Avignon, for in the years 1382–96 he produced Aragonese versions of the speeches from Thucydides' history, John Zonaras' *Epitome historiarum,* and the *Chronicle of Morea.*[78] These were the earliest works of their kind to be translated into the vernacular.

Overall, this investigation of Fourteenth Century Hellenic studies has identified about twenty westerners who knew classical Greek, and a dozen Greek men of letters who visited the West. Among all these there were twelve who devoted themselves to the task of translating, and whose collective efforts made available to the Latin world a total of more than eighty separate Greek works—a not un-impressive figure.

By the fourteenth century, then, the knowledge of Greek in Western Europe had not become lost. Rather, there had been simply a shift in the purposes it served. In the preceeding century Robert Grosseteste (d. 1253), bishop of Lincoln and chancellor of Oxford University, had mastered Greek thoroughly, and with a team of Sicilian translators had rendered several works of Aristotle into Latin. Even more prolific as a translator had been William of Moerbecke (d. 1286), and following him, Roger Bacon (d. 1294). But for them the language had served merely as a tool with which to unlock the knowledge of the ancients. Once the entire Aristotelian corpus had been rendered into Latin, Greek practically disappeared from the philososphy faculties of the universities. But that does not mean that it vanished entirely. In the fourteenth century its study merely came to be pursued by interested parties with radically different purposes: medical doctors eager to learn more about curing man's ills, missisonary orders dedicated to saving man's soul, and humanists fascinated by the heights to which the rediscovered beauty of Greek literature could elevate man's spirit.

# NOTES

1. Kenneth M. Setton, "The Byzantine Background to the Italian Renaissance," *Proceedings of the American Philological Society* 100 (1956) 50 n. 49; Hans Baron, *From Petrarch to Leonardo Bruni* (Chicago, 1968), p. 166.

2. Setton, loc. cit.

3. *v*, e.g., Charles Homer Haskins, *The Renaissance of the Twelfth Century* (New York, 1927, 1955), pp. 280, 291–303; Richard C. Dales, *The Intellectual Life of Western Europe in the Middle Ages* (Lanham, Md., 1980), pp. 97–98, 111–12; Robert Weiss, *Medieval and Humanist Greek* (Padua, 1977); Walter Berschin, *Griechisch-Lateinisches Mittelalter von Hieronymus zu Nikolaus von Kues* (Berne, 1980). The interest here is, of course, in Greek belles lettres. Demotic Greek was used by diplomats and merchants in contact with Byzantium, but it exerted no significant influence on scholarship and therefore is of no concern here. For comments on the latter, *v* Deno J. Geanakoplos, *Greek Scholars in Venice* (Cambridge, Mass., 1962), p. 25; Manussos Manussacas, "Un poeta cretense ambasciatore di Venezia a Tunisi e presso i Turchi: Leonardo Dellaporta e i suoi componimenti poetici," in *Venezia e l'Oriente fra tardo medioevo e rinascimento*, ed. Agostino Pertusi (Venice, 1966) pp. 284–87; Antonio de Stefano, "Jacopo Pizzinga, protonotario e umanista siciliano del sec. XIV," *Bolletino Centro di studi filologici e linguistici siciliani* 5 (1957) 183–87; Nicholas Jorga, *Philippe de Mézières 1327–1405* (Paris, 1896).

4. "Greek in Western Europe at the End of the Middle Ages," *Dublin Review* 119 (1955) 68.

5. *Renaissance in Italy*, 2 vols. (New York, 1935), I, pp. 371–2; *v* also Edward McNall Burns, *Western Civilizations, Their History and Their Culture*, 7th ed. (New York, 1969), p. 201.

6. *The Western Experience*, 4th ed. (New York, 1987), p. 433. Similarly, Paul MacKendrick, Deno J. Geanakoplos, J. H. Hexter and Richard Pipes, in *Western Civilization*, edited by William L. Langer, 2 vols. (New York, 1968), I, pp. 679–83, quote Petrarch's explanation of what a Hellenist he would have been if fate had not removed his teacher prematurely, even though it was demonstrated half a century ago that the cessation of these studies had been the poet's own doing (*v* n. 63 below).

7. Crane Brinton, John B. Christopher, and Robert Lee Wolff, *Civilization in the West*, 4th ed. (Englewood Cliffs, N.J., 1981), p. 219.

8. A similar statement is found in Thomas H. Greer, *A Brief History of the Western World*, 5th ed. (New York, 1987), p. 280.

9. Georg Voigt, *Die Wiederbelebung des klassischen Altertums, oder das erste Jahrhundert des Humanismus.* 2 vols. (Berlin, 1893), II, p. 106.

10. Weiss, "Greek in Western Europe," p. 68; Berthold Altaner, "Die Kenntnis des Griechischen in den Missionsorden während des 13. und 14. Jahrhunderts," *Zeitschrift für Kirchengeschichte* 53 (1934), p. 441.

11. "Non sunt quatuor Latini, qui sciant grammaticam Hebraeorum et graecorum et Arabum . . . Multi vero inveniuntur qui sciunt loqui Graecum et Arabicum et Hebraeum inter Latinos, sed paucissimi sunt, qui sciunt rationem grammaticae ipsius, nec sciunt docere eam," *Opus tertium* cap. 10, ed. J. S. Brewer, *Fr. Rogeri Bacon opera quaedam hactenus inedita* (London, 1859), p. 33. *v* also Altaner,

"Kenntnis," p. 440; Lynn Thorndike, *A History of Magic and Experimental Science*, 8 vols. (New York, 1923) 2.644–45.

12. Berthold Altaner, "Sprachkenntnisse und Dolmetscherwesen im missionarischen und diplomatische Verkehr zwischeen Abendland (Päpstliche Kurie) und Orient im 13. und 14. Jahrhundert," *Zeitschrift für Kirchengeschichte* 55 (1936), p. 85; "Sprachstudien und Sprachkenntnisse im Dienste der Mission des 13. und 14. Jahrhunderts," *Zeitschrift für Missionswissenschaft und Religionswissenschaft* 50 (1931), p. 131.

13. Altaner, "Kenntnis," (at n. 10), p. 440; Maud F. Jerrold, *Francesco Petrarca, Poet and Humanist* (London, 1909), p. 61.

14. The fourteenth century saw considerably less Greek activity in Southern Italy than the preceding one, during which there had been, for instance, a respectable output of Greek verse, sometimes with contemporary political reference. (*v* Marcello Gigante, ed., *Poeti italobizantini del secolo XIII* [Naples, 1953] and *Poeti bizantini di Terra d'Otranto nel secolo XIII* [Naples, 1979].) Nevertheless, in Calabria and Terra d'Otranto many towns still spoke Greek and worshipped according to the Greek rite. Monasteries practised the Basilian rule. Mixed localities had separate Greek and Latin speaking clergy, though bilingual liturgy was not uncommon. Legal documents were drawn up by bilingual notaries who doubled as interpreters and translators. Classical Greek was also known here. Almost all the secular Greek authors were represented in fourteenth-century South Italian archives. It was probably from here that Simon Atumanus obtained an *Odyssey* written in a Terra d'Otranto hand. *v* Robert Weiss, "The Greek Culture of South Italy in the Later Middle Ages," *Proceedings of the British Academy* 37 (1951), pp. 24–25; 30–33; Alexander Turyn, *Dated Greek Manuscripts of the Thirteenth and Fourteenth Centuries in the Libraries of Italy*, 2 vols. (Chicago, 1972), I, pp. 104–5, 214; J. Gay, "Notes sur la conservation du rite grec dans la Calabre," *Byzantinische Zeitschrift* 4 (1895) 59–66; Agostino Pertusi, "Italo-Greci e Bizantini nello sviluppo della cultura italiana dell' umanesimo," in *Venezia e l'Oriente fra tardo medioevo e rinascimento*, ed. Agostino Pertusi (Venezia, 1966), p. 36; "La scoperta di Euripide nel primo umanesimo," *Italia Medioevale e Umanistica* 3 (1960), p. 102. For names of South Italian Greeks who copied manuscripts in the fourteenth century, *v* Turyn, I, pp. xxx-xxxv.

15. Robert himself did not know Greeek, but he showed a great interest in the acquisition and translation of manuscripts, especially medical treatises. At least twice he dispatched search parties southward to look for Greek manuscripts. *v* Robert Weiss, "The Translators from the Greek of the Angevin Court of Naples," *Rinascimento* 1 (1950), pp. 205–8; 214.

16. Ibid., p. 208.

17. Ibid., pp. 212–15; George Sarton, *Introduction to the History of Science*, 3 vols. (Baltimore, 1947), III, pp. 448–49; Walter Goetz, *König Robert von Neapel (1309–1343): seine Persönlichkeit und sein Verhältnis zum Humanismus* (Tübingen, 1910), p. 36.

18. Weiss, "Translators," (at n. 15), pp. 216–26; Lynn Thorndike, "Translations of Works of Galen from the Greek by Niccolò da Reggio," *Byzantina Metabyzantina* 1 (1946), 220–33; Sarton, op. cit., III, pp. 446–47.

19. Weiss, "Translators," p. 211.

20. Ibid., p. 204.

21. A manuscript in the hand of the monk Joseph Melendytes bears the date 1299/1300; Turyn, (at n. 14) I, p. xxx.

22. Geanakoplos, op. cit., (at n. 3), p. 25 n. 40.

23. Sarton, (at n. 17) III, p. 1377.

24. Robert Weisss, "Lo studio del Greco all' Abbazia di San Dionigi durante il Medioevo," *Riviste di Storia della Chiesa in Italia* 6 (1952), pp. 435, 438.

25. Charles Jourdain, "Un collège oriental à Paris au treizième siècle," *Revue des Sociétés Savantes* 6 (1861), 66–68.

26. Robert Weiss, "Lo studio del greco all' Università de Parigi alla fine del Medioevo," *Convivium* 23 (1955), 146–49; Altaner, "Sprachstudien," (at n. 12), p. 126; Guiseppe Di Stefano, "L'Hellénisme en France à l'orée de la renaissance," in *Humanism in France at the End of the Middle Ages and in the Early Renaissance*, ed. A. H. T. Levi (Manchester, 1970), pp. 35, 37; Geanakoplos, (at n. 3), p. 21 n. 28.

27. Jourdain, (at n. 25) pp. 69–70, 72; Altaner, "Sprachstudien," p. 126; Guiseppe Di Stefano, *La découverte de Plutarque en Occident: aspects de la vie intellectuelle en Avignon au XIVe siècle* (Turin, 1968), p. 9. For other problems at Paris, *v* George R. Stephens, *The Knowledge of Greek in England in the Middle Ages* (Philadelphia, 1933), p. 88.

28. Thorndike, *Magic* 2.877; Sarton, (at n. 17) III, p. 439.

29. Lynn Thorndike, "Translations of the Works of Galen from the Greek by Peter of Abano," *Isis* 33 (1942) 649–53; Sarton, III, p. 441–42; John E. Sandys, *A History of Classical Scholarship*, 3 vols. (Cambridge: Cambridge University Press, 1921), 1.606; J. T. Muckle, "Greek Works Translated Directly into Latin before 1350," *Mediaeval Studies* 5 (1943), p. 104.

30. V. Laurent, "Un théologien unioniste de la fin du xiii . . . eme siècle: le métropolite d'Adrianople Théoctiste," *Revue des Études Byzantins* 11 (1953), 191–93.

31. Sandys, (at n. 29) 1.595.

32. Setton, (at n. 1) p. 62. For a discussion of Greek books and their use at this time, *v* Robert Weiss, "The Study of Greek in England During the Fourteenth Century," *Rinascimento* 2 (1951), 219–25.

33. Weiss, op. cit., p. 222. Sandys (p. 602) thought that Richard's knowledge of Greek was limited to a meager vocabulary.

34. Weiss, op. cit., pp. 223, 238–39; M. R. James, "The Catalogue of the Library of the Augustinian Friars at York," in *Fasciculis Joanni Willis Clark dicatus* (Canterbury, 1909), p. 13

35. Weiss, op cit., pp. 234–36; Andrew G. Little, *The Grey Friars in Oxford* (Oxford, 1892), p. 249; Altaner, "Kenntnis," (at n. 12), p. 488.

36. Weiss, op. cit., pp. 236–38; Anton Neumann, "Über die orientalischen Sprachen seit dem 13. Jahrhundert, mit besanderer Rücksicht auf Wien," in *Die feierliche Inauguration des Rektors der wiener Universität für das Studienjahr 1899/1900* (Vienna, 1899), p. 110 n. 33.

37. Robert Weiss, "England and Council of Vienne on the Teaching of Greek, Arabic, Hebrew, and Syriac," *Bibliothèque d'Humanisme et Renaissance* 14 (1952) 3–7.

38. Heinrich Denifle, *Die Entstehung der Universitäten des Mittelalters bis 1400* (Berlin, 1885), p. 307; Altaner, "Kenntnis," (at n. 12) p. 488; Setton, (at n. 1) p. 35.

39. Altaner, "Sprachstudien," (at n. 12), pp. 124–25.

40. For a biographical sketch of this intriguing personality, *v* Katherine Walsh,

*A Fourteenth Century Scholar and Primate: Richard FitzRalph in Oxford, Avignon and Armagh* (New York, 1981), p. 153.

41. Altaner, "Sprachstudien," (at n. 12), pp. 124–25; Denifle, (at n. 38), p. 310. On the question of the failure of the language programs at the major universities, *v* Berthold Altaner, "Die Durchführung des Vienner Konzilsbeschlusses über die Errichtung von Lehrstühlen für orientalische Sprachen," *Zeitschrift für Kirchengeschichte* 52 (1933) 226–36.

42. Charles Molinier, "Guillem Bernard de Gaillac et l'enseignement chez les Dominicains à la fin du XIIIe siècle," *Revue Historique* 25 (1884), 254–56.

43. Ibid., p. 262.

44. Ibid., p. 271; Altaner, "Kenntnis," (at n. 12), pp. 474–75; Setton, p. 34.

45. Altaner, "Kenntnis," p. 387.

46. Ibid., p. 457; Turyn, p. 153–55.

47. Altaner, "Kenntnis," p. 483.

48. Decima L. Douie, *The Nature and Effect of the Heresy of the Fraticelli* (Manchester, 1932), pp. 56–60.

49. Douie, op. cit., pp. 69–70, 260–61. Muckle (at n. 29), p. 113, has some of the translations being made around 1280, but Angelo did not begin to learn Greek until 1295. *v* also Altaner, "Kenntnis," (at n. 12), p. 484.

50. Altaner, "Kenntnis," pp. 485–86.

51. Douie, (at n. 48), p. 67.

52. For John of Montecorvino (1305), Matthew of Cortona (1323), Bernardus, Theobald della Casa (1381), Francis of Camerino, Richard (1333), Hugh Gaspert and William Emergani (1350), *v* Altaner, "Kenntnis," pp. 457–58, 460, 488–89. Raphael, Bishop of Arcadia, and Nicolaus, both interpreters for a Byzantine embassy at Avignon in 1348–52, are discussed in Berthold Altaner, "Sprachkenntnisse," (at n. 12), p. 93. Amico di Bonamico (1348) is covered in Robert Weiss, "Lo studio di Plutarco nel Trecento," *La Parola del Passato* 8 (1953) 338, and John Ciparissiota (1376) in Angelo Mercati, "Giovanni Ciparissiota alla corte di Gregorio XI (Novembre 1376-Dicembre 1377)," *Byzantinische Zeitschrift* 30 (1930) 496–501. It is interesting that Amico, Bernardus and Theobald were Florentines, as were Jordan da Rivalto and Francesco Bruni.

53. Francesco Lo Parco, *Gli ultimi oscuri anni di Barlaam e la verità storica sullo studio del greco di Francesco Petrarca* (Naples, 1910), pp. 21–23; Ernest H. Wilkins, *Life of Petrarch* (Chicago, 1961), p. 34.

54. Robert Weiss, "Petrarca e il mondo greco," *Atti e Memorie dell'Accademia Petrarca di Lettere, Arti e Scienze di Arezzo*, n.s. 36 (1952–53), p. 71.

55. Robert Weiss, "Per la storia degli studi greci del Petrarca: il 'Triglossos'," *Annali della Scuola Normale Superiore di Pisa* 21 (1952), pp. 252–55; 260–61.

56. Ibid., p. 263.

57. Agostino Pertusi, *Leonzio Pilato fra Petrarca e Boccaccio* (Venice, 1964), pp. 3–4; Geanakoplos, (at n. 3) p. 21; Setton, (at n. 1) p. 53; Raymond J. Loenertz, "Ambassadeurs grecs auprès du pape Clément VI (1348)," *Orientalia Christiana Periodica* 19 (1953) 195.

58. Pertusi, "Italo-Greci," (at n. 14), p. 36, and *Leonzio*, p. 119; E. Franceschini and Agostino Pertusi, "Un'ignota Odissea Latina dell'ultimo Trecento," *Aevum* 33 (1959) 323–355; "Scoperta de Euripide," (at n. 14), pp. 123–24 and plates 8–10;

Robert Weiss, "Notes on Petrarch and Homer," *Rinascimento* 4 (1953) 267, 270; Sarton, (at n. 17), III, p. 1377; Geanakoplos, (at n. 3) p. 22 n. 29.

59. Pertusi, "Italo-Greci," (at n. 14), pp. 36–37, 152; *Leonzio*, (at n. 57), p. 119.

60. Pertusi, *Leonzio*, pp. 433–34; "Scoperta de Euripide," p. 151. An improved text of Homer was prepared by Antonio Loschi, a young friend of Coluccio Salutati, around 1393; *v* Weiss, "Greek in Western Europe," p. 71.

61. Wilkins, (at n. 53), pp. 162, 190.

62. Hastings Rashdall, *The Universities of Europe in the Middle Ages*, rev. ed., 2 vols. (Oxford, 1936), II, p. 49; Pier Giorgio Ricci, "La prima cattedra di greco in Firenze," *Rinascimento* 3 (1952) 160, 165. For the interest in Greek by Florentines before Leontius, *v* Robert Weiss, "Gli inizi dello studio del greco a Firenze," *Medieval and Humanist Greek*, pp. 227–254.

63. Wilkins, (at n. 53), p. 371; Voigt, 2.106; Vittore Branca, *Boccaccio: the Man and his Works*, trans. Richard Monges, co-trans. and ed. Dennis J. McAuliffe (New York, 1976), pp. 33–35, 49, 115–19.

64. Weiss, "Greek Culture," (at n. 14), p. 47; Setton, (at n. 1), pp. 47–52; Pertusi, "Scoperta de Euripide," (at n. 14), pp. 108–110; Giorgio Fedalto, "Per una biografia di Simone Atumano," *Aevum* 40 (1966) 445–67.

65. Turyn, (at n. 14) p. 209; Weiss, "Studio di Plutarco," (at n. 52), p. 325.

66. Turyn, p. 213–14; Fedalto, (at n. 64) p. 456.

67. Fedalto, (at n. 64), pp. 448, 452.

68. Weiss, "Studio di Plutarco," p. 322; Di Stefano, *Découverte*, pp. vii, 28; Dean Putnam Lockwood, "Plutarch in the Fourteenth Century: New Evidence Concerning the Transition from Middle Ages to Renaissance," *Transactions and Proceedings of the American Philological Association* 65 (1933) lxvi–lxvii.

69. Setton, pp. 47–52; Robert Weiss, "Gli studi greci di Coluccio Salutati," in *Miscellanea in onore di Roberto Cessi*, 2 vols. (Rome, 1958), 1.350.

70. Pertusi, "Scoperta de Euripidee," (at n. 14), p. 113; Gino Mercati, "Se la versione dall' ebraico del codice veneto greco VII sia di Simone Atumano archivescovo di Tebe," *Studi e Testi* 30 (Rome, 1916) 41. The translation from the Hebrew may have been made possible by the large Jewish population of Thebes, from whom he could have learned Hebrew.

71. Setton, p. 52; Di Stefano, *Découverte*, pp. 29–31. For the extent of Raoul's knowledge of Greek, and his plans for teaching it, *v* P. Cunibert Mohlberg, *Radulph de Rivo, der letzte Verträter der altrömischen Liturgie*, 2 vols. (Louvain, 1911), 1.19–25.

72. Setton, pp. 45–46; Altaner, "Kenntnis," (at n. 12), pp. 462–65.

73. Sandys, p. 423; Setton, pp. 46–47. Demetrios had, of course, been preceded by an even greater translator of Latin, Maximos Planudes.

74. Setton, pp. 54–56.

75. From around this time dates a letter, codex Bodl. ms. gr. misc. e. 4, foll. 2v, written by Chrysoloras to Coluccio Salutati in answer to a request for information on Greek breathings. See A. R. Littlewood, "An 'Ikon of the Soul': the Byzantine Letter," *Visible Language* 20 (1976) 214–5.

76. G. Pesenti, "La scuola di greco a Firenze nel primo rinascimento," *Atene e Roma* 12 (1931) 86.

77. Setton, pp. 46–47, 65; Altaner, "Sprachstudien," p. 134. This Nicholas may be identical with the Nicholas "Arenopolitanus" who was in Rome in 1369.

78. Anthony Luttrell, "Greek Histories Translated and Compiled for Juan

Fernàndez de Heredia, Master of Rhodes, 1377–1396," *Speculum* 35 (1960) 404; Weiss, "Studio di Plutarco," (at n. 52), pp. 327–32; Setton, pp. 64–68.

# WARRIOR INITIATION AND SOME SHORT CELTIC SPEARS IN THE IRISH AND LEARNED LATIN TRADITIONS

William Sayers
Council of Ontario Universities

# WARRIOR INITIATION AND SOME SHORT CELTIC SPEARS IN THE IRISH AND LEARNED LATIN TRADITIONS

In an influential public lecture that has weathered well since 1964, Kenneth Jackson employed a visual image in his title, *The Oldest Irish Tradition: A Window on the Iron Age*.[1] He then turned a temporal telescope on the corpus of early Irish epic texts known as the Ulster cycle to show the manuscripts carrying these tales as the products of the twelfth and later centuries, while the texts reflected the language of the seventh to ninth centuries and, at even greater remove, the material culture and social organization of the Celts in the second to fourth centuries. The medieval Irish antiquarians themselves placed the events of the epics in the age of Christ. This deep native perspective, undistorted by any Graeco-Roman prism, permits us to study the evolution of traditional oral and literary phenomena over an extended period, although it does not immediately follow that the critical stages in such developments can be dated with certainty. Such a lengthy tradition affects the literary *personae* and their narrative contexts in rather different fashion.

The biography of an epic hero is by its very nature exceptional, and this is particularly true of his first years. Paternity, circumstances of conception and birth, fosterage in the wilderness or under servile conditions, precocity or its antithesis, special relationships with the divine and supernatural, reception of insignia or other recognition of future role, initiatory exploits—all these serve to define and situate the special, often "outsider" status of the youthful hero who comes or is called to the succor of his threatened society.[2] Later, anomalies of behaviour, Dumézil's "sins of the warrior," may result from the hero being drawn between poles of supernatural power, e.g., natural vs. cultural forces, when he becomes the stake or pawn in a divine tug-of-war.[3] To exceptionalities that are fundamental to the conception of the epic figure may be added others that are consequences of conscious or unconscious syncretism and synthesis. Does the figure of Cú Chulainn in the Ulster cycle, for example, exhibit cultural features suggestive of a merger of and resolution between Celtic and pre-Celtic peoples in early Ireland, or even more particularly between relatively late Celtic immigrants from northern Britain and previous inhabitants of Ireland?[4] Or does the career of this hero, and indeed the Ulster cycle as a whole, reflect a purposeful manipulation of pseudo-historical and literary material by revisionist Uí Néill compilers in the service of expansionist claims on the kingdom of Ulster?[5]

As concerns the narrative context, as an epic figure begins to dominate a story-telling tradition, he exerts a magnetic attraction on other traditional matter not firmly attached to a comparable figure. Thus, in the tales of the Ulster cycle, we find Cú Chulainn, to the near exclusion of other heroes, associated with, for example, *búada* 'gifts' (exceptional sensory powers and other skills), physical particularities (supernumerary pupils and digits, the pre-battle distortion, *riastrad*), the list of *cles* or martial feats practised by the Ulster warriors, and so on. Most of these are also attributed, at one time or another and in piecemeal fashion, to figures like Conall Cernach and Lóegaire Búadach, but almost invariably in conjunction with Cú Chulainn, so that the latter is given even more prominence through the devices of comparison and accumulation. Once the basic association of hero and attribute is in place, the latter can evolve according to the internal dynamic of the literary form, as does Cú Chulainn's *riastrad*, which becomes more detailed as the epic *Táin Bó Cúailnge (The Cattle-Raid of Cooley)* develops. Not surprisingly, the paramount hero is often credited with unique weapons and equipment, retained from childhood or special acquisitions, native and central to the tradition, like Cú Chulainn's *carpat serrda*, 'scythed chariot' (although later interpreted as *serda* 'Syrian'), which is simply an exponential rhetorical expansion on the description of the early Celtic war-cart, or more or less fossilized remnants from an earlier era, or even with their ultimate orgin outside the native tradition.

It is perhaps in one of the two latter categories that we may place Cú Chulainn's unique spear, the *gae bolga*. In addition to the cryptic name, there are the particular, near surrealistic conditions of its use: 1) (only) against an otherwise invulnerable or superior opponent, 2) caught between the toes, or even thrown with them across or through the water, after some kind of preparation in the water by the hero's charioteer, 3) a degree of guile or deceit in its employ, and 4) the expansion and multiplication of the single spear point into twenty-four barbs inside the victim's body so that the weapon must be cut free. All these have caused a considerable flow of scholarly ink. Without attempting a full survey here, one may note T. F. O'Rahilly's association of the arm with the lightning bolt and a Celtic weather god *Bulga*, J. Pokorny's identification with the harpoon, throwing stick, line and float of the Inuit, and E. Hamp's derivation of the second element of the name from a common Celtic *\*balu-gaisos* 'death spear' (cf. OIr. *at.bail* 'dies'), which reduced to *bolga* and was then amplified and explained by the reintroduction of *gae* 'spear'. Against these speculations, E. MacNeill's derivation of the name from an original *\*gabul-gai* 'forked spear' holds up very well,[6] although the development suggested by Hamp and Mac Neill assumes the lenition of the *-g-*, which is not assured. A weapon less widely commented on but equally mysterious is Cú Chulainn's *deil chlis*.

While a more detailed comment on the name will follow below, its elements may be initially identified as *deil* 'split piece of wood', hence 'wand, rod, goad', and *cles* '(martial) feat or trick'. Although the use of the *gae bolga* informs three narrative episodes in the Ulster cycle, Cú Chulainn's single combats against Lóch and Fer Diad (actually doublets) and against his son Connla (to disregard one isolated use against a giant in an aerial duel), the *deil chlis* is shown in action on only a single occasion, supported by a passing reference in a typically ornate descriptive passage.

The fuller mention is in the "Macgnimrada" ("Boyhood Deeds of Cú Chulainn"), as recounted by Fergus early in *Táin Bó Cúailnge*. The seven-year-old Cú Chulainn has duped Conchobar into arming him on a day promising a brief but glorious martial career for one then initiated into warrior status. Brandishing and breaking successive sets of weapons, comprising spear and shield in the Lebor na h-Uidhre (LU) version (two spears, shield and sword in the Book of Leinster, LL), until he is given the king's own arms, while possibly retaining some of his own, he sets out on a foray with the king's charioteer in the royal chariot that culminates in combat against the three sons of Nechta Scéne.[7] This episode has been compared by Georges Dumézil to the hero's combat with a triple-headed ophidian in a common Indo-European myth.[8]

In the LU recension of the *Táin*, the three sons are called Fóill, Fannall, and Túachell, suggesting the significations 'sly', 'swallow,' and 'cunning', respectively. Although the special warrior skill of Fanall (variant Faindle) is to skim across the water like a swallow or swan, one may speculate that this opponent, too, originally represented a quality ethically indefensible in the warrior initiand, e.g., a name deriving from *fann* 'weak, powerless', *fainne* 'weakness' or *foindel*, var. *fainnel* 'roving, vagrancy; frenzied, erratic behaviour' (for the mother's name, cf. *scén* 'fright, terror'). There may be a trace of mnemonic concerns in the sequence Fóill-Fannall-Túachell. The particular qualities of Fóill and Túachell are that the former can be killed only with a first blow because of his evasiveness and that the latter is invulnerable to weapons; here we must understand conventional weapons. Cú Chulainn dispatches his three opponents as follows: Fóill with the first thrust of Conchobar's broad-bladed spear, Fannall by wrestling with him in the water and drowning him, before taking his head, Túachell by throwing his *deil chlis*. The third encounter is presented as follows, after the charioteer's warning of the opponent's invulnerability: '*Ondar dó-ssom in del chlis dia mescad, conid nderna retherderg de,*' or *Cú Chulaind. Sréthius fair iarom in sleig conid rallá ina chomsudiu. Dolluid a dochum iarom 7 benaid a chend de* (ll. 750-53). Editor Cecile O'Rahilly translates: " 'Here is the *deil chlis* for him to confound him so that it may riddle him like a sieve.' Then he cast the spear at him and knocked him down. He went towards him and cut off his head." From this we may, for the moment, retain the identification of the *deil chlis* as a spear (*sleig*), and some possible devious or surprise element in its use ("to confound him"). Other commentators have seen 'red running (of blood)' in *retherderg*, rather than 'sieve hole' (i.e., *derg* 'red' as opposed to *derc, derg* 'hole'; see the further discussion below). Finally, there is no clear statement that the blow of the *deil chlis* was fatal. Stunned and knocked to the ground, Túachell may have been slain with the sword.

The rhetorically fuller account of the LL recension of the Táin structures the three single combats somewhat differently. The paradigm is as follows: Fóill, invulnerable to weapons, killed with the thrown *deil cliss*; Túachall, evasive, killed with first spear throw; Faindle, advancing across the water, drowned. Thus, while the sequence of names and defensive strengths varies somewhat from that of the

LU recension, the match between Cú Chulainn's offensive tactics and the defences remains. It is tempting to see here another expression of the trifunctional ideology of the Indo-Europeans as defined by Dumézil, where the three estates of kings/priests, warriors, and providers may also find elaboration within a given function, e.g., a lawgiver king succeeded by a warrior king, then by a pacific ruler devoted to the material well-being of his subjects. In a synchronic view, successful Irish kings, whose panfunctionality parallels that of the goddess of territorial sovereignty, establish basic legitimacy in the first function through the justice of their rule, tend to be untroubled defenders of their land and people, and rule over fine weather, rich harvests, multiplying flocks. It then seems justified, for heuristic purposes, to see in the warrior sons of Nechta Scéne three fundamentally second function figures who also have attributes of the three functions. Their functionally specific defences will be overcome by appropriate weapons and techniques.

Fóill's magical invulnerability suggests the first function of druids and he is conquered with a unique (and perhaps magical) aerial weapon. Túachell, the defensive fighter *par excellence* (second estate), is killed with a conventional warrior's spear made of iron and wood and thus of terrestrial origin (which would fit the pattern most neatly if thrust, i.e., earth-based, rather than cast; the verbs used seem to lie on middle ground between a short throw and thrust). Lastly, the third estate, herdsmen, agriculturalists, fishermen and other material providers, is represented by Faindle, who uses neither magic nor martial skills, but only bodily strength. He is defeated on his own terms, by brute physical strength, in his own element, water. Thus arrayed, the three fatal combats suggest what I hold to be the original three-fold death of Irish and Indo-European tradition: 1) falling/hanging (aerial), 2) wounding with a weapon/burning (terrestrial), and 3) drowning°nterment (aquatic/subterranean). The conventional expression in Irish language and tradition refocused this as wounding, drowning, and burning (*guin 7 bádud 7 loscud*), with only residual traces of hanging/falling.[9] Whether this information can be brought to bear on the identification of the *deil chlis* is another matter. It does, however, underline the special quality or status of the arm if it is seen as used against a magically protected opponent. In being employed against the otherwise invincible warrior and with guile or unexpectedness, not untypical of the Varunaic/Odinnic aspect of the first function, the *deil chlis* shares some characteristics with the *gae bolga*. Both are unique arms of the last resort.

Returning now to Cú Chulainn's encounter with Fóill, we find in the LL *Táin* a fuller account than in LU, after the charioteer's significantly expanded warning that neither "*points* nor weapons nor *sharp edges*" (emphasis added) would harm him: "*Dobér-sa mo láim fón deil chliss dó .i. fón n-ubull n-athlegtha n-iarnaide, 7 tecéma i llaind a scéith 7 i llaind a étain 7 béraid comthrom inn ubaill dá inchind tria chúladaig co ndingne retherderg de fria chend anechtair combat léiri lésbaire aeóir triana chend*" (ll. 1102–06). " 'I shall take in hand for him my *deil cliss*, that is, the round ball of refined iron, and it will land on the flat of his shield and the flat of his forehead and carry out through the back of his head a portion of brain equal to the iron ball, and he will be holed like a sieve so that the light of the air will be visible through his head.' "

Here the *deil cliss*, while still thrown, is clearly not a simple spear, perhaps not a spear at all. The phrase "round ball of refined iron" certainly suggests more than a conventional spear head. The problematic *retherderg* is still with us, seemingly traditionally attached to the episode, perhaps more so than the exact identity of the weapon, but with no further clue as to its signification. Although the editor leaves the term *deil chlis/cliss* untranslated and without comment in notes to both editions thus far considered, the glossary to her earlier edition of the Stowe recension of the *Táin*, which follows the Book of Leinster for this incident, identifies the *deil cliss* as a staff sling.[10] This equation is supported by the *Contributions to a Dictionary of the Irish Language* but is traceable to Ernst Windisch's edition of the LL *Táin* where he translates "Kunststück-Schwippstock", but with no further discussion.[11] It may be objected that the staff sling seems the true weapon and could conceptually be referred to *deil* 'rod, wand', but it is the missile, the iron ball, that has the fatal effect and is more directly equated in the text with the name. Pending the further discussion, it cannot be ruled out that the weapon, or at least the compiler's conception of it, was some kind of mace with a rounded iron head or flail with a ball flexibly attached to a handle. In any case, the compiler of the LL recension seems to have resolved the paradox of invulnerability to weapons of the LU account by amplifying yet limiting it to encompass points, edges, and weapons and then introducing a pointless, edgeless sphere. The expanded description of the missile, with the conscious alliteration of *ubull athlegtha iarnaide* ("resmelted iron apple [ball]") also advises caution in taking the characterization too literally.

Before leaving this incident with the *deil chlis*, we should recall the general context within which it occurs: a coherent complex of highly significant and culturally archaic initiation events: choice of heroic destiny, first arms, first foray and facing down of adult/peer (the encounter with Conall guarding the frontier), first combats and spoils, the hunting and capture of wild animals and birds, the return in full chariot flight to Emain Macha, the battle-maddened defiance of and challenge to its inhabitants, the disconcerting and conciliatory reponse of Conchobar in the form of naked female emissaries and vats of water to cool the hero's ardor and, finally, Cú Chulainn seated, clothed and combed, at Conchobar's knee. Here we find yet another illustration of the states of separation, liminality, and aggregation by which van Gennep characterized the rites of passage.[12]

This summary of one episode from the "Boyhood Deeds" masks two important considerations, one, that the incidents, seven in the LU account, three in LL, are, as Melia has shown, by and large variations on the tripartite theme of van Gennep's thesis,[13] but may reciprocally cast light into dark textual corners like the *deil chlis* question, and another, that the protagonist is still only seven years old. Thus, other well known scenes, such as Cú Chulainn's initial approach to the king's seat at Emain Macha carrying a ball and (hurley?) playing stick, wooden shield, and "toy javelin" (*bunsach*, LU *TBC*, ll. 415f.), during which he throws the javelin ahead, then runs and catches it before it hits the ground, or the fight against the smith Culann's hound, in which he casts his ball through the beast's open maw and out through its body, underline his propensity, well documented in later exploits, to use weapons more appropriate to childhood activities or other less conventional arms—large stones, stakes, the butt end of spears.[14] In the particular heroic persona of Cú Chulainn, destined to die young and glorious, precocity in adult arms is matched by the equivalent heroic anomaly of a retention of boyhood arms into young adulthood. This dialectic is exploited for the purposes of narrative variation when some opposing warriors initially refuse to meet a beardless youth in single combat.[15] It is then possible that the *bunsach* 'wand, staff; toy javelin' and *deil chlis* 'wand of feats' were originally one and the same, or a child's and adolescent's respective version of the same arm, although the latter name gave greater opportunity for a fanciful development once the link with the true identity of the equipment had been lost.

The other mention of the *deil chlis* in the *Táin* comes in the "Breslech Mór Muirthemne" episode ("The Great Battle on the Plain of Muirthemne"), whose motifs have clear links with the "Macgnímrada" and which, like them, is an interpolation in the larger work, although less skillfully integrated than Fergus's account of Cú Chulainn's youthful exploits. The text is substantially the same in all versions of the *Táin* and is in the full-blown style of the LL recension. After a healing sleep imposed by his divine father Lug, Cú Chulainn, now, it should be emphasized, a young warrior of seventeen years, learns of the death of the boy-troop which, not subject to the debilitating malady, the *ces noínden*, of the other Ulstermen, had advanced into battle. He rises to attack the host, since the agreement to meet only in single combat has been violated by the enemy's engagement with the young warriors. The description of Cú Chulainn's leather armour and multiple arms is an elaborate set piece and clearly goes beyond the limits of reality. His weapons consist of eight small swords and his ivory-hilted sword, eight little spears (*slegíni*) and his five-pronged spear (*sleig cóicrind*; these may be rearward facing barbs), eight little javelins (*gothnatha*) and his ivory-shafted (or battle) javelin (*goth néit*), eight little darts (*cletíni*) and his *deil cliss*, eight shields and one huge, sharp-edged shield (LU *TBC*, ll. 2229–36). With this arsenal of nine sets of weapons stowed in his chariot, Cú Chulainn then undergoes his distortion, which is here given its most elaborate description.[16] In this passage circumstantial evidence would identify the *deil chlis* as a kind of small spear (*cleittín[e]*, var. *cletín*). The sequence of arms suggests that they were among the smallest of such missiles, although as in the other "eight small plus one large" sets, the *deil cliss* was somehow distinctive and larger within its sub-category.

*Cleittíni* are mentioned fairly frequently in the epic texts. As his enemies often claimed that without his spear Cú Chulainn would be no more formidable than any other warrior, one may be inclined to assume that it is the *gae bolga* or *deil chlis* that is meant when, for example, the satirist Redg makes what he hopes will be an irresistible request for his *cleittíne* (LU *TBC*, ll. 1511ff.). Within this same narrative context we find the arm also called *gae* (although not in LL) and may note the presence of the term *clessín*, rendered "strange feat" by the editor/translator, but perhaps closer to a snide "little trick." On the other hand, when Cú Chulainn "gives" Redg the weapon, in the form

of a fatal cast, there is no aquatic adjunct, i.e., it is not thrown over
or through the water, suggesting that the *deil chlis* was intended, or
perhaps simply some other valuable small spear. In this instance the
weapon is identified as having a bronze head and is linked in typical
Irish fashion to the toponym of the site where the encounter was
reported to have occurred (Umarrith < *Umasruth*, 'bronze stream').
*Cleittíne* may then have served as a generic term, with a variety of
small spears subsumed in it.

The ample account of Cú Chulainn's encounter with his fos-
ter-brother Fer Diad that is given in the LL *Táin* also presents a
hierarchy of arms, although there is no explicit reference to the *deil
chlis*, since it will be the *gae bolga* which proves the decisive weapon.
By mutual agreement, the two champions undertake during the first
half-day of battle to present themselves equipped with a *sciath chlis*
'feat shield,' eight *ocharchliss* (?), eight javelins (*clettíni*), eight ivory-
hilted blades (*cuilg ndet*, spear blades on a short shaft seem meant),
and eight battle darts (*gothnatha neit*; ll. 3093ff.). In what seems the
portion of the combat conducted from chariots and at greatest distance their defences were so good that neither was wounded. Later
in the day they fight with their flaxen-thonged spears (*sleg*), these too
thrown. Now both suffer wounds. The second day is devoted to thrusting spears (*manaís*), the third to swords. In the above, *ocharchliss* oc-
cupies the approximate slot where we might have expected the *deil
chlis*. It appears a conflated, late form.[17]

Attention was earlier called to the twenty or so martial feats
that Cú Chulainn and other warriors learned from their female
teacher, Scáthach, in Alba. Classical authors' accounts of the Celts'
pre-battle showmanship in chariots and on their poles (e.g., Caesar,
*Bell. Gall.*, IV.33) match well with descriptions in the Old Irish texts
of feats performed as the hosts advance, on the training ground outside the king's hall, or even in it. In *Tochmarc Emire (The Wooing of
Emer)* the Ulster warriors are described as doing three feats while
balanced on ropes stretched from the door across the hall. *No clistis
errid Ulad for súanemnaib tarsnu ón dorus co 'raile isin tig i nEmain.
. . . Trí clessa dognítis ind errid .i. cless cleitenech 7 uballchless 7 fóeburchless.*[18]
Cú Chulainn surpasses them all in quickness and dexterity. These
three skills recur in the full list of feats as given in the various works,
albeit in a slightly different sequence. The feats which head the list
are *ubullchles, fáeborchles, fáenchles*, and *cles cletenach*. The 'apple feat',
'edge feat', 'horizontal feat' and 'feat of spear(s)' can be determined

with fair certainty as juggling, twirling, and other patterned movement with 1) spherical missiles, 2) sword(s), 3) shield (held perpen-
dicular to the body?) and 4) small spear(s)—the basic arms of the early
Irish warrior. Perhaps smaller versions of certain weapons were used
in these exercises.[19] Thus we have a degree of lexical interlocking
when the *deil chlis* 'rod of feats' is equated with *cleittíne* and the lexical
root of this term figures in turn in *cles cletenach*. Complicating the
matter is the 'ball' (recalling the iron ball of one identification of the
*deil chlis*) in close proximity to the *cleittíne* in the first four skills, with
*cor ndelnd* 'putting of wands (?)' given as a separate feat later in the
list.[20]

Even with the exaggeration of the description of Cú Chulainn's arms-taking in the "Breslech Mór Maige Muirthemne" passage,
there is evidence that the Celtic warrior carried both a larger spear,
chiefly for thrusting, plus one or more short throwing spears. In
*Togail Bruidne Da Derga (The Destruction of Da Derga's Hostel)*, for example, Conall Cernach is described as leaving the field at the end of
the day with the fragments of his two spears, shield and sword.[21] Celtic
weapons seemed to have been widely recognized as distinctive. In
Virgil's description in the *Aeneid* of the prophetic shield with its scene
of Gauls attacking the Capital we find *duo quisque Alpina coruscant /
gaesa manu, scutis protecti corpora longis* (VIII.662)—not only pairs of
spears but even a term loaned from Celtic for their description. The
*gaesum* was not the only foreign weapon the Romans faced, nor is this
the only name taken into Latin. Virgil is the first to name another
particularized spear as well. Of certain Campanian warriors he writes:
*teutonico ritu soliti torquere cateias* (VII.741). Later authors, such as Aulus
Gellius, Silius Italicus, C. Valerius Flaccus, ascribed the *cateia* not to
the Teutons, but to the Scythians, Persians and others. It is now
generally recognized that the *cateia* too was a Celtic weapon.

In his commentary on Virgil, Servius (fourth-fifth centuries)
provides the following description: *cateiam quidam asserunt teli genus
esse tale quale aclydes sunt, ex materia quam maxime lenta, cubitus longitudine,
tota fere clavis ferreis illigata, quas in hostem iaculantes lineis, quibus eas
adnexuerant, reciprocas faciebant."*[22] Leaving the *aclydes* for the later discussion, the *cateia*, a cubit (45–55 cm) in length, seems within the same
size range as the smallest Irish spears, *cleittíni* (leaving to one side the
'darts' *gothnatha*). The flexibility of the shaft (*ex materia . . . lenta*) recalls the Irish term *deil* whose original sense, it will be recalled, was
'split length of wood.' Iconographical and other evidence suggests

that the *cateia* was thrown with the aid of a leather strap (Lat. *amentum*) like the barbed *tragula*, also known to the Romans (Caesar, *Bell. Gall.*, V.48), perhaps ultimately of Celtic origin as well.[23] By winding the thong around the shaft, the spear could be given a rotary motion during flight.[24] Similarly, both larger and smaller Irish spears carried thongs or straps (*sreng, súainem*).[25] With reference to Servius's description one should also note the literary motif and perhaps actual Celtic practice of catching spears and throwing them back.[26] Another special feature in Servius's description also warrants attention: the nails which stud thee length of the *cateia*. A description of the Battle of Clontarf, fought near Dublin on Good Friday in 1014 between King Brian bóruma and the Dublin, Hebridean and Orkney Norse and their Leinster allies, includes among an extensive listing of Irish arms "terrible sharp darts, with variegated silken strings, thick set with bright, dazzling, shining nails." Despite the full-blown prose there is no reason to doubt the relvance of the descriptive detail.[27] There is no generally accepted etymology for *cateia*. Walde rejects Fick's derivation from the Celtic antecedent of OIr. *cath* 'battle' as *"farblos"*, and suggests a root *\*kat-* 'gekrümmt' (*v infra*).[28] A Gaulish *\*catu-gaisos* 'battle spear' could be theoretically postulated (cf. Hamp's *\*balu-gaisos*), but seems somewhat tautological and unlikely to become attached to an apparently highly specific spear type.

The idea of special Celtic javelins and missiles, retrieved, returned by the enemy, or with other exceptional aerodynamic properties, underwent an interesting development in the works of postclassical authors, one which has gone largely uncontested by modern commentators. For example, Walde's standard reference work on the Latin language defines the *cateia* as "ein mit Nägeln beschlagener Holzspiess, der vermöge einer Einhölung auf der einen Seite und der gebogenen Konstruktion von selbst in seinem Lauf in einem Bogen zurückkehrt."[29] Tracing the origins of this Celtic boomerang takes us first to Silius, who makes the otherwise unsubstantiated claim that the weapon was bowed (*panda manus est armata cateia*),[30] then to Servius's commentary on Virgil, where the *cateia* was likened to the *aclys* (pl. *aclydes*). This weapon, the name borrowed from the Greek αγκυλιρ 'thong' (hence 'thonged javelin'),[31] is also mentioned in the *Aeneid*, in the hands of Oscan warriors: *teretes sunt aclydes illis tela, sed haec lento mos est aptare flagello"* (VII.730, some 60 verses before the mention of the *cateia*). The name *aclys* seems to have originally designated a short, perhaps all wooden spear but later moved to semantic middle ground between spear and throwing club. Commentators are divided as to whether *teretes* in Virgil's mind referred to the rounded head of the weapon or the tapering shaft, but the mention of curvature recalls Silius's use of *panda* with the *cateia*. According to Servius, the *aclys* was a cubit and a half long, pointed at the ends and equipped with a line. While the line might have permitted the weapon to be recovered after a throw, it may also have served to force an opponent to drop a shield in which it was embedded, or even bring him down if caught in armour. A certain scepticism is perhaps appropriate in the consideration of later writers' comments on exotic and archaic weapons, and one may wonder whether the recovery line is not a literary development on a thong used to throw the *aclys*, as in the case of the *cateia*. In any case, we have another example of the "returning weapon," not a spear thrown back but not quite a boomerang.

Other classical authors also commented on unique Celtic weapons. In addition to the sword, shield, and spear, all characterized by length, Strabo (IV.4.2) names the *madaris* 'a kind of javelin' (cf. OIr. *maide* 'stick, staff'). After also mentioning bows and slings, he describes a wooden weapon resembling the Roman *grosphus*, thrown by hand and not by means of a strap. It had a range greater than an arrow, and was used in fowling as well as in battle. While Strabo does not credit the arm with boomerang-like properties, these would certainly be attractive in a long-range missile that might miss its mark. This immediately calls to mind the many instances of bird hunting in the Irish texts, often with a view to stunning rather than killing, although no special arm, other than spear or sling, is described there.

A further step in the evolution of the "returning weapon" motif is found in Isidore of Seville's *Etymologiae*, where he writes in his chapter on spears, "De hastis": *Clava est qualis fuit Herculis, dicta quod sit clavis ferreis invicem religata, et est cubito semis facta in longitudine. Haec et cateia, quam Horatius caiam dicit. Est enim genus Gallici teli ex materia quam maxime lenta, quae iacta quidem non longe propter gravitatem evolat, sed quo pervenit, vi nimia perfringit; quod si ab artifice mittatur, rursum redit ad eum qui misit* (XVIII.7.7).[32] Here, several shifts appear to have taken place. The nails embedded the length of the *cateia* have been transferred, or at least first ascribed, to the *clava*, a wooden club, as has the length of the *aclys* (according to Servius). Although the shaft is flexible, the arm is now very heavy. While this justifies its great percussive force, this too perhaps borrowed from the *aclys*, neither the weight nor the short flight accords well with the supposed aerodynamic performance that would bring the weapon back to the thrower. Given its striking power, being on the return flight path must have been hazardous! As noted, other long-range weapons of the Celts, like the fowling stick, may have had such properties. In this conflated account we should not, however, neglect the fact that Isidore designates the *cateia* as a Celtic weapon.

In suggesting the similarity if not full identification of the continental Celtic *cateia* with some Irish short spears and perhaps the *deil chlis*, with a degree of interference in the written tradition from the *aclys* and other specifically Celtic weapons, we can summarize as follows. The *cateia* and *aclys*, both non-Roman weapons, had a number of (assumed) similarities: length, curvature (linear or terminal), flexibility (of construction or in use), throwing strap, thong, or line, "revertibility" (retrieved, returning, or perhaps thrown back), and possibly an unusual flight pattern. They are expressly associated by later writers, perhaps when the weapons were no longer current in the Roman world. The presence of a throwing strap on the *cateia* would provide greater opportunities for manipulating the arm in displays of weapons-handling skill and may possibly have contributed to its special flight characteristics. If a relatively heavy metal point were mounted on a light flexible rod and impetus were provided via a strap wound around the middle or toward the rear of the shaft, some kind of disconcerting sinuous or spiral motion may have resulted. A number of these features are associated with smaller Irish javelins and the *deil chlis*, or are inherent in the term *deil*.

Both Latin terms, *cateia* and *aclys*, and the somewhat imprecise relation between them, could have been known in Irish monastic circles. Virgil's mention of *aclydes* is quoted by Priscian and this in turn was singled out by the Irish glossator at St. Gall who equates them with *cletecháin*.[33] While the dimunitive is rare, it seems reasonable to consider it a variant on *cleittíni*. It may be that Isidore's *Etymologiae* played a role not so much in the introduction of the spear types in Ireland, if we assume a degree of cultural continuity with the continent, but in the subsequent blurring of the image of the *deil chlis*, with its reminiscences of both *cateia* and *aclys* in the various recensions of the *Táin*.[34] One is hesitant to assign any importance to the superficial phonetic similarities of *aclys* and (*deil*) *chlis* or of *aclydes* and *cleitínni*, but some conscious juxtaposition cannot be ruled out, given the etymologizing and paronomastic approach of the Irish learned caste to lexicon.[35] Some or all of these factors, plus the proximity of *ubullchles* and *cles cletenach* in the feats lists, may have led one compiler of the *Táin* to resolve the perhaps self-imposed problem of Fóill's invulnerability to weapon points and edges by making the *deil chlis* an essentially percussive missile, while other mentions of the weapon place it more squarely in the family of small spears.

Finally, we may return to the image, if image it is, of *retherderg* which stuck tenaciously to the *Táin* acount of the *deil chlis*. *Rether from OE *hridder* 'riddle, sieve' is a rather unlikely lexical import or literary borrowing when OIr. had a common word *criathar* for 'sieve', and the consistent spelling *derg* makes 'red' a more plausible meaning than 'hole' (*derc*).[36] *Rether-* appears more likely to derive from OIr. *ríathor* 'torrent' and the compound would mean 'torrent red', an image for a streaming wound (cf. the comparable phrase with a different color adjective, *riathair ruamannda* 'red torrents').[37] This would be an appropriate and potentially traditional descriptive phrase for a jagged wound caused by a weapon mounted with a set of sharp nails as opposed to the type of incision made by a sharpened blade. This interpretation, if convincing, would make the LU the carrier of the internally more consistent version of this single combat.

The evidence—archaeological, ethnographical, and literary—is fairly coherent as concerns the Celts' use of spears in battle, with a broad distinction between thrusting lances and various sizes of javelin. Types with special features and distinctive names may have been particular to one or more tribes, or to certain categories of warriors, such as unmarried young men.[38] Compared to sword and thrusting spear, javelins may have been considered consumables, not always recovered after being thrown. As a consequence not all may have beene so elaborateley decorated as other arms, and thus did not receive the full description in the literary tradition accorded to more valuable weapons. Because of their short length, the *cateia* and other like-sized spears may have been among the hunting and training arms used by Celtic youngsters. In the Nechta Scéne episode, such a spear, like the bladeless 'toy javelin' (*bunsach)* of the "Boyhood Deeds," may have been retained by Cú Chulainn after receiving adult weapons from Conchobar. The unexpected use of a juvenile arm or one otherwise restricted in its use may explain why Cú Chulainn counted on it confounding his adversary. If the weapon differed appreciably from those normally used in combat, it may have qualified, according to the logic of the folktale, as a weapon that was not a weapon and thus have enabled Cú Chulainn to vanquish his opponent.

With time, some Celtic missiles must have become obsolete due to changes in technology and warfare. In Ireland certain arms may have lived on in the antiquarian tradition. An archaic spear, retaining some of its special features, could be transformed into an extraordinary weapon and assigned to the dominant hero in the literary tradition, to figure in pre-eminent narrative and descriptive contexts, as in the "Boyhood Deeds" and "Great Battle on the Plain of Muirthemne," respectively. During this development the arm, under its original or perhaps a new name, is subject to interference from other learned tradition, native, like the list of feats, or imported, like Isidore's conflated conception of the *cateia*. The result is a polysemous interpretation of the nature and effects of the weapon.

In much of this the *deil chlis* would have paralleled the *gae bolga*, although the ultimate historical antecedents and cultural provenance of the two spears may differ. In competition for status as the hero's unique, invincible weapon, the *gae bolga* appears to have carried the day, perhaps because of the more ample volume of exotic features. While Cú Chulainn's youth may have played a role in attracting the two weapons to him in the story-telling tradition, it is culturally significant that short spears are given this exceptional treatment in the early Irish epic texts, and not the Celtic sword. Yet the latter weapon, perhaps due to the importance of its counterpart in the Norman and general European arsenal, was to undergo in partially derivative literary traditions an unarrested and expanding development from Fergus's Caladbolg (*Táin Bó Cúailnge*) and Arthur's Caledfwlch (the Welsh tale *Culhwch ac Olwen*), to Caliburnus (Geoffrey of Monmouth's *Historia Regum Brittaniae*), Escalibor (Old French romance) and Excalibur.

## NOTES

1. Kenneth Jackson, *The Oldest Irish Tradition: A Window on the Iron Age*, The Rede Lecture 1964 (Cambridge: Cambridge University Press, 1964). Credit for the now familiar image must, however, go to Aodh de Blácam who, in his *Gaelic Literature Surveyed* (Dublin, 1929) wrote: "In the older portion [of the literature written in Gaelic] is found a window into the early Iron Age, wherein European civilization was founded" (p. xi). I should like to thank readers of an earlier draft of this paper for comments that have assisted in tightening its argument. Such weaknesses as persist are stubbornly my own.

2. For the specifically Irish expression of such a career, *v* Daniel F. Melia, "Parallel Versions of the 'Boyhood Deeds' of Cúchulainn," *Forum for Modern Language Studies* 10 (1974), 211–26, reprinted in *Oral Literature: Seven Essays*, ed. Joseph J. Duggan (Edinburgh: Scottish Academic Press, 1975), pp. 25–40; Joseph F. Nagy, "Heroic

Destinies in the *Macgnímratha* of Finn and Cú Chulainn," *Zeitschrift für celtische Philologie* [*ZCP*] 40 (1984), 23–39, and *The Wisdom of the Outlaw: The Boyood Deeds of Finn in the Gaelic Narrative Tradition* (Berkeley, 1985); Tomás O Cathasaigh, *The Heroic Biography of Cormac mac Airt* (Dublin, 1977), and "Between God and Man: The Hero of Irish Tradition," *The Crane Bag* 2 (1978), 72–79.

3. Georges Dumézil, *Heur et malheur du guerrier: aspects mythiques de la fonction guerrière chez les Indo-Européens* (Paris, 1969). For more recent studies, both theoretical and applied, *v* Jaan Puhvel, "The Stakes of the Warrior," *Journal of Indo-European Studies* [*JIES*] 10 (1982), 1-2, and "The Warrior at Stake," in *Homage to Georges Dumézil*, ed. Edgar C. Polomé, JIES Monograph Series 3 (Washington: Journal of Indo-European Studies, 1982), pp. 25–33; Udo Strutynski, "*Honi Soit Qui Mal Y Pense:* The Warrior Sins of Sir Gawain," *Homage . . . Dumézil*, pp. 35–52.

4. "In addition to the fundamental exploration of this theory in Thomas F. O'Rahilly's *Early Irish History and Mythology* [*EIHM*] Dublin, 1946), *v* Joseph Weisweiler, *Vorindogermanische Schichten der irischen Heldensage* (Tübingen, 1953), reprinted from *ZCP* 24 (1953), 10–55, 165–97; for a juxtaposition of archaeological, linguistic, and literary evidence, J. P. Mallory, "The Sword of the Ulster Cycle," in *Studies on Early Irish History: Essays in Honour of M. V. Duignan*, ed. B. G. Scott (n. p., 1981), pp. 99–113, at p. 107; and for some parallels with northern Eurasian culture, William Sayers, "The Smith and the Hero: Culann and Cú Chulainn," *Mankind Quarterly* [*MQ*] 25 (1985), 227–60.

5. *v* Joan N. Radner, "Fury Destroys the World: Historical Strategy in Ireland's Ulster Cycle," *MQ* 23 (1982–83), 41–60.

6. O'Rahilly, "The *Gai Bolga* and its Kin," in *EIHM*, pp. 58–74; Julius Pokorny, "Beiträge zur ältesten Geschichte Irlands: 2. Der *gae bolgae* und die nördliche, nicht-iberische Urbevölkerung Irlands," *ZCP* 12 (1918), 195–231; Eric Hamp, "*At.bail(1), (gae) bulga*," *Ériu* 24 (1973), 179–82; Eóin Mac Neill, *Celtic Ireland* (Dublin and London, 1921), p. 48, n., and "*De origine scotiae linguae*," *Ériu* 11 (1932), 121.

7. *Táin Bó Cúailnge: Recension I*, ed. and trans., Cecile O'Rahilly (Dublin, 1976), ll. 700ff., and *Táin Bó Cúalnge from the Book of Leinster*, ed. and trans. O'Rahilly (Dublin, 1967), ll. 1060ff. The passage is not found in the C recension.

8. *Heur et malheur du guerrier*, pp. 134ff.

9. For a close focus on the Irish material, *v* Joan N. Radner, "The Significance of the Threefold Death in Celtic Tradition," in *Celtic Folklore and Christianity: Studies in Honor of William W. Heist*, ed. Patrick K. Ford (Santa Barbara, 1983), pp. 180–200. Evidence for my rather different triad is assembled in a forthcoming article, "*Guin 7 Crochad 7 Gólad:* The Earliest Irish Threefold Death".

10. *The Stowe Version of Táin Bó Cúailnge*, ed. Cecile O'Rahilly (Dublin, 1961), s. v. Dineen offers an imaginative solution to the *deil chliss* problem in his *Irish-English Dictionary:* "A missile weapon (perh. resembling the bolas)", the set of balls and thongs of the Argentine gaucho.

11. *Contributions to a Dictionary of the Irish language* [*DIL*], incorporating fascicules issued as *A Dictionary of the Irish language*, gen. ed. E. G. Quin (Dublin, 1913–76). *Die altirische Heldensage Táin Bó Cúalnge*, ed. and trans. Ernst Windisch (Leipzig, 1905), p. 154.

12. Arnold van Gennep, *Les rites de passage* (Paris, 1909, repr. New York, 1969).

13. Melia, op. cit.

14. Cú Chulainn repeatedly uses the sling in battle (e.g., LU *TBC*, ll. 916ff.), but this

is more a question of relative emphasis since the sling was clearly not excluded as an early Irish battle weapon. On other occasions in the *Táin* he uses a holly shoot he had withdrawn from his foot (ll. 1780ff.), his bare hands, crushes the victim against a rock (ll. 2544ff.), and finally, in the last cataclysmic encounter, wields the framework of his chariot (ll. 4093ff.). In *Aided Con Chulainn (The Death of Cú Chulainn)*, satirists' importunate demands for Cú Chulainn's spear, intended to deprive him of his particular advantage (*v* discussion, infra), are met with the spear cast butt end first, with nonetheless fatal results; ed. and trans. Whitley Stokes, *Revue Celtique* 3 (1887), 175–85, since re-ed., *The Book of Leinster*, eds. R. I. Best, Osborn Bergin, M. A. O'Brien and Anne Sullivan, 6 Vols. (Dublin, 1954–83), II, pp. 442–57.

15. Opponents' honor-motivated reluctance to meet a beardless youth recur at ll. 1449f., 1700f., 1877f., 2530f.

16. *v* Sayers, "The Smith and the Hero" (at n. 3) for the blacksmithing imagery of this passage and its affinities with the Eurasian shamanistic tradition.

17. For a discussion of *ocharchless, v* William Sayers, "Martial Feats in the Old Irish Ulster Cycle," *Canadian Journal of Irish Studies* 9 (1983), 45–80, at p. 57. In the episode preceding the encounter with Redg, Cú Chulainn employs a *certgae* against Bude mac Báin. While 'short spear' is doubtless the correct reading rather than 'proper' or 'fine' spear, i.e., as opposed to more unusual weapons such as the *gae bolga* and *deil chlis*, this term too seems to have been drawn into a close, near-exclusive association with Cú Chulainn. *v* O'Rahilly, *TBC from the Book of Leinster*, note on l. 1784, on the development of the episode, and, for other instances of the term, *DIL*. It is also a *certgae* that Cú Chulainn throws at Fer Diad to distract him before sending the fatal *gae bolga* through the water (LL *TBC* only, l. 3350; O'Rahilly translates here as "fine spear").

Irish terminology for spears was relatively rich, as we have seen. As well as differences in shaft length and weight, we must assume a variety of lengths, shapes and special features for the heads (barbs, fluting). In addition to the lance (*manaís, laigen*), we find among missiles *sleg, gae, croisech, cleittíne* and *goth*, plus diminutive forms and (largely literary) compounds. *Goth* was also used of an insect's sting and in this parallels Lat. *spiculum*, which occurs frequently in the *Hisperica Famina* (vv. 29, 234, 236, 604), with its many Irish affinities (note too the simile of the flight of bees for missiles, v. 42, which also has counterparts in the vernacular); *The Hisperica Famina: I, The A-Text*, ed. and trans. Michael W. Herren (Toronto, 1974). For the same kind of entomological imagery for darts, cf. OFr. *wibete* < Lat. *vespetta*, as found in Wace's *Roman de Rou*. The *gaveloc* in Geiffrei Gaimar's *Estoire des Engleis* may also have had Celtic antecedents: v Alexander Bell, "Notes on Gaimar's Military Vocabulary," *Medium Ævum* 40 (1971), 93–103. The Gaulish cognate of OIr. *gabul* 'fork' has also been suggested as a possible source of OFr. *javelle, javelot*, and this adds further credibility to Mac Neill's derivation of *gae bolga* from *gabul gai*. Cf., as well, the short, barbed Teutonic javelins called *angon* in AS; David Wilson, *The Anglo-Saxons* (London, 1960), p. 124.

A survey of Irish weapons is found in the uncompleted study of Helmut Bauersfeld, "Die Kriegsaltertümer im Lebor na hUidre," *ZCP* 19 (1933), 294–345, although reliance on a single compilation vitiates his observations on relative frequency of the terms, e.g., *goth* occurs there only once but in fact the term is far from infrequent in the OIr. corpus as a whole. A portion of this study has been superseded by Mallory's article (n. 3). While I fault Bauersfeld for his single source, I am acutely aware that the present study lacks chronological specificity, to use Mallory's term, and that the telescoping process affects more than a millenium. Mallory's study, however, shows the difficulties of trying to relate the archaeological and iconographical evidence to the literary. My principal concerns here are the survival of weapons terminology in the learned traditions, which led a life increasingly detached from the early material reality.

18. *Tochmarc Emire in Compert Con Culainn and Other Stories*, ed. A. J. van Hamel, Mediaeval and Modern Irish Series 3 (Dublin, 1956), par. 4. For a general discussion of the feats, *v* Sayers, n. 16.

19. Further to the *sciath chliss* used by Cú Chulainn and Fer Diad in conjunction with light spears, *v Fled Bricrend*, par. 42, where Cú Chulainn performs feats with *nói n-ubla clis ocus nói cletíne clis ocus nói scena clis*, nine each of feat balls, spears and shields, to entertain the Ulster ladies.

20. Sayers, "Martial Feats," p. 54. Just prior to the list of feats in the *Taín* (LU, 11. 1725f.; LL, 11. 1847f.), Cú Chulainn kills Cúr when interrupted in the exercise of the ball feat. He casts the ball through both Cúr's shield and head, the same effect as the *deil chlis* in its non-spear manifestation. Further interference from and interdependence with other traditional material is illustrated by the inclusion of *immorchor ndelend* 'projection of wands, goads' among the three *búada* or 'gifts' of the charioteer; *v* William Sayers, "Three Charioteering Gifts in *Táin Bó Cúailnge* and *Mesca Ulad: immorchor ndelend, foscul ndiriuch, léim dar boilg*," *Ériu* 32 (1981), 163–67.

21. *Togail Bruidne Da Derga*, ed. Eleanor Knott, Mediaeval and Modern Irish Series 8 (Dublin, 1975), 11. 1510ff. More light-hearted evidence of Celtic tastes in weaponry is found in Chrétien de Troyes' *Perceval* where the departing young hero's mother recovers two of his customary three javelins lest he appear too Welsh to Arthur's courtiers; *Le conte du graal (Perceval)*, ed. Félix Lecoy, 2 Vols. (Geneva and Paris, 1972), vv. 600–611. Note too the frequency of multiple spears in continental Celtic grave goods.

22. Maurus Servius Honoratus, *Servii Grammaticii qui feruntur in Vergilii carmina commentarii*, eds. Georg Thilo and Hermann Hagen, 3 Vols. (Leipzig, 1881–87).

23. The weapon was used for hunting and fishing as well as warfare and is also mentioned by Plautus; *v The Complete Encyclopedia of Arms and Weapons*, eds. Leonid Tarassuk and Claude Blair (New York, 1982). Cú Chulainn is also seen hunting fish with a line attached to a spear in a short introduction to *Ces Noinden Ulad (The Debility of the Ulstermen)*, ed. by Kuno Meyer as "Die Ursache von Noinden Ulad," *ZCP* 8 (1912), p. 120.

24. A variety of twisting and holding techniques is illustrated on Greek vases and reproduced in Tarassuk and Blair, p. 20. Arrian (*Tact.* 37.4, 42.4, 43.2) gives three specifically Celtic ways of throwing the javelin.

25. Flaxen thongs are mentioned on the spears employed by Cú Chulainn and Fer Diad (LL *TBC*, 1. 3108). The term *gothsreng* 'spear thong' occurs in the St. Gall incantation as a metaphorical name for some ailment (stomach cramps, cancer?): *Thesaurus Palaeohibernicus*, eds. Whitley Stokes and John Strachan, 2 Vols. (Cambridge, 1901–03), II. 249.5. *v* also *DIL*, s. v. *súainem*. In the story of Diarmaid and Gráinne, fitting the finger in the spear thong is singled out for special mention. It is of interest that this reference occurs in a context of martial feats: Diarmaid

keeping his footing on a cask rolling down a hillside, making a running leap and "walking" along the edge of a sword blade, and performing a running vault or handstand over an upright spear (cf. the last feat in the Ulster cycle feat list); *Tóruigheacht Dhiarmada agus Ghráinne: The Pursuit of Diarmaid and Gráinne*, ed. and trans. Nessa Ni Shéagdha, Irish Texts Society 48 (Dublin: Irish Texts Society, 1967), 1. 750ff.

26. In *Scéla Mucce Meic Dathó [The Tale of Mac Dathó's Pig]*, ed. Rudolf Thurneysen, MMIS 6 (Dublin, 1935), pars. 10ff. Cet Mac Mágach boasts of catching spears on his shield and returning them, and the same spear is cast back and forth in Cú Chulainn's fatal combat with Lugaid in *The Death of Cú Chulainn*. The motif is found in Welsh literature, in Culhwch's encounter with the giant Ysbaddaden, where three stone spears, apparently with forged iron heads, are thrown at the intruders who catch and hurl them back, wounding their host; *The White Book Mabinogion*, ed. J. Gwenogvryn Evans (Pwllheli: priv., 1907), p. 228.

The idea of stone weapons, which occurs in Norse tradition as stone arrows, may be related to the primitive believe in a stone heaven and stone weapons thrown down to earth: *v* Mircea Eliade, *The Forge and the Crucible*, 2nd ed. (Chicago, 1978), pp. 20ff. Note, too, the popular Irish tradition of "fairy darts", aeroliths thrown down at cattle and humans; *Siscéalta ó Thír Chonaill: Fairy Legends from Donegal*, coll. Seán Ó hEochaidh and trans. Máire Mac Neill (Dublin, 1977), No. 23.

27. *Bera bodba biraithi, co suathnemaib sita, sainemail, congran tairngnib, glana, glorda, glaindi; Cogadh Gaedhel re Gallaibh*, ed. and trans. James. H. Todd (London: H.M.S.O., 1867, repr. New York, 1965), p. 159. The ornate style, where series of alliterating adjectives are frequent, may have encouraged the retention in the learned tradition of a possibly archaic detail no longer characteristic of the spears in use at Clontarf. Spear shafts with nails are also mentioned in poems from the Hisperic corpus; *The Hisperica Famina II: The Related Poems*, ed. and trans. Michael Herren (Toronto, 1987), p. 82, 1. 54.

28. *Lateinisches etymologisches Wörterbuch*, ed. A. Walde, 3rd rev. ed., 2 vols. (Heidelberg, 1938), s. v.

29. Walde, ibid.

30. Silius Italicus, *Punica*, ed. J. D. Duff, 2 Vols. (CCL, 1934), 3.277.

31. Walde gives "ein kurzer, mittels eines Riemens geschleuderter Speer", Tarrasuk and Blair, a "javelin" and also a "short, spiked mace". The etymology has also been related by Walde to αγκαλις, "weil die Wurfwaffe dem gebogenen Arm ähnlich gewesen sei wie der Boomerang."

32. No commentary on the *cateia* is offered in the most recent full edition and translation of Isidore's work, *Etimologias*, eds. José Oroz Reta and Manuel A. Marcos, 2 Vols. (Madrid, 1983). The editors have chosen to translate *est enim genus Galli teli ex materia quam maxime lenta* as "es un tipo de arma arrojadiza propria de los galos, fabricada con un material enormemente pesado." *Lentus*, certainly 'flexible' in Servius' commentary on Virgil from which Isidore's wording has been taken, and perhaps ultimately traceable to Virgil's description of the *aclys (haec lento mos aptare est flagello)*, has been ascribed its alternative meaning 'slow, sluggish', and these flight characteristics attributed to the weight. Isidore is more likely to have intended flexibility, although the idea of great weight accords well enough with the striking force. In *Lateinisches and Romanisches aus den Etymologiae des Isidorus von Sevilla* (Hildesheim and New York, 1975), Johann Sofer identifies the *caia* in this

passage as 'Keule, Wurfkeule, Prügel' (p. 39), but for *cateia* is content to cite Georges Dottin's *Manuel pour servir á l'étude de l'antiquité classique* (Paris, 1915), p. 277: "La *cateia* est vraisemblablement une hache de jet comparable à la francisque des Germains." This is the conclusion reached by Salomon Reinach in *Les Celtes dans les vallées du Pô et du Danube* (Paris, 1894), pp. 194–99. In the light of the other evidence, this identification lacks conviction, as the technique required to throw a light axe effectively would be ill served by a flexible handle. *v* also Bertrand's contribution in the same volume, "L'amentum et la cateia sur une plaque de ceinture en bronze avec figures du cimitière gaulois de Watsch (Garniole)," pp. 188–93.

33. *Thes. Pal.*, II. 120.

34. *Cateia* also occurs in the Anglo-Saxon Ælfric's early 11 c. glossary, lumped together with clubs as in Isidore, in an entry reading *clava vel cateia vel teutona: anes cynnes gesceot* ("missiles of a kind"); *Anglo-Saxon and Old English Vocabularies*, ed. Richard P. Wülcker, Vol. 1 (London, 1884; repr. Darmstadt, 1968), p. 143.

35. On the reception and influence of Isidore in Ireland, see the introductory comments to Rolf Baumgarten's "A Hiberno-Isidorean Etymology," *Peritia* 2 (1982), 225–28, and appended bibliography.

36. This interpretation on the part of Cecile O'Rahilly stems from her ed. of the Stowe recension where *rether* is glossed as 'sieve', with reference to 1. 1141.

37. *DIL*, s. v. *ríathor*. The verb 'riddles' *críathraid* is also used of the effects of weapons on the human body in typical martial descriptions; *DIL* s. v.

38. In "Werewolves, Cyclopes, *Díberga* and *Fíanna*: Juvenile Deliquency in Early Ireland," *Cambridge Medieval Celtic Studies* 12 (1986), 1–22 (at 19), Kim McCone cites Polybius (2.28–30) for a battle between Romans and Gauls where transalpine *Gaisatai* 'spearmen' fought naked in the front line, protected only by shields. The description suggests that these were young warriors in their prime. The name also occurs in Strabo, 5.1.6.

# THE CRISIS OF THE
# SALZBURG MINISTERIALAGE,
# 1270–1343

John B. Freed
Illinois State University

# THE CRISIS OF THE SALZBURG MINISTERIALAGE, 1270–1343

The nobility of the medieval principality of Salzburg was composed of three distinct strata: the old free nobility that had largely died out or entered the archiepiscopal ministerialage by 1200; the ministerials who composed the *de facto* nobility of the High Middle Ages; and the knights of the Later Middle Ages.[1] The ministerials were the functional successors and probably the biological descendants of an elite group within the archiepiscopal *familia* who belonged by the middle of the eleventh century to a quasi-hereditary estate, but it was only during the Investiture Contest that the ministerials, identified as such, formed into distinct lineages named after their preferred residence, often a castle or fortified tower. In spite of the ministerials' wealth and political importance (ministerials participated in the election of all but one of the archbishops between 1147 and 1256), scribes distinguished carefully in the twelfth century between nobles and ministerials. Although ministerials, particularly women and benefactors of ecclesiastical foundations, could be styled as nobles in unofficial documents in the twelfth century, it was not until after 1270, when the last surviving noble family in the principality, the Walchens, had entered the archiepiscopal ministerialage, that ministerials were identified as nobles in archiepiscopal charters.

Approximately twenty of the ministerial lineages in the twelfth century can be classified as greater ministerials (*ministeriales maiores*), that is, ministerials who had their own servile vassals or *milites* as they were generally called in Salzburg. No nobleman or prominent archiepiscopal ministerial was identified before 1200 as a *miles* in an archiepiscopal charter or in the codices of traditions of the cathedral chapter or of the Benedictine abbey of St. Peter's in Salzburg. After 1180, however, lesser ministerials (*ministeriales minores*), that is, ministerials who had no vassals of their own but who could themselves be vassals of the greater ministerials, began to be called knights as well. In the first half of the thirteenth century, the lesser ministerials, the retainers of extinguished noble lineages who had entered the archbishop's service, and the servile vassals of the greater ministerials began to form a separate estate of knights.

Just as the Investiture Contest had provided the chief impetus for the rise of the greater ministerial lineages, so the so-called *Salzburger Interregnum* (1246–70) gave the knightly lineages, whose ancestry can usually be traced at best to the late twelfth century, an opportunity to improve their position. For instance, Werner of Lengfelden, the ancestor of one of the important late-medieval knightly lineages, the Thurns, served intermittently as the master of the archiepiscopal kitchen between 1241 and 1268; Werner's grandson, Jakob II of Thurn, was in the 1320s the vidame of Salzburg, the official charged with administration of the archbishop's financial and judicial affairs north of the Tauern.[2] Although Archbishop Frederick III (1315–38) still distinguished in 1327, when he levied the first general tax in the principality, between "unsers gottshaus dienstman, ritter und knecht,"[3] the greater ministerials, who began to be called knights themselves after 1270, were coalescing with the knights to form a single estate, the *Ritterstand* of the Later Middle Ages. By the end of the fourteenth century, only two of the approximately twenty greater ministerial lineages (the Felbens and Törrings)—too few to constitute a separate estate—survived and continued to reside in the principality.

The principality, the creation of Archbishop Eberhard II (1200–46), consisted, roughly, of the modern Austrian province of Salzburg and the Rupertiwinkel, a strip of territory on the left bank of the Salzach between the Saalach and Tittmoning, which was ceded to Bavaria in 1816. In addition, the archbishops were the temporal rulers of Mühldorf in Upper Bavaria, Friesach, the largest city in thirteenth-century Carinthia, Pettau (now Ptuj, Yugoslavia), and a territory of approximately three-hundred square kilometers around and including the city of Rann (Brežice, Yugoslavia), outside the archiepiscopal province and more than four hundred kilometers from Salzburg. The diocese itself stretched from the Inn River and its tributary the Isen in southeastern Bavaria, across the modern Austrian provinces of Salzburg, Carinthia, and Styria, as far south as the Drava in Yugoslavia.

The social structure of the late-medieval duchy of Styria, most of which was under the archbishop's spiritual jurisdiction, was very different than the principality's. The Styrian nobility was divided into two estates: the *Herrenstand* or estate of lords, which consisted around 1300 of approximately three surviving lineages of comital or free noble status and twenty-two families of ministerial rank, some of whom like the Styrian Liechtensteins were themselves of noble origin; and a separate estate of knights. While the lords of noble and ministerial status were considered equal under territorial law, they were not equal in feudal law because a lord of ministerial rank could be a vassal of a noble, whereas a noble could not be the vassal of a ministerial. The differences between the ranks within the nobility are graphically illustrated by the size of a woman's dowry (*Heimsteuer*). The amount of a woman's dowry and of a widow's dower, which were intended to provide a couple or a widow with an annual income commensurate with their estate, was fixed by custom within very narrow limits. The dowry of a count's daughter was twice that of a bride who belonged to one of the great ministerial lineages, whose dowry was in turn approximately six times the amount a bride of knightly status received.[4]

There were also two estates of nobles in the late medieval duchy of Austria, the lords and the knights. The Austrian *Herrenstand* was composed of the few surviving lineages of comital or noble rank, the descendants of the Babenberg ministerials, and a few ministerial families whose ancestors had served extinguished comital dynasties. Intermarriages between the lords and the knights were exceptional before 1400, and the most important families of lords, namely, the few dynasties who were legally free and the former Babenberg ministerials, rarely intermarried with those lords whose ancestors had been comital retainers.[5] The formation of a single noble estate, the *Ritterstand*, consisting of both ministerials and knights, in the late-medieval principality of Salzburg was thus an anomaly.

Herbert Klein attributed the absence of an estate of lords in the ecclesiastical principality to the early extinction of most of the ministerial lineages,[6] but Heinz Dopsch pointed out that the number of lordly lineages declined rapidly in Styria too—only ten of the twenty-five lineages in 1300 survived a century later. The key was, according to Dopsch, that the archbishops, whom the Avignonese popes ranked second in wealth among the bishops of Christendom,[7] unlike the Habsburg dukes, turned the extinction of the great min-

isterial houses to their own advantage. The Habsburgs were too preoccupied with imperial politics and financially embarrassed to prevent
the Styrian lords, who married only among their peers, from profiting
from the extinction of their fellows. The surviving dynasties inherited
or bought the possessions of their extinguished colleagues, and the
gap between the Styrian lords and knights widened. Indeed, the Habsburgs were often forced to sell or to pledge properties and rights to
the lords. In contrast, the archbishops concentrated their attention
and considerable resources after 1270 on their principality. They
forced the ministerials to recognize the archbishop's overlordship and
then enforced their feudal rights to obtain the fiefs of extinguished
lineages, bought the lands and rights of impoverished families, and
ruthlessly crushed insubordinate dynasties.[8]

The extinction of both noble and ministerial families was, of
course, a common occurence and had been happening for centuries.
It was due to a combination of factors: restrictions on the numbers
of sons who married, clerical celibacy, the postponement of marriage
by men, a violent life-style, and failure to sire a male heir. For instance,
the following families of greater archiepiscopal ministerials, among
others, had already died out in the male line in the twelfth century:
Seekirchen (1138/39), Högl (1151), Siegsdorf (1171), and Surberg
(1204). Henry of Högl, whose four maternal uncles, the Seekirchens,
did not have a surviving heir, had only a daughter Diemut, Salzburg's
most-sought-after heiress. Her four marriages, including her marriages to Meginhard of Siegsdorf and Megingod II of Surberg, were
childless. Meginhard and his married but childless brother Henry
were killed under unknown circumstances, and Megingod's only
nephew Sigiboto II of Surberg, a bachelor, never returned from the
Third Crusade.[9]

There were two crucial differences between these earlier
family tragedies and what occurred after 1270. First, the archbishop
did not benefit directly from the extinction of these families. Their
property passed via heiresses like Diemut of Högl to another lineage
or the last member or members of a family left their properties to
one or more religious foundations within the archdiocese. For example, most of the Seekirchen-Högl-Surberg fortune was eventually
divided among the cathedral chapter, St. Peter's, and the Nonnberg,
a Benedictine convent in Salzburg. Admittedly, such bequests were
also advantageous to the archbishop because these houses were archiepiscopal proprietary foundations. Dopsch cited the case of the

Gutrats as an early attempt by Archbishop Eberhard II to curb the power of a ministerial lineage.[10] Eberhard confiscated in the 1230s the property of Karl of Gutrat because he had married an Austrian ministerial without the archbishop's permission,[11] but Eberhard restored most of Karl's possessions to his sons Kuno V and Otto II in 1243.[12] On the whole, the archbishops, five of whom came between 1164 and 1270 from princely houses,[13] were too preoccupied with imperial affairs during the High Middle Ages to devote all of their attention to their principality.

Starting with Archbishop Frederick II of Walchen (1270–84), the prince-archbishops were largely recruited from the ministerial and knightly families of southeastern Germany.[14] They were familiar with the affairs of the principality before their elevation to the see of St. Rupert (Frederick II was a member of the last noble family in the principality to enter the archiepiscopal ministerialage and had been the provost of the cathedral chapter), but the late-medieval archbishops also had a more parochial, political perspective than their princely and noble predecessors. The establishment of the Wittelsbachs in Bavaria in 1180 and of the Habsburgs in Austria and Styria in 1282 and in Carinthia in 1335 assured Salzburg's survival for centuries as a buffer state but limited the archbishops' opportunities for further territorial expansion. The boundary between Bavaria and Salzburg was fixed in two agreements in 1254 and 1275,[15] and the modern border between Salzburg and Styria in the Enns valley was established in 1297 after a decade of warfare.[16] The survival of the principality as an independent entity depended upon the elimination of the greater ministerial lineages who had established ties through enfeoffment and marriage to the Wittelsbachs, the Habsburgs, and their retainers. The *Landgerichte*, courts within the principality, where great ministerial families like the Gutrats exercised high justice as vassals of such magnates as the counts of Plain or the dukes of Bavaria, were a special threat to the security of the principality. The archbishops pursued, therefore, after 1270 a systematic policy of eliminating the great ministerial lineages by taking advantage of their familial difficulties, political miscalculations, and financial problems.[17]

The second crucial change after 1270 was the ministerials' growing financial embarrassment. All of the great ministerial lineages who died out in the twelfth century were wealthy at their extinction. Much of our information about them comes from the bequests they made to religious foundations and the disputes this caused. The scribe who recorded Henry of Högl's deathbed bequest to St. Peter's described him, for example, as "predives," exceedngly rich.[18] I know of only one fairly prominent ministerial lineage, the Steinbrünnings, that appears to have been in financial difficulty in the twelfth century. The cause of the Steinbrünnings' trouble was that they permitted at least four out of six sons in the first half of the twelfth century to marry and to alienate some or all of their share of the family patrimony; by 1250 the Steinbrünnings had been reduced to the status of knights.[19] In contrast, the history of many of the ministerial lineages after 1270 is one of mounting debts and property alienations. The beneficiaries of the ministerials' indebtness were the archbishops and some of the knightly families like the Kuchls who enjoyed the archbishops' favor.

While Dopsch was aware of the ministerials' financial difficulties,[20] he did not explain why families that had prospered for two centuries were suddenly in such trouble around 1300. The problem is that we have few records that describe the ministerials' income or expenditures. The evidence for their financial difficulties is simply the documents in which they pledged or sold their property and rights to the archbishop, various churches, or other families.

Since the formation of the *Ritterstand*, a single noble estate that included both ministerials and knights in Salzburg, depended upon the elimination, politically and/or biologically, of the greater ministerial lineages and their replacement, politically and socially, by knightly families, this article will study the political and financial crisis that confronted the greater ministerial lineages after 1270 in the following manner. The first section is concerned with the extinction of the Gutrats in the male line in 1304. The Gutrats were chosen for such special scrutiny because the lists of the Gutrats' archiepiscopal fiefs that were drawn up in conjunction with the Gutrats' pending extinction and the division of their Austrian holdings between the sisters of the last male Gutrat, Kuno VI, provide the best information we have about the properties, rights, and income of a greater ministerial lineage at the end of the thirteenth century. It should be stressed that the Gutrats, unlike some other lineages, were still extremely wealthy and powerful at their demise. The removal of families like the Gutrats was a political necessity if the archbishops wanted to be the real masters of their principality.

The second and third sections are about the Kuchls, a knightly lineage whom Dopsch described as the richest family in fourteenth-century Salzburg[21] and who replaced the Gutrats as the most powerful family in the area around Hallein. The second section is about the lesser ministerials and other individuals who employed the toponymic surname Kuchl before 1250. It is impossible to determine how these Kuchls, some of whom were presumably the ancestors of the later knightly lineage, were related to each other or the later knights. The obscurity that surrounds these petty ministerials contrasts with the considerable information we have about the Gutrats, who were at the same time one of the wealthiest and most influential families in the principality. The Kuchls may even have been vassals of the Gutrats. The third section is largely the story of the meteoric career of one remarkable man, Conrad II of Kuchl, who was for four decades the trusted servant and adviser of four archbishops. Conrad amassed a fortune, which his sons used first to entrench themselves in the Salzach valley south of Salzburg, in the area where the Gutrats had once been the dominant lineage (Kuchl is about nine kilometers south of the Gutratsberg), and then to build in the Rupertiwinkel, what the modern historian of the Kuchls, Walter Brugger, called "a state within a state."[22] Conrad III and Hartneid I of Kuchl utilized the disappearance of the Gutrats, the financial difficulties of some of the other greater ministerial lineages, the temporary financial embarrassment of Archbishop Frederick III after the defeat of the Habsburg party at Mühldorf in 1322, and the election of their cousin Ortolf of Weissenegg (1343–65) as archbishop to create their lordships.

Brugger's otherwise excellent study did not place the story of the Kuchls into the broader context of the decline of the greater ministerial lineages and the formation of a single noble estate, the *Ritterstand*, in the late-medieval principality of Salzburg. The fourth section will examine, therefore, what the history of the Kuchls reveals about the financial and political problems of the greater ministerials after 1270 and will discuss some possible causes of their distress. The ministerials' financial problems, it will be suggested, may have been the cause as well as the consequence of their opposition to the consolidation of archiepiscopal authority after 1270. Several factors may have been involved: a change in family strategy that permitted more than one son in each generation to marry, an extravagant life style, the destructive effects of late-medieval warfare, and a change in the climate that reduced their income. A powerful *Herrenstand*, which would have limited archiepiscopal authority, did not form in the principality of Salzburg because the archbishops possessed both the determination and the resources to exploit the ministerials' familial and financial misfortunes.

As we have seen, the election of Archbishop Frederick II in 1270, followed by the accession of the Habsburgs in Austria and Styria,[23] marks a turning point in the history of Salzburg. The other terminal date, 1343, was chosen because the published sources for the principality end with the accession of Archbishop Ortolf in 1343. The investigation of the history of the few surviving ministerial lineages after 1343 will require considerable archival work; but the ministerials' fate had been sealed by 1343 in any case.

I.

The Extinction of the Gutrats

The Gutrats, whose original home was in Schnaitsee, Upper Bavaria, belonged at the beginning of the twelfth-century to the ministerialage of the counts-palatine of Bavaria. To bind the Schnaitsees to Salzburg, Archbishop Eberhard I (1147–67) entrusted in 1163 Kuno I of Schnaitsee, who had married an archiepiscopal ministerial, with the castellany of Hohenwerfen, the archbishops' main castle south of the city of Salzburg. The Schnaitsee-Gutrats held this office until the 1230s. As the burgraves of Werfen, the Schnaitsee-Gutrats also served as the archiepiscopal judges in the Pongau. After Berchtesgaden started to mine salt around 1190 on the Tuval (known today as the Gutratsberg), north of Hallein, Archbishop Adalbert II (1168–77, 1183–1200) authorized Kuno III to construct a castle on the Tuval to protect Salzburg's interests. The output of the newly rediscovered salt deposits on the nearby Dürrnberg (they had been mined by the Celts and Romans), southwest of Hallein, quickly surpassed those on the Tuval; and Hallein, thirteen kilometers south of Salzburg, became the chief salt-producing center in the eastern Alps and a major source of the archbishops' wealth. Kuno III of Schnaitsee built a second larger castle further down on the Tuval and adopted in 1209 the surname Gutrat. The Gutrats were the only laymen who owned a *Sudhaus*, a facility for evaporating water from the brine, in Hallein (the other eight *Sudhäuser* belonged to the archbishop and various churches). In addition, the counts of Plain had enfeoffed the Schnaitsees with the courts (*Landgerichte*) situated in the Salzach valley between Salzburg and Pass Lueg, thirty kilometers to the south. It was thus only after the Plains' fiefs escheated to the archbishop in 1260, that the Gutrats administered high justice in this stretch of the Salzach valley as vassals of the archbishop. The Gutrats were at the beginning of the thirteenth century the most powerful lords in the upper Salzach valley.[24]

As has already been mentioned, Archbishop Eberhard II declared in 1239 that all of Karl of Gutrat's archiepiscopal fiefs had automatically escheated to the church of Salzburg because he had married without the archbishop's permission an Austrian ministerial, Margaret of Zöbing.[25] Since Karl appeared in the archbishop's entourage until 1234,[26] even though he had married Margaret before November 22, 1230,[27] Karl's extrinsic marriage had merely been a convenient legal pretext to seize the holdings of a ministerial whose divided loyalties threatened the security of the principality after Archbishop Eberhard had sided with Emperor Frederick II against Duke Frederick II of Austria.[28] After Karl's death, the archbishop and the duke, who had joined in the interim the Hohenstaufen party, agreed in 1243 to the division of Karl's sons. Kuno V was to be an archiepiscopal ministerial, Otto II an Austrian retainer. They regained all of their father's possessions, except for the castellany of Hohenwerfen and the court in the Pongau. If either of the brothers died, the other was to obtain the entire inheritance; but the children of the survivor were to be divided equally between the two princes.[29] The first attempt to eliminate a powerful ministerial lineage had been at best a limited success because the needs of the Hohenstaufen party took precedence over the consolidation of archiepiscopal authority within the principality.

Kuno V served the archbishops faithfully for several decades. He was identified in 1266 and again in 1278 as the archiepiscopal seneschal and appears to have occupied this largely ceremonial court office for the rest of his life.[30] Kuno served in 1268 as both the burgrave and captain (*Hauptmann*) of Salzburg[31] but had been replaced as the castellan of Hohensalzburg by 1276 at the latest.[32] The archbishops appointed a captain to command their forces only during an emergency, and Kuno is, in fact, the only person who is known to have held the office during the thirteenth century. Kuno along with the cathedral provost, Frederick of Walchen, and their co-ministerials, Gebhard I of Felben and Conrad V of Kalham-Wartenfels, governed the principality during the absence of Archbishop Ladislaus (1265–70), who had assumed in 1266 the regency of the duchy of Silesia-Breslau for his nephew. After Frederick became archbishop in 1270, Kuno and his colleagues were the archbishop's chief advisers.[33]

Archbishop Rudolph (1284–90) started in the winter of 1288/89 a bitter, ten-year war with Duke Albrecht of Austria, the future King Albrecht I, about, among other things, their respective rights in the upper Enns valley.[34] On January 11, 1290, during peace negotiations in Vienna, the archbishop agreed that Kuno, who had supported the duke, could continue to serve Albrecht but without prejudice to the archbishop's lordship and jurisdiction.[35] It is worth noting that Kuno employed the next day the toponym Senftenberg,[36] the name of one of his mother's Austrian castles. Kuno must have decided that he owed his primary allegiance to the duke rather than the archbishop. Kuno's disloyalty was especially dangerous for the archbishop because Duke Leopold VI had appointed Kuno's grandfather Kuno III around 1200 as the protector of Admont's property contiguous to his own in the upper Enns valley,[37] that is, in the very area that was in dispute. This incident must have alerted the archbishops to the very real threat that the Gutrats posed to the security of Salzburg.

The extinction of the Gutrats in the male line provided Archbishop Conrad IV (1291–1312) with his opportunity. Kuno V's brother Otto II announced on January 8, 1296, that he had voluntarily surrendered to Conrad all of his alods situated within the archdiocese, including people, lands, and castles, and that he and his son Henry had then been enfeoffed by the archbishop with their former alods and other fiefs. Otto acknowledged that the alods had been *Inwärtseigen*, alods that could be alienated only to other members of the archiepiscopal *familia* or to archiepiscopal proprietary foundations. It was agreed that if Otto and Henry died without an heir, their fiefs would escheat to the church.[38] After his father's death Henry declared on January 27, 1299, that he had resigned his alods, including the two castles on the Gutratsberg with their appurtenances, to the archbishop and that Conrad IV had enfeoffed him and any male heirs he might yet father with the lineage's former alods. Henry also surrendered all his rights to the advocacy in the upper Enns valley,[39] that is, the subadvocacy over Admont's property that Duke Leopold had conferred to Otto's grandfather.

The latter provision was directly related to the end of the war between the archbishop and duke. On September 24, 1297, Duke Albrecht had surrendered to Conrad IV the advocacy over Admont's properties situated west of the Mandling, a tributary of the Enns.[40] This was the advocacy that Conrad IV obtained from Henry in 1299. The Mandling still forms the border between the modern provinces of Salzburg and Styria in the Enns valley. The childless Henry was dead by November 3, 1299, and his fiefs escheated to the archbishop.[41]

The chief targets of these agreements were Henry's cousins, the children of Otto's brother Kuno V, who had died sometime between March 10, 1294, and September 14, 1296.[42] On March 16, 1304, Archbishop Conrad IV settled his unspecified differences with Kuno V's children: Kuno VI, who had been a minor at his father's death,[43] Herburg, who was married by 1296 to the Bavarian ministerial Walter of Taufkirchen;[44] and Elsbeth, who was married by 1304 to the Austrian ministerial, Eberhard the Younger of Wallsee. The latter was the son of Eberhard the Elder, the *Landrichter* of the Land ob der Enns, the chief Habsburg official in Upper Austria.[45] Kuno VI, like his uncle and cousin, surrendered to the archbishop all his alods, including the two castles on the Gutratsberg, situated within the archdiocese (the Gutrats' possessions in the duchy of Austria were specifically excluded) and received them back in fief along with the fiefs that had belonged to Henry. It was stipulated that Kuno would forfeit his fiefs if he married someone who did not belong to the archiepiscopal *familia* or if he permitted the archbishop's enemies to use his castles. In return, Conrad IV agreed to treat Kuno as an *Amtmann* (the official charged with the administration of one of the manorial offices to which the archbishops' estates were assigned), seneschal, and ministerial of the church. If Kuno died without an heir, his archiepiscopal fiefs were to escheat to the archbishop, who was to pay Kuno's sisters and their heirs 400 marks of pure silver (if one of the sisters died without heirs, the other would receive the entire amount). Herburg and Elsbeth were required to renounce all their rights to Kuno's archiepiscopal fiefs, except for the Gutrats' ancestral domain, Schnaitsee, which Herburg of Taufkirchen possessed, because it was an *Inwärtseigen*.[46] Besides, Schnaitsee was situated within the duchy of Bavaria. The terms of this agreement suggest that the cause of the archbishop's displeasure had been Herburg's and Elsbeth's marriages outside the archiepiscopal *familia* and the threat that these marriages, which would have installed Wittelsbach and Habsburg ministerials in the Gutrats' place, posed to the principality's security.

Although this agreement does not mention Kuno VI's health, it appears to have been prompted by the expectation that he would soon die unmarried and without an heir. On August 17, 1304, the Taufkirchens and Wallsees divided the Gutrats' holdings that were situated outside the ecclesiastical principality, basically, the inheritance of Margaret of Zöbing in Lower Austria. It consisted of two castles (Senftenberg and Zöbing), two market towns, three villages, the patronage of six churches, and assorted properties and vineyards.[47] The Taufkirchens sold their share of this Austrian inheritance to the Wallsees in 1314 for 2,250 pounds.[48]

Henry of Gutrat had compiled in 1299 a list of the fiefs he had inherited,[49] and the archiepiscopal chancellery drew up a more detailed list of the Gutrats' fiefs after Henry's death.[50] According to these lists, the Gutrats held the following fiefs from the archbishop: the courts at Gaissau and in the Kuchltal, that is, on both banks of the Salzach between Salzburg and Pass Lueg, thirty kilometers to the south, and at Abtenau on the Lammer, a tributary of the Salzach; advocatorial rights over ecclesiastical property in the Styrian Ramsau, that is, east of the Mandling in the Enns valley, in Plankenau (south of St. Johann in the Pongau in the upper Salzach valley), and in Abtenau and Gaissau; tithes in the Ramsau, in the valley of the Grossarl (a tributary of the Salzach in the Pongau), in St. Johann in the Pongau, and in Reut in the Pongau; and various other properties. These rights and properties paid in a good year, according to the second list, approximately 210 Salzburg pounds in addition to considerable payments in kind; but the second list did not include several fiefs that Henry mentioned in his own list, most notably, the *Sudhaus* in Hallein and the two castles on the Gutratsberg. However, the Kuchls purchased the *Sudhaus* in 1330 for 1,500 Salzburg pounds.[51] If we figure, as was done in calculating the value of an annual income, that the income represented one-tenth of the value of a property,[52] then the *Sudhaus* would have provided the Gutrats with an annual income of approximately £150.

We can thus arrive at a rough estimate of the Gutrats' annual income. Their properties in the ecclesiastical principality would have paid at least 360 Salzburg pounds. If we assume that the Taufkirchens had obtained half of the Gutrats' Austrian possessions, which they sold in 1314 for 2,250 (Viennese?) pounds, then the total value of the Austrian lands would have been £4,500, which would have provided the Gutrats with an annual income of £450. Since the Taufkirchens had acquired the Gutrats' ancestral holdings in Schnaitsee, whose value is in any case unknown, it is possible that the Wallsees' share of the Austrian inheritance was worth more than £2,250. We can conclude, therefore, that the Gutrats' estimated annual income of £810 errs on the conservative side. Moreover, this figure does not include the value of the payments they received in kind.

To place this figure into some sort of perspective, it is worth noting that the Bavarian *Landfrieden* of 1244, 1256, 1281, and 1300, which were also in effect in Salzburg,[53] stipulated that a knight required a minimum annual income of thirty pounds to maintain a castle, that is, to live in a manner that befit his estate.[54] The figures reveal the chasm that separated a greater ministerial lineage like the Gutrats from the knights in the thirteenth century.

The history of the Gutrats shows how Archbishop Conrad IV used his position as the ministerials' feudal and service lord (*Dienstherr*) to eliminate a powerful ministerial lineage. It also reveals why it was so important for the archbishops to prevent the ministerials' marriages to "foreigners" and, if possible, to exclude the greater ministerials altogether from the affairs of the principality. The Gutrats' courts and advocacies gave them extensive judicial rights in the upper Salzach and Enns valleys, which they exercised independently from the archbishop's authority until 1260 and 1297, respectively; the two castles on the Gutratsberg posed a potential threat to the archiepiscopal saltworks in Hallein; and the Gutrats' advocacy in the upper Enns valley controlled an invasion route into the principality. Moreover, the Gutrats' loyalty, as Kuno V's behavior after 1288/89 indicates, was uncertain. The establishment of Wittelsbach and/or Habsburg ministerials in the Gutrats' place in the principality would have made a bad situation intolerable. The disinheritance of Kuno VI's sisters was the only solution. The archbishops could not be the masters of their principality until they had broken the power of dynasties like the Gutrats.

The Gutrats were hardly, however, in financial difficulty in 1304, perhaps because the *Sudhaus* provided them with an unusual but lucrative source of income. It is worth noting in this context that the Cistercian abbey of Raitenhaslach exchanged or sold most of its salt from its *Sudhaus* in Hallein in Krems, the center of the Austrian wine-producing area in the Wachau.[55] Since the Gutrats' Austrian holdings were situated in this region—Senftenberg is five kilometers northwest of Krems and Zöbing eleven kilometers to the northeast—one can only wonder if the Gutrats shipped salt via the Salzach, Inn, and Danube to Lower Austria and imported wine to Salzburg.

Other ministerial families were not, as the history of the Kuchls will show, as fortunate. The Kuchls replaced the Gutrats not only as the owners of the *Sudhaus* in Hallein but also as the most powerful lineage in the upper Salzach valley between Salzburg and Pass Lueg. We will have to investigate in particular how the Kuchls, the most important of the knightly families who rose to prominence after 1270, acquired their great wealth and why many of the greater ministerial lineages were, unlike the Gutrats, in such financial difficulty by the beginning of the fourteenth century.

2.

The Early Kuchls

While the Gutrats were one of the most powerful families in the principality by the second half of the twelfth century, little is known about the Kuchls before 1250. Some of the individuals who employed the toponymic surname Kuchl before the Interregnum were archiepiscopal ministerials, but it is impossible to establish how they were related to each other or to the later knights. Two other prominent fourteenth-century knightly lineages, the Lengfelden-Thurns and the Wiesbachs, were the direct descendants of lesser ministerials of the twelfth century who had been vassals, that is, *milites*, of the greater ministerials who served as the burgraves of Hohensalzburg.[56] Since some of the early Kuchls appear to have been members of the garrison of Hohenwerfen, it is possible that the ancestors of Conrad II of Kuchl were vassals of the Gutrats who were the castellans of that fortress between 1163 and the 1230s. This is, however, an educated guess. Essentially, the history of the Kuchls as a lineage begins only in 1249/50 with Conrad I, the probable father of Conrad II.

Megingoz, who has listed as a witness before 1140 after several archiepiscopal ministerials, was the first person to employ the surname Kuchl. His placement in the witness list indicates that he may have been a ministerial.[57] Ozo of Kuchl appeared in a group of ministerials in 1122/47, when an archiepiscopal ministerial gave the cathedral canons an alod.[58]

Archbishop Eberhard I referred specifically to Hartwig of Kuchl as an archiepiscopal ministerial in 1160/63, when Eberhard settled Hartwig's dispute with his stepson Manegold of Kellau (three kilometers southeast of Kuchl) about an alod that belonged to Manegold's mother. Eberhard I of Kuchl was among the witnesses, but there is no indication that Hartwig and Eberhard I were kinsmen.[59]

The archiepiscopal ministerial Eberhard of Kuchl and his wife Wernburg renounced the world in 1170/83 and gave the cathedral chapter, which they presumably joined as a lay brother and sister (a convent was attached to the chapter), two alods they owned in Upper Bavaria and in an unidentified *Puchschach*. His brothers Adalmann and Wolfker gave their consent.[60] There is no other reference to Wolfker, but the cathedral canons remembered Adalmann on September 21.[61] Eberhard had a third brother Eppo, who was mentioned in 1163/66.[62]

Brugger thought that the Kuchls might have come originally from the Pongau because Eberhard's brothers Eppo and Ortolf lived there.[63] Brugger based his argument on the witness list in the charter in which Archbishop Eberhard settled Hartwig of Kuchl's dispute with his stepson. It reads: "Eberhardus de Cuculis, Eppo Eberhardi frater de Pongou, Dietmarus de Einode, Ortolfus frater Epponis et Eberhardi de Pongou."[64] While it seems strange, if Brugger is right, that the scribe did not simply note the presence of Eberhard of Kuchl and his brothers Eppo and Ortolf and referred to Eberhard himself by two different names, Eberhard of Kuchl did have, as we have already seen, a brother named Eppo. In addition, Provost Gerhoch of Reichersberg (1132–69) noted in the *Annales Reicherspergenses* that Archbishop Eberhard I permitted his ministerials in 1159 to give property to the Augustinian canons of Seckau in Styria and that Ortolf of Kuchl gave the canons his property in *Puochsachen*.[65] Archbishop Adalbert II confirmed this donation in 1197.[66] We can conclude, one, that Eberhard I of Kuchl who owned property in *Puchschach* had a fourth brother Ortolf of Kuchl who possessed property in *Puochsachen* and, two, that Eberhard of Kuchl and Eberhard of the Pongau, both of whom had brothers named Eppo and Ortolf, were the same person. But I cannot explain why the scribe gave Eberhard two different surnames in the same charter.

It is less certain, however, that the Kuchls came from the Pongau. As we have seen, Eberhard I owned property in Upper Bavaria, though it could have belonged originally to his wife, and *Puchschach/Puochsachen* has been identified as either Buchschachern on the Thalgauberg, northeast of Salzburg, or as Puchschachen, four kilometers northwest of Seckau, Styria.[67] Eberhard I and his brothers can thus be linked to other areas besides the Pongau. The Kuchls' association with the Pongau may indicate, instead, that they performed garrison duty at Hohenwerfen, the archbishop's chief castle in the Pongau, which was situated sixteen kilometers south of Kuchl. The charter of Archbishop Eberhard that Eberhard I and his brothers Eppo and Ortolf witnessed was issued in fact in Hohenwerfen. Since Kuno I of Schnaitsee became the castellan of Hohenwerfen shortly after the charter was drafted,[68] the Kuchls may have been for several decades vassals of the Schnaitsee-Gutrats.

Several other individuals employed the surname Kuchl in the second half of the twelfth century. During of Kuchl was listed in 1151/63 after the archiepiscopal ministerials, During of Diebering, Kuno I's predecessor as the burgrave of Hohenwerfen, and Eckart of Tann in an entry in the cathedral canons' codex of traditions.[69] During's placement in the list indicates that he, too, may have been a ministerial who was assigned to the garrison of Hohenwerfen, and his name, which was not very common, suggests that he may have been a godson of During of Diebering. Towards the end of the twelfth century, Willibirg of Thalgau, who belonged to the archiepiscopal *familia*, gave the monks of St. Peter's two serfs as altar dependents (*censuales*). Etich of Kuchl and Lembert of Kuchl and his son Lembert followed the abbatial cook Gunther as witnesses.[70] As we have seen, the Kuchls' property at *Puchschach/Puochsachen* may have been situated on the Thalgauberg. Willibirg could thus have been a kinswoman of the Kuchls, but Etich's and the Lemberts' placement after the abbatial cook suggests that they were members of the abbatial *familia* rather than archiepiscopal ministerials. This was certainly true of Henry, the bailiff (*preco*) of Kuchl, and Frederick of Kuchl who witnessed an entry in the monks' *Traditionsbuch* in 1188/93.[71]

There are fewer references to the Kuchls in the first half of the thirteenth century. Gottschalk I of Kuchl served as a witness in 1204. He was listed between Wolfram of Eichham, a prominent archiepiscopal ministerial, and Hermann, a knight and the illegitimate son of Megingod II of Surberg, a powerful ministerial who had been from 1166/67 until his death in 1193 the burgrave of Hohensalzburg.[72] Gottschalk could thus have been either a ministerial or knight. The widow Tuta of Kuchl gave St. Peter's in 1199/1214 with the consent of her sons, Eberhard II and Ulrich, a quarter of their property situated north of Teisendorf, Bavaria, when her son Conrad became a monk.[73] The cathedral canons celebrated Tuta's anniversary on February 18.[74] While one of Tuta's sons Eberhard II bore the same name as one of the earlier Kuchls and while the extremely common name Conrad was the leading name of the later knightly lineage, this evidence is not sufficient to link these Kuchls to either the earlier ministerial Eberhard I and his wife Wernburg who had renounced the world in 1170/83 or to the later Kuchls. Henricus Chucheler was a monk in St. Peter's around 1228.[75] Finally, Bertha of Kuchl joined the cathedral canons' prayer fraternity around 1200.[76]

In conclusion, a number of archiepiscopal ministerials lived in Kuchl in the twelfth century: Hartwig and Eberhard I and his four brothers Adalmann, Eppo, Ortolf, and Wolfker. Several others individuals who employed the surname Kuchl before 1250 were in all probability ministerials as well: Megingoz, Ozo, During, Gottschalk I, Tuta and her sons Eberhard II, Ulrich, and Conrad, the monk Henricus Chucheler, and Bertha. It is impossible to arrange their names in a meaningful family tree. At least some of these men appear to have performed garison duty at the archiepiscopal castle of Hohenwerfen in the Pongau and may have been vassals of its burgraves, the Dieberings and the Schnaitsee-Gutrats. In addition, the abbey of St. Peter owned property in Kuchl, and some of its men used the name Kuchl: Henry, the bailiff of Kuchl; Frederick; Etich; and Lembert and his son Lembert. The best guess is that the later Kuchls were the descendants of one or another of the lesser ministerials, the "ministeriales et militares minores" as they would be called in 1262,[77] even if we cannot establish the genealogical connection; but the members of the later knightly estate were of such diverse origin that it is also conceivable that the later Kuchls were the descendants of one of the abbey's retainers, say, the bailiff Henry.[78] The difference between the early Kuchls and the Gutrats, whom the early Kuchls may have served and whom the later Kuchls replaced, is striking.

3.

### The Knights of Kuchl

Just as the greater ministerials suddenly appeared during or immediately after the Investiture Contest, so the Kuchls, the richest and most powerful of the new knightly lineages, emerged in the person of Conrad II, seemingly out of nowhere, after the *Salzburger Interregnum* (1246–70). Conrad became the chief adviser of four archbishops as they consolidated their authority within the principality and amassed a personal fortune in the process. In fact, Conrad I, who was probably Conrad II's father, may have laid the financial basis for his son's career through his involvement in the production of salt.

The history of the later Kuchls begins with Conrad I, "miles de Chuchil," who represented the cathedral chapter in 1249/50 on a commission of arbitration that settled the canons' dispute with St. Peter's about the boundaries of their properties in Scheffau and Abtenau, southeast of Kuchl.[79] Conrad's designation indicates that he was a member of the nascent knightly estate.

The next reference to a Conrad of Kuchl occurs only in 1270, but it is a highly significant one. The brothers Ulrich II and Henry III of Radeck, who belonged to a prominent family of archiepiscopal ministerials,[80] announced on April 21, 1270, that they had settled their dispute with Ulrich II of Wiesbach, Conrad of Kuchl, and their associates about the castle of Radeck and certain other issues. Henry of Radeck agreed to pay the consortium 250 Salzburg pounds in installments, namely, £20 on June 24 and £30 on September 8. He pledged the castle of Radeck and an annual income of £20 to cover the remaining £200.[81] This agreement reveals that a prominent lineage of archiepiscopal ministerials was already in considerable financial difficulty by 1270 and that the Kuchls were individuals of some means before they entered, as far as we know, the archbishop's service.

We do not know which Conrad of Kuchl was involved in the 1270 transaction. Brugger and Dopsch identified him as Conrad II, the son of the Conrad who had served as an arbiter in 1249/50;[82] but there is no definite evidence to prove either assertion. There is no question that there were two different Conrads because the younger man lived until 1324/25.[83] Even if we assume that Conrad II was only twenty in 1270, he would have been seventy-five in 1324/25. This is possible, but was the man who lent the Radecks money a teenager? Since there are only two other references to a Conrad of Kuchl before 1285—in 1278 and in 1281[84]—it is just as conceivable that Conrad I was still alive in the 1270s. While Conrad II was called a ministerial on two occasions,[85] he was classified as a knight in a 1286 charter that still distinguished carefully between ministerials and knights.[86] The later Kuchls were thus lesser ministerials and knights.

What was the source of the money that Conrad I or II of Kuchl lent to the Radecks? Once again, there is no definite answer, but two pieces of circumstantial evidence suggest that the Kuchls may have been involved in the production of salt in Hallein. First, the other individual who represented the cathedral chapter on the commission of arbitration in 1249/50 was Brother Albert, the manager of the chapter's *Sudhaus* in Hallein. Could Conrad I have been connected with that operation as well? Second, Archbishop Rudolph leased for a year in 1285 the four archiepiscopal *Sudhäuser* in Hallein for £1,250 to a consortium of ten individuals who included Gottschalk II of Kuchl.[87] Could Conrad I and/or Conrad II have engaged in similar transactions? In any case, Conrad II and his sons subsequently became involved, in the production and transportation of salt.

Brugger thought that Gottschalk II and Gerhard of Kuchl, whom Henry of Gutrat enfeoffed in 1299 with three properties, with which Gottschalk II's son Pilgrim had previously been enfeoffed,[88] were the sons of Conrad I and the brothers of Conrad II.[89] This supposition is not supported by any documentary evidence. As the 1299 enfeoffment shows, Gottschalk II and Gerhard were associated with the Gutrats. For instance, Gottschalk II was mentioned for the first time in 1271, when Kuno V of Gutrat compensated St. Peter's for injuries he had caused the abbey. Gottschalk was listed on this occasion after the Gärrs, knightly vassals of the Gutrats.[90] All that we can say with any degree of certainty is that Gottschalk II and Gerhard like Conrad II were probably the descendants of some of the individuals who had used the surname Kuchl before 1250 and were linked like the earlier Kuchls to the Gutrats.

Conrad II raised himself and his descendants from these comparatively humble origins to the highest rank of Salzburg society through forty years of service to four archbishops. He became in essence the archbishops' chief adviser in temporal matters. Conrad was identified on July 6, 1285, as the vidame of Salzburg.[91] Archbishop Rudolph sent Conrad on a diplomatic mission to Vienna in October 1286.[92] By December 1, 1286, Conrad was the captain of Kropfsberg, which was situated on the western border of the principality at the confluence of the Ziller and Inn Rivers. Conrad may have been sent there because the archbishop's position had been threatened by the illegal construction of a new castle in the Zillertal.[93] He was back in Salzburg by April 20, 1287, when he witnessed as the urban judge of Salzburg, the chief archiepiscopal official in the city, the *Sühnebrief*, in which Archbishop Rudolph reconciled the "rich" and "poor" burghers and granted Salzburg its first municipal charter (*Stadtrecht*).[94] Archbishop Rudolph must have recalled Conrad to help restore order in the city. Conrad was reinstated sometime between February 29 and

December 26, 1288, as the vidame of Salzburg[95] and held this position during the archbishops' long war with Duke Albrecht of Austria.

As the vidame, Conrad may have been involved in one of the major incidents during the war. After a rumor reached Salzburg in November 1295 that Duke Albrecht had died, Archbishop Conrad IV ordered the burghers of Salzburg and Hallein, accompanied by one hundred armed men, under the command of an unnamed vidame to destroy the Habsburgs' saline in Gosau, Upper Austria, about thirty kilometers east of Kuchl. The Salzburgers caused an estimated three thousand pounds in damages.[96] Franz Martin thought that the vidame in question was either Conrad of Kuchl or Rudolph III of Fohnsdorf.[97] The latter was the archiepiscopal vidame in Friesach, Carinthia and the commander of the archiepiscopal forces during the war. Rudolph was identified in the *Österreichische Reimchronik* as Archbishop Conrad IV's closest blood relative.[98] The destruction of Gosau would certainly have been in keeping with Rudolph's other actions, and he would have had a personal motive to do so—Duke Albrecht had destroyed the castle of Fohnsdorf in 1289;[99] but since the men who destroyed Gosau came from Salzburg and Hallein, it is more likely that Conrad of Kuchl was in charge. Moreover, Conrad also had a personal motive for destroying Gosau: Archbishop Conrad IV had enfeoffed Conrad with a share in the corporation that possessed a monopoly for transporting salt on the Salzach.[100] The works at Gosau were thus a threat to Conrad's own income. Conrad's role in this incident may explain why he was replaced as the vidame of Salzburg shortly after Archbishop Conrad IV made peace with Duke Albrecht in September 1297—the first reference to Conrad's successor, Provost John of Berchtesgaden, who had supported the Habsburgs during the war,[101] occurs on November 20, 1297.[102]

While Archbishop Conrad IV may have removed Conrad from his office for diplomatic reasons, Conrad retained his influence. He had been one of four individuals who were identified in 1291 as members of the archiepiscopal council,[103] the first time that body was specifically mentioned;[104] and he belonged to the council for the rest of his life.[105] Conrad served again from 1306 to 1312 as the *Stadtrichter* of Salzburg.[106] While the archbishop appointed the judge, the *Stadtrichter* had to be a burgher of Salzburg and live within the city.[107] Conrad did own a house on the market square in Salzburg, from which he assigned to the cathedral canons in 1304 an annual income of two pounds to say a mass on the anniversary of his death.[108]

Archbishop-Elect Weichart (1312–15) appointed the cathedral provost Frederick of Leibnitz on April 28, 1312, as his general vicar in spiritual and temporal matters during his absence at the curia and selected the "discrete man" Conrad of Kuchl as the provost's adviser and assistant in the administration of the temporal affairs of the church.[109] This appointment may explain why Conrad was identified on May 21, 1312, as the *Hauptmann* of Salzburg,[110] the first reference to the captaincy since Kuno V of Gutrat had served in 1268 as the captain during the absence of Archbishop Ladislaus. Conrad's appointment is one example of how the Kuchls took the place once held by the Gutrats. Provost Frederick must have been equally impressed with Conrad's abilities because as archbishop-elect he sent instructions from Orange in Provence on May 1, 1316, to his vicars, namely, the dean of the cathedral chapter and the vigorous knight (*strennuo militi*) Conrad of Kuchl, and to the other unnamed members of the council to avoid a war with King Louis of Bavaria in Frederick's absence in spite of Bavarian provocations.[111] Conrad II must have been an extraordinarily capable man, and his career is even more spectacular if we remember that he was a *novus homo.*

Conrad's second marriage and the marriages of his daughters reveal how far the Kuchls had risen. His first wife Diemut, whose family of origin is unknown, was mentioned in 1298; they had at least one daughter.[112] This unnamed daughter was in all probability the Diemut who was married by 1318 to Ekk of Felben, the scion of a noble family in the Pinzgau that had entered the archiepiscopal ministerialage at the beginning of the thirteenth century.[113] Conrad married in 1302 Margaret of Weissenegg, the daughter of Otto I of Weissenegg, a Carinthian ministerial of the bishop of Bamberg, who had been in 1283 the judge and captain of the bishop of Bamberg in Villach, Carinthia, but who had served in 1289 as the archiepiscopal burgrave of Friesach.[114] This marriage proved highly advantageous to the Kuchls when Margaret's nephew Ortolf of Weissenegg became archbishop in 1343.[115]

Archbishop Conrad IV must have attached great importance to this marriage because he gave the couple one hundred Salzburg pounds as a wedding present. If the marriage was childless and if Conrad predeceased her, Margaret was not to remarry without the archbishop's permission. If she did, she would forfeit the £100. Conrad assigned her an annual income of £150 from his lands as her widow's dower and gave her £100 as her *Morgengabe.* The widow's dower was to revert to the children of Conrad's first marriage after Margaret's death if she did not have children of her own. In return, Margaret renounced any rights she might have to Conrad's fiefs, houses, and moveable property.[116]

Margaret and Conrad did in fact have two sons, Conrad III and Hartneid I, who was named after one of her brothers, and at least one daughter,[117] perhaps Agnes who was married to Frederick II of Törring, a member of the only lineage of archiepiscopal ministerials that survives today (they have been counts since 1630).[118] Conrad's second marriage and the marriages of his daughters are indicative of his status in Salzburg society. Such marriages between ministerials and knights contributed to the formation of a single knightly estate within the principality, just as marriages between ministerials and noblewomen in the twelfth century had been a factor in the gradual ennoblement of the ministerials.[119]

Conrad does not appear to have made any major property acquisitions before 1318,[120] but during the last six years of his life he was concerned with providing for the well-being of his children. His son-in-law Ekk of Felben had incurred considerable debts, secured by various properties and rights in the Pinzgau and Pongau in the upper Salzach valley. A document of September 26, 1318, indicates that Conrad had redeemed pledges of 210 Salzburg pounds, 70 Aquileian marks (70 Salzburg pounds), £75, and £35 as they had come due and that Ekk had retained the right until September 29, 1319, to buy back the properties and rights from his father-in-law.[121] Ekk did not and sold the properties to Conrad on April 22, 1324.[122] Since no price was indicated, the latter transaction was probably a formality. Archbishop Frederick III enfeoffed Conrad II and his son and daughter, Conrad III and Diemut, with Ekk's former holdings on April 29.[123] Conrad provided in this way for his daughter after her husband's bankruptcy.

Conrad purchased in 1319 two properties located north of St. Johann in the Pongau and an annual rent of a pound from Wulfing I of Goldegg, who belonged to the most important ministerial lineage in the Pongau.[124] Conrad made several other acquisitions as well.[125] It should be stressed that most of Conrad's acquisitions were confined to the area south of Salzburg, particularly in the Pinzgau and the Pongau. He was still alive on July 4, 1324, but had died by October 2, 1325.[126] The cathedral canons celebrated on August 27 the anniversary of the knight of St. Rupert's, Conrad of Kuchl, who had joined the canons' prayer fraternity along with his first wife Diemut and sister Mechthild during his tenure as vidame.[127]

Conrad's sons, Conrad III and Hartneid I, served the archbishops in a variety of capacities and greatly expanded the family's holdings. The focus of the Kuchls' acquisitions and interests shifted gradually from the upper Salzach valley northward. The brothers took advantage not only of the financial difficulties of the great ministerial lineages, but also of the temporary financial embarrassment of Archbishop Frederick III, who had sided in 1322 with the losing Habsburg party at the battle of Mühldorf, which cost the Habsburgs the throne for more than a century. Frederick was forced to raise considerable sums to ransom his men.[128] Conrad III and Hartneid reached the height of their power in the mid-fourteenth century when their first cousin Ortolf of Weissenegg was archbishop.

Since Conrad and Hartneid were still rather young when their father died (Hartneid was a minor who lacked his own seal in 1325 and 1326),[129] their mother acted as the actual head of the lineage. Archbishop Frederick announced on October 2, 1325, that Conrad, Hartneid, and Margaret had paid him 300 Salzburg pounds for the lifelong possession of the castle of Golling, situated four kilometers south of Kuchl, an annual income of twelve pounds from the saltworks in Hallein, and assorted cultivated properties, most of which were situated around Kuchl. The Kuchls were responsible for keeping the castle of Golling in proper repair.[130] Golling was in the fourteenth century the seat of the Gutrats' old court in the Kuchltal.[131] The Kuchls had thus taken the place of the Gutrats in the Salzach valley between Salzburg and Pass Lueg. The Kuchls retained Golling until 1375.[132]

The next day Archbishop Frederick sold the castle of Staufeneck on the left bank of the Saalach in Bavaria, eleven kilometers southwest of Salzburg and four kilometers northeast of Bad Reichenhall, with its appurtenances, including the court at Aufham, four kilometers northwest of Staufeneck, to Conrad and Hartneid for 1,500 Salzburg pounds. As the lords of Staufeneck, the Kuchls exercised high justice on the left bank of the Saalach between Bad Reichenhall and the Salzach. The Kuchls were to keep the castle in proper repair, though the archbishop was to compensate them if the castle burned or collapsed, to defend it with the archbishop's assistance, to keep it at the archbishop's disposal, and not to employ it against the archbishop. The archbishop retained the right to redeem Staufeneck,[133] which Archbishop Conrad IV had purchased in 1306 from the Staufenecks, a heavily indebted lineage of archiepiscopal ministerials.[134] Archbishop Ortolf regained the castle and court two decades later.[135] The Kuchls were entrenched for the time being in the Salzach and Saalach valleys, though Archbishop Frederick III was careful to safeguard the archbishopric's rights to both Golling and Staufeneck.

The Kuchls joined Rüdiger V of Radeck, the grandson of the man to whom their father or grandfather had lent money in 1270, on March 25, 1326, in an even more spectacular loan of £1,850 to the archbishop. In return, Archbishop Frederick III appointed Rüdiger and Conrad III as the coburgraves of Hohensalzburg, the archbishops' chief castle, where they were required to live. The archbishop was to pay them a pension of £450 the first year and £400 thereafter; in exchange, Rüdiger and Conrad were to serve the archbishop with twenty men. If the archbishop decided to remove Rüdiger and Conrad from their office, he would no longer be required to pay them their pension and they would be free of their obligation to serve the archbishop. The debt was then to be paid from the properties and rights that the archbishop had pledged to them, namely, £1,000 from the saltworks in Hallein and the remainder from the tolls in Salzburg, as soon as both were unencumbered. Rüdiger of Radeck was to serve as the vidame of Salzburg until all three men had been repaid. If Conrad and Hartneid died without heirs, the archbishop would be responsible for providing their unnamed sisters, the daughters of both of Conrad II's marriages, with dowries.[136]

In spite of Rüdiger V's loan to the archbishop, the Radecks must have been in growing financial difficulty. In 1326 Rüdiger of Radeck and his brother Henry IV sold their share of some properties in the Pongau, which they had owned jointly with the Kuchls, to Conrad and Hartneid for £100.[137] The Radecks sold in 1334 their half of the castle of Radeck to the archbishop for 1,025 Salzburg pounds. Archbishop Frederick III deducted from this amount the £125 that Archbishop Frederick II had lent Ulrich II of Radeck in 1273.[138] The Radecks then assigned 100 of the remaining £900 to Henry IV's wife as her widow's dower and repaid a loan of £150 they owed the Kuchls.[139]

In 1338 the Kuchls took advantage of the political and financial problems of the Goldeggs. On November 2 Conrad and Hartneid purchased for £500 from Frederick of Goldegg various properties, advocatorial rights, and serfs near Wagrain in the Pongau and in the valley of the Gastein, a tributary of the upper Salzach.[140] The next day Frederick of Goldegg sold to Conrad and Hartneid for £1,500 the *Sudhaus* in Hallein, with which the Goldeggs had been enfeoffed after the extinction of the Gutrats. The Kuchls paid Frederick £500 in cash and assigned the income from farmland that the archbishop had granted them to cover the remaining £1,000.[141] Conrad III's and Hartneid's purchases and loans between 1325 and 1330 indicate that they must have inherited a substantial amount of liquid capital from their father.

We have one clue to the source of Conrad II's wealth. As has already been mentioned, Archbishop Conrad IV granted Conrad in 1295 a vacant position among the *Schiffherren* of Laufen, which Conrad III and Hartneid inherited.[142] The *Schiffherren*, a consortium composed originally of twenty-seven burghers of Laufen, possessed a monopoly on the transportation of salt on the Salzach. Each member was allowed to own two large ships and one small one. The salt had to be unloaded and reloaded in Laufen, seventeen kilometers downstream from Salzburg, because of the rapids in the Salzach.[143] The possession of a share was thus a highly lucrative privilege, especially after the Kuchls acquired the *Sudhaus* in Hallein in 1330. It is worth noting in this regard that Archbishop Frederick III granted another share in the consortium in 1322 to Jakob II of Thurn, a member of another prominent knightly lineage when he served as the vidame of Salzburg in 1322.[144] As Archbishop Conrad's wedding present to Conrad II and Margaret shows, the archbishops undoubtedly found other ways to reward their chief officials for their services.

The Kuchls' interests shifted north of Salzburg in the 1330s. Conrad III purchased in 1339 from Eckart of Tann, who belonged to a powerful ministerial lineage that possessed the *Landgerichte* northeast of Salzburg, various scattered properties situated on both banks of the Salzach between Laufen and Tittmoning, eighteen kilometers downstream from Laufen. No prices was given.[145] The archiepiscopal ministerial Conrad II of Oberndorf sold to Conrad in 1340 for £535 various properties located for the most part in the Rupertiwinkel, the section of the principality situated on the left bank of the Salzach between the Saalach and Tittmoning.[146] The same year Archbishop Henry (1338–43) and the other owners of *Sudhäuser* in Hallein purchased a mill in Hallein from Conrad and Hartneid. The archbishop enfeoffed them in exchange with a manor in Mülln on the northern outskirts of the city of Salzburg, where the Kuchls built a suburban residence.[147] IN 1343 Conrad and Hartneid with their mother's approval sold to Archbishop Henry an income of £43 from the saltworks in Hallein for £430.[148]

The shift in the Kuchls' interests became even more apparent a few years later. In 1345 their cousin Archbishop Ortolf gave Abtsee, Abtsdorf, and Steinbrünning to Conrad and granted the advocacy of Triebenbach to Hartneid in exchange for the brothers' possessions in the mountains, that is, in the Pinzgau and the Pongau, and a mill at Stuhlfelden in the Pinzgau. The Kuchls' new possessions were situated a few kilometers south of Laufen. A decade later Ortolf gave Conrad, who was the captain of Salzburg, and Hartneid permission to build castles, respectively, at Abtsee and at Triebenbach. These castles became the center of the Kuchls' new lordship in the Rupertiwinkel.[149]

Like their father, Conrad III and Hartneid served the archbishops in a variety of ways. As we have already seen, Conrad became the coburgrave of Hohensalzburg in 1326. He was by 1330 the burgrave of Tittmoning, the town on the northern border of the principality with Bavaria.[150] Conrad's personal interest in the Rupertiwinkel may date from this appointment. He was identified for the first time as the captain of Salzburg in 1337[151] and may have held this office until his death sometime between 1365 and 1373,[152] that is, throughout Ortolf's archiepiscopate. As Conrad's long tenure as captain shows, the office began to be filled on a permanent basis in the fourteenth century. The late-medieval captain of Salzburg replaced the vidame as the chief archiepiscopal official in the principality when the captain assumed the vidame's jurisdiction in capital cases while continuing to serve as the commander of the archiepiscopal forces.[153] Hartneid, who was overshadowed by his brother, was by 1343 the *Pfleger* of Tittmoning, the archiepiscopal official who exercised both military and judicial functions in the *Landgericht* of Tittmoning in the northern part of the Rupertiwinkel; but Hartneid had been replaced as *Pfleger* by 1345.[154] The Kuchls succeeded the Felbens as the hereditary marshals of Salzburg in 1369. The Kuchls' appointment to this ceremonial court office, which they held until their own extinction in the male line in 1436, shows in symbolic terms how the knights had taken the place of the ministerials as the nobility of the late medieval principality.[155]

Conrad's and Hartneid's marriages to Wittelsbach retainers may have been the result of the new focus in the Kuchls' interests.

Emperor Louis the Bavarian announced in 1341 that Elizabeth, the daughter of his servant Ulrich, the butler aus der Au, had married Conrad and that he was giving Elizabeth to the church of Salzburg. If she outlived Conrad and returned to Bavaria, she was to be again subject to Louis's jurisdiction.[156] In 1342 the emperor, for the benefit of his soul and in recognition of Hartneid's services, gave the church of Salzburg Hartneid's wife Sophia, the daughter of Louis's retainer Seifried of Frauenberg.[157] The emphasis on the servile status of Conrad's and Hartneid's wives is striking and stands in sharp contrast to the Kuchls' actual position as the wealthiest and one of the most influential noble lineages in fourteenth-century Salzburg.

The history of the Kuchls is the story of the almost meteoric rise of a family of obscure lesser ministerials. Their success was largely due to one remarkable man Conrad II who was for forty years the trusted adviser of four archbishops. Conrad accumulated a vast fortune that enabled his sons Conrad III and Hartneid I to succeed the Gutrats, whom their ancestors had once probably served as knights, as the most powerful lineage in the Hallein area and then to establish in the 1330s and 1340s a new lordship near Laufen in the Rupertiwinkel. We can now analyze what the history of the Kuchls reveals about the rise of the knights and the concomitant decline of the greater ministerial dynasties.

4.

The Causes of the Ministerials' Financial Problems

The striking feature in the story of the Kuchls is the number of once powerful ministerial lineages who were in varying degrees of financial difficulty by the beginning of the fourteenth century and whose property and rights the Kuchls obtained: the Felbens, Goldeggs, Oberndorfs, Radecks, and Staufenecks. Any attempt to explain the causes of the ministerials' problems must be speculative because we have no account books that list their income or expenditures; the only evidence for the ministerials' financial distress is the liquidation of their estates.

Roger Sablonier has classified explanations for the late-medieval nobility's financial difficulties into three categories. The first set of explanations attributes the problems to the nobility itself, for instance, excessive donations to churches, extravagance, the fragmentation of the family patrimony among too many heirs, etc. While such explanations may account for the problems of an individual family, they do not provide, according to Sablonier, an adequate explanation for what happened to the nobles as a group and they treat the nobility's problems in a social and political vacuum. The second group of explanations blames the nobility's difficulties on external causes, most notably, the constant warfare of the Later Middle Ages and the late-medieval agrarian crisis. These explanation are plausible in theory but hard to prove in practice. Sablonier argues instead for a model of societal change that places the nobility's problems into the context of overall structural changes in society caused by such things as the agrarian crisis, demographic decline, and the growth of the territorial state. He cautions that regional and chronological differences and gradations within the nobility must always be considered.[158] After all, the Kuchls prospered while the great ministerial lineages were ruined. To what extent can Sablonier's model be applied to Salzburg?

Some ministerial lineages were, as the case of the Staufenecks shows, in great financial difficulty by 1300. Henry I and William III, the son of Henry's first cousin, acknowledged on September 4, 1301, that Staufeneck was an archiepiscopal fief rather than an alod as they had claimed.[159] Four days later William pledged his share of the castle and the family's Austrian and Bavarian holdings to Archbishop Conrad IV for £142.[160] Pope Boniface VIII ordered the prior of St. Peter's on March 15, 1302, to investigate the complaints of the cathedral chapter about the Staufenecks' debts.[161] Archbishop Conrad lent William £24 on May 25 and another £30 on July 8. Staufeneck and the family lands served as the collateral.[162] The loans resumed in 1305. On January 28 the archbishop lent William £104, secured by Staufeneck, for ten years; on February 24, £20, secured by various advocacies over property that belonged to the cathedral chapter, on April 24, £10; and on June 2, £60.[163] Finally, on September 20 William acknowledged that he was bankrupt and sold Staufeneck and its appurtenances to Archbishop Conrad IV for £560. The next day the archbishop promised to give William an annual lifelong pension of £30—the minimum amount required by Bavarian territorial law to maintain a noble life style—to pay for his housing; in return, William promised to place his children under the archbishop's jurisdiction and to grant the archbishop the right to purchase first any remaining property William wished to sell.[164] While there is no evidence that Henry of Staufeneck had incurred any debts of his own, he shared in his cousin's ruin. He sold his share of Staufeneck to the archbishop on February 24, 1306, for £600.[165]

Even the loss of their ancestral castle did not stop the Staufenecks' ruinous course. In 1307 William sold his annual pension of £30 to the archbishop; the same year Henry sold two gardens and a meadow for an unspecified amount; in 1308 William sold various advocacies for £25; in 1309 Henry surrendered various scattered properties to the archbishop, so that Henry's wife and son could be enfeoffed with them in an apparent attempt to salvage something of the family patrimony; in 1314 Henry sold whatever rights he had to another property for five and a half pounds; and finally in 1319 Henry and his son Frederick—the last time they are mentioned—sold a forest to the archbishop for five pounds.[166] The Staufenecks disappear completely from the sources after a William of Staufeneck— William III?—acknowledged in 1335 that Archbishop Frederick III had settled all of William's claims to the properties he had sold the archbishop.[167] As Dopsch pointed out, we do not know whether the Staufenecks like the Gutrats died out or whether they were so impoverished that they simply disappeared from the extant sources.[168] Politically and socially it amounted to the same thing: a once powerful ministrial lineage had been eliminated. The Staufenecks were an extreme case but not unique. For instance, the Oberndorfs, who sold various properties to Conrad III of Kuchl in 1340 for £535, disappeared completely from the sources after 1343.[169]

William of Staufeneck was the only individual who offered an explanation for why he was borrowing money. He needed £60 in 1305 to pay for his sister's marriage. Shortly thereafter he sold his half of Staufeneck because, he said, providing her with a dowry had left him hopelessly indebted.[170] His explanation is less than convincing. It is not very likely that a family would ruin itself in order to provide a daughter or sister with a dowry.

Harald Bilowitzky's study of late-medieval marriage contracts in Styria indicates that the payments were designed to provide a couple or childless widow with an income befitting their station in life without ruining either family. The dowry (*Heimsteuer*) was usually paid in cash to the husband, who was expected to invest the money in real estate. An annual return of ten percent was considered normal. The husband could not alienate the property without his wife's express consent. If the couple was childless and the husband survived the wife, he retained the income until his death, when the property reverted to her

heirs. The groom gave the bride a *Morgengabe* if it was her first marriage and designated the properties that would form her widow's
dower (*Widerlage*). The woman, whether or not she had any children,
could dispose of her *Morgengabe* freely, but the *Widerlage* reverted to
the husband's heirs after her death. In the thirteenth century the
amount of the bride's dowry equalled the combined *Widerlage* and
*Morgengabe*. Thereafter, the size of the dowry declined relative to the
husband's contribution. The amount of the respective payments was
fixed by custom within fairly narrow limits and was determined by
the couple's estate. The bride's family lost the dowry, of course, if the
couple had children, but the underlying principle behind the system
was that the loss entailed by a daughter's marriage would be recouped
by a son's marriage.[171] It remains to be seen if similar arrangements
were made in the principality of Salzburg, but Conrad II's marriage
to Margaret of Weissenegg in 1302 fits the pattern.

The most obvious explanation for the ministerials' financial
difficulties after 1270 is that lineages who resisted the consolidation
of archiepiscopal authority within the principality lost the archbishops'
favor and paid for their opposition. Once again, the Staufenecks are
a case in point. The Staufenecks, who had been the burgraves of
Plain, built the castle of Staufeneck, before 1248. After the extinction
of the counts of Plain in 1260, the Staufenecks became legally archiepiscopal ministerials because the Plains' fiefs, including their ministerials, escheated to the archbishop.[172]

The Staufenecks refused to accept, however, the archbishop's
lordship. Ulrich of Staufeneck agreed in 1283 to compensate the
church of Salzburg for all the damages his late father had caused it
so that William II could receive Christian burial.[173] Ulrich and his
cousin Henry acknowledged in 1285 that Archbishop Rudolph had
excommunicated them on account of the injuries they had caused the
church while they had been in the service of Duke Henry XIII of
Lower Bavaria (1253–90). They admitted that they had not served
the archbishop as faithfully as their fellow ministerials and promised
to do so in the future. If they violated their promises and attached
themselves to another lord, they would forfeit their fiefs. Henry also
agreed to marry within a year a woman who belonged to the archiepiscopal *familia*; if he did not, the archbishop was to select a wife for
Henry.[174]

These promises remained unfulfilled. Bishop Henry of Re-
gensburg, who was serving as the arbiter between Archbishop Conrad

IV and Duke Henry's son Duke Otto III, stipulated in 1291 that Henry of Staufeneck should go to the archbishop's court and seek to pay him homage. If Henry was not restored to the archbishop's favor, then Duke Otto was to intervene on Henry's favor. If that failed too, then the matter was to be settled by judicial means. The Staufenecks' court, advocacies, alods, and fiefs were at stake.[175] On March 29, 1293, Henry swore that he would submit to the archbishop by marrying a member of the archiepiscopal *familia* by November 11, 1294. He provided a bond of £50; fidejussors offered additional bonds totaling £350. After Henry had submitted, he and the archbishop were to select arbiters who were to rule about the injuries he had caused the church so that Henry could regain the archbishop's grace.[176] On October 12, 1294, Henry assigned to Elizabeth of Felben, to whom he was betrothed, an annual income of £30 as her widow's dower.[177] Henry was thus finally reconciled with the archbishop, and by 1299 he was serving as the archiepiscopal burgrave and judge in Raschenberg.[178] Still, it is not difficult to see why a family that had opposed the archbishop for so long was in financial trouble at the beginning of the fourteenth century and why Archbishop Conrad IV exploited the Staufenecks' problems. It is worth observing that Henry of Staufeneck's submission to archiepiscopal authority took the form of an acknowledgement of his servile legal status, namely, the requirement that he could marry only within the archiepiscopal *familia*.

The story of the Felbens is not very different from that of the Staufenecks. Gebhard II of Felben, the father of Ekk, the son-in-law of Conrad II of Kuchl, sided with the Habsburgs against Archbishop Rudolph in 1289–90 but was formally reconciled with Rudolph's successor in 1292.[179] Twenty-four fidejussors provided in 1320 an enormous bond of 1,000 marks of silver, Salzburg weight (2,000 Salzburg pounds), that Ekk's brother Otto would keep the peace for ten years with Archbishop Frederick III and the men who had assisted the archbishop in imprisoning Otto. Otto acknowledged that he owed Frederick III £1,000 for the injuries he had caused the archbishop and his burghers and peasants. Otto pledged his share of the castles of Wildenwart, near Rosenheim, Bavaria, and of Kaprun in the Pinzgau to cover the debt and agreed to assign to the archbishop an income of £40 to pay the salaries of the castellans of the two castles.[180] Since Otto had acquired a castle in Bavaria and since most of Otto's bondsmen were Bavarians, Otto had probably supported Louis the Bavarian's candidacy for the German throne while the archbishop was backing the Habsburgs. In 1333 Otto's son Henry acknowledged that his late father had broken the terms of his reconciliation and had lost all his possessions in the principality.[181] We do not know whether Ekk shared his brother's political views, but it is more than possible that his debts in 1318 were connected to his brother's disloyalty. In any case, Ekk surrendered to Archbishop Frederick III in 1332 his half of the castle of Felben and received back half of the castle of Kaprun, which Ekk had given to the archbishop as security that the archbishop would suffer no injury from the castle of Felben.[182] Obviously, the archbishop trusted Ekk as little as he did Ekk's brother Otto.

The Goldeggs were another lineage that was often at odds with the archbishop and in financial trouble. Conrad II of Goldegg, whose son Frederick sold the Goldeggs' *Sudhaus* in Hallein to the Kuchls in 1330, also supported Duke Albrecht in 1289–90.[183] Conrad II's brother Otto VI in a remarkable example of a family hedging its bets remained loyal to the archbishop and even served with Conrad II of Kuchl on the archiepiscopal council.[184] Otto VI's loyalty during this crisis may explain why Archbishop Conrad IV enfeoffed the Goldeggs with the Gutrats' *Sudhaus* after the Gutrats' extinction. John I of Goldegg, the son of Conrad II, sold, however, his share of his paternal inheritance on account of his great need to his cousin Wulfing I, Otto VI's son, in 1312 for £450.[185] Wulfing sold the castle and court of Taxenbach in the Pinzgau to Archbishop Weichart in 1314 for £800. Wulfing's cousins, John I, John II, and Frederick, the sons of Conrad II, consented. Wulfing retained the right to redeem Taxenbach for the same amount five years later; if he did not, it was to belong permanently to the archbishop.[186] In 1318 and 1319 the Goldeggs sold various properties.[187] The dates of these transactions suggest that the Goldeggs were trying to raise funds to redeem Taxenbach when the loan came due in 1319, which, judging by subsequent events, they did.

Archbishop Frederick III then accused Wulfing of being responsible for damages that two Bavarians had caused the archbishop in the Ziller valley. Arbiters ruled in 1320 that the archbishop was to forgive Wulfing, who was to serve the archbishop for a year with twenty men within Bavaria and with ten men outside Bavaria. If Wulfing did not fulfill his obligations, the archbishop would have the right to seize Taxenbach and Wulfing's other properties. Wulfing was required to swear that he would not fight against the archbishop for anyone, except when Louis the Bavarian went on a campaign personally.[188] Wulfing did in fact fight for Louis against the archbishop and the Habsburgs at the decisive battle of Mühldorf on September 28, 1322.[189] The archbishop's revenge was swift. He destroyed Taxenbach and the Goldeggs' ancestral castle near Goldegg. On March 6, 1323, Wulfing sold Taxenbach with his cousins' consent to the archbishop for £2,500. In return, the archbishop gave Wulfing permission to build a new castle at Goldegg.[190] In spite of what had happened, Wulfing retained the castellany of the castle and town of Tittmoning, which he betrayed to the Bavarians on August 22, 1324.[191] Archbishop Frederick III was forced to pay Louis in 1327 £6,500 to regain Tittmoning.[192] Once again, the archbishop's punishment of Wulfing's treason was remarkably lenient, perhaps because Wulfing had the support of the victorious Louis. Wulfing's cousin Frederick sold, however, with his relatives' consent his comital rights and court in the Gastein valley and the castle of Klammstein at the lower end of the valley to the archbishop in 1327 for £1,000.[193] Frederick's sales to the Kuchls followed in 1330. It is hard to tell whether financial or political necessity or both motivated these sales.

On the other hand, the archbishops were prepared, as the case of the Kuchls shows, to reward families who served them faithfully. As we have seen, Archbishop Conrad IV provided Conrad II of Kuchl with a share in the consortium that monopolized the transportation of salt on the Salzach and subsidized his marriage to Margaret of Weissenegg.

The Radecks, the first of the greater ministerial lineages that seems to have been in financial trouble, are another example of a family that enjoyed the archbishops' favor. As we have seen, Ulrich II and Henry III of Radeck had been forced already in 1270 to pledge Henry's half of their ancestral castle to a consortium of knights that included the Wiesbachs and Conrad I or II of Kuchl. In spite of their problems, the Radecks served the archbishops faithfully in the following decades. Henry III represented Archbishops Frederick II and Conrad IV on boards of arbitration in disputes with the dukes of Lower Bavaria.[194] Henry's nephew Gerhoch III played a prominent role in the affairs of the principality between the 1280s and 1320s. A few examples will suffice. He was one of the seven archiepiscopal ministerials who witnessed in 1287 Salzburg's first municipal charter, and he was one of four archiepiscopal ministerials who accompanied Archbishop Conrad IV to the peace negotiations with Duke Albrecht in Vienna in 1297.[195] Gerhoch was specifically identified in 1306 and again in 1320 as a member of the archiepiscopal council,[196] and he served from at least 1307 to 1312 as the captain of Mühldorf, an archiepiscopal enclave within the Wittelsbach duchy.[197] As we have already seen, Gerhoch's son Rüdiger V along with Conrad III and Hartneid I of Kuchl lent Archbishop Frederick III £1,850 in 1326; and Rüdiger became the vidame of Salzburg and the coburgrave of Hohensalzburg. Nevertheless, Rüdiger and his brother Henry IV had to sell the other half of Radeck to Archbishop Frederick III in 1334 for £1,025.

Although loyal service to the archbishops did not end the Radecks' financial problems, the archbishops did in fact help the Radecks. Archbishop Frederick II purchased in 1273 for £350 Henry III's half of the castle of Radeck, which he had pledged to the consortium of knights in 1270. The archbishop agreed to redeem Ulrich II's half of Radeck, which had been pledged for £125 to the knight Ulrich II of Wiesbach, and to return it to Ulrich II of Radeck as soon as he repaid the debt.[198] In fact, the Radecks regained Radeck without paying the £125, which were deducted in 1334 from the £1,025 that Archbishop Frederick III paid for the castle.[199] Henry IV continued to live after 1334 in Radeck as its burgrave.[200] It may be that the Radecks concluded that their financial difficulties left them with no other alternative than to serve the archbishops.

If the retention or loss of the prince-archbishop's favor was the chief factor in determining a lineage's financial well-being, the ministerials' financial difficulties cannot be attributed solely to their political miscalculations. The negative consequences of such mistakes are clearest in the case of the Goldeggs in the 1320s, but John I complained of his great need when he sold his share of the Goldegg patrimony to his cousin Wulfing in 1312, and Wulfing was forced to pledge Taxenbach to the archbishop in 1314, that is, before Wulfing joined the Wittelsbach party. The Radecks, who served the archbishops faithfully, were the first greater ministerial lineage to fall on troubled times. This suggests that the ministerials' financial problems may not have been simply the result of their political mistakes but may rather have driven some of them to support the Wittelsbachs or Habsburgs against the archbishop in a vain attempt to salvage their positions.

Four other factors may have contributed to the ministerials' financial troubles: the fragmentation of their patrimony among too many heirs;

an extravagant life style; the devastating effects of war; and the late-medieval agrarian crisis. A significant change in family strategy can be detected among many ministerial lineages in the second half of the thirteenth century. Before 1250 many of the greater ministerial lineages had permitted only one son in each generation to marry and to sire children; after 1250 it became customary for more than one son to marry.

For example, Otto VI (1270–93) and Conrad II (1250–99), who belonged to the sixth generation of the Pongau-Goldegg lineage, were the first pair of Goldegg brothers to marry and father children. Otto had only one son Wulfing I who married, but two of Conrad II's sons, John I and Frederick, married. Kuno IV (1211–55) and Karl (1219–1239/43), members of the fourth generation of the Schnaitsee-Gutrats, were the first brothers in that family to wed. Gebhard I (1231/41–1272) and Frederick I of Felben (1247/57-1300/07), who represented the fourth generation of their house, were the first Felben brothers to marry. Gebhard I's son Gebhard II had two sons who married: Otto and Ekk, the son-in-law of Conrad II of Kuchl. Frederick I had three sons and a daughter Elizabeth, who married Henry I of Staufeneck. Finally, Archbishop Frederick II and his brothers Otto (1252–82) and Adalbero II (1254–87) belonged to the fifth generation of the Walchens; Otto and Adalbero II were the first brothers in that dynasty to marry. Otto had only one daughter who married a ministerial of the bishop of Freising, but Adalbero II had two sons who married.[201]

While it is possible that this apparent change in family strategy is only a function of the surviving documentation, the twelfth-century *Traditionsbücher* of St. Peter's, the cathedral chapter, and the other ecclesiastical foundations in the archdiocese provide considerable information about the ministerials' families because the benefactors were likely to mention their spouses, parents, children, and other kinsmen in making pious donations. I do not think, therefore, that it is simply a coincidence that the evidence suggests that some of the greater ministerial lineages altered their family strategies in the middle of the thirteenth century and arranged for more than one son in each generation to marry.

It is more difficult to ascertain why this change occurred. I have proposed elsewhere that an important reason why so many noble and ministerial lineages died out in southeastern Germany during the twelfth and thirteenth centuries was because they permitted only one son in each generation to marry, so that the family patrimony would not be divided among too many heirs. The son who was designated to continue the lineage was often in his thirties or even forties before he married. If he died or was killed before he could marry or if he failed to father a son, the lineage was extinguished, at least in the male line.[202] Contemporaries were aware of the phenomenon. Abbot Hermann of Niederalteich (1242–1273, d. 1275) listed forty-one important Bavarian noblemen, including the dukes of Andech-Meran, and the counts of Bogen, Falkenstein, and Wasserburg, who died without heirs and whose domains were acquired by Dukes Louis I (1183–1231) and Otto II (1231–53) of Bavaria.[203] Could the greater ministerial lineages have realized after 1250 the dangers of such a strategy and deliberately adopted a new policy of allowing more than one son to marry? Could the carefully contrived system of dowries and widows' dowers, which Bilowitzky detected in late-medieval Styria, have been a response to the change in family strategy, a device that permitted more than one son to marry and to live in a manner that befit his estate without bankrupting the lineage? These questions merit further scrutiny.

Whatever the reason for the change in family strategy, the result was the division of a lineage's patrimony among brothers, uncles and nephews, and cousins. This fragmentation of a lineage's property and rights among too many heirs made it easier for the archbishops to acquire the individual pieces one by one. Such a division may have been at the heart of the Radecks' problems. The Radecks were a cadet branch of the Bergheims who had already demonstrated a tendency in the twelfth century to allow more than one son to marry. Gerhoch II of Bergheim adopted the surname Radeck in 1247 when he built that castle, while his brother Markwart II was the ancestor of the later Bergheims. The Bergheims were one of the unruliest lineages and were finally forced to sell the castle and court of Bergheim in 1295.[204] Both the Bergheims' misconduct and the Radecks' loyal service to the archbishop may have been responses to their financial problems. I suspect that such a division of a dynasty's inheritance may also have been at the heart of the Goldeggs' problems in the second decade of the fourteenth century. John I, who sold his share of his paternal inheritance to his cousin Wulfing in 1312 because he was in great need, would have possessed only about one-sixth of the domains that had belonged to his paternal grandfather, assuming that the Goldeggs' holdings had been divided equally. John could not have afforded the same life style as his grandfather.

The problem is that some individuals may not have realized this. It is impossible to prove that the ministerials were guilty of extravagance because we have no records of their personal expenditures, but I wonder what William III of Staufeneck did with all the money he borrowed from Archbishop Conrad IV in the first decade of the fourteenth century. We have a bit of circumstantial evidence that the nobles of southeastern Germany may have been living considerably beyond their means. The account books of the sons of Count Meinhard II of the Tyrol, Otto (1295–1310), Louis (1295–1305) and Henry (1295–1335), who were also the dukes of Carinthia, present a picture of ruinous extravagance. Their agents brought back from one of many expeditions to Venice, for instance, 42 bolts of baldachin, 10 gilded necklaces set with precious stones, 13 expensive belts, 141 pieces of cloth of different colors, 143 pieces of silk, furs, 123 pairs of gilded spurs, 120 swords, and an equal number of gilded bridles and reins.[205] Princes who lived in such a fashion were presumably not surrounded by noble courtiers dressed in homespun *Loden*.

The Tyrol and Carinthia are not Salzburg, but it is hard to believe that Salzburg was totally unaffected by what was occurring in two neighboring principalities, particularly because Carinthia was part of the archdiocese and because there were many family connections between the nobility of Salzburg and Carinthia—after all, the second wife of Conrad of Kuchl, Margaret of Weissenegg, belonged to a lineage of Bamberg ministerials from Carinthia who had entered the archbishop's service. It is worth noting in this regard that the members of the archiepiscopal council, including Conrad II of Kuchl, were presented after the death of Archbishop Rudolph in 1290 with an unpaid bill of 111 marks of silver that the late archbishop owed a tailor, Master Werner of Oppenheim. The council was forced to pledge the tolls in Salzburg for a year to pay the bill.[206] Did some of the ministerials try to demonstrate their superiority to upstarts like the Kuchls by ostentatious displays of wealth and ruin themselves in the process? There is no way of knowing for certain.

A third cause of the ministerials' financial difficulties may have been the incessant warfare in southeastern Germany after the extinction of the Babenbergs in 1246. Ottokar II of Bohemia (1253–78) obtained the vacant duchies of Austria and Styria and hoped to acquire Carinthia as well after the death of his childless cousin Duke Ulrich III of Carinthia (1256–69). Salzburg became involved because Styria and Carinthia were under the archbishop's spiritual jurisdiction and because Archbishop-Elect Philip hoped to succeed his childless brother as the duke of Carinthia and refused ordination. Pope Alexander IV finally deposed Philip in 1257 for not taking holy orders and transferred Bishop Ulrich of Seckau, whom the canons and ministerials had already elected as Philip's successor, to Salzburg. Philip, supported by his brother Ulrich and cousin Ottokar, refused to accept his deposition, while Duke Henry XIII of Lower Bavaria backed Ulrich, who never managed to establish himself in the archbishopric and resigned in 1265. The future of the duchies was finally resolved when Rudolph of Habsburg enfeoffed his sons in 1282 with Austria and Styria. Thereafter the principality, sandwiched between Bavaria and Styria, was drawn into the dynastic rivalries between the Wittelsbachs and Habsburgs.[207] As we have seen, the ministerials, due to their own family connections, were more than willing to support one of the rival princes against the archbishop.

Much of late-medieval warfare consisted of burning and pillaging an opponent's land. Georges Duby thought that it was the lords' dwellings with their appurtenances that suffered most from such tactics and that warfare was thus a major cause of the decline of the late-medieval manorial economy.[208] The Salzburg cathedral canons who compiled the *Annales sancti Rudberti* often commented on the destructive effects of war: in 1256 Archbishop-Elect Philip burned and pillaged lands located both within and outside the mountains that belonged to the church; Philip devastated in 1257 the lands situated in the mountains that belonged to the church and to ministerials who had elected Bishop Ulrich of Seckau to replace him; Philip did the same thing in 1258; in 1262 Duke Henry of Lower Bavaria plundered and burned the portion of the city of Salzburg located on the right bank of the Salzach (the main part of the city with the cathedral is on the left bank), captured Hallein, and built a castle above Hallein; in 1263 Duke Henry besieged the city of Salzburg; in 1266 the Bohemians burned Bad Reichenhall, southwest of Salzburg; in 1275 Ottokar of Bohemia seized and destroyed the possessions of the church and caused an estimated 40,000 marks in damages; and in 1285 Duke Henry burned and occupied Mühldorf.[209] The canons stopped making entries in their annals after 1286 but resumed in 1308 in the *Continuatio canonicorum S. Rudberti Salisburgensis.* It contains the following reports: in 1310 Austrian and archiepiscopal forces stationed in Tittmoning burned and pillaged in Lower Bavaria and in the Ru-pertiwinkel, and in 1319 Duke Frederick of Austria burned and pil-laged Lower Bavaria as it had never been devastated before.[210] Frederick agreed in 1320 to pay the archbishop 1200 marks for the injuries Salzburg had suffered during this campaign.[211]

As Sablonier pointed out, it is difficult to link the problems of individual lineages with such generalized accounts of destruction, though it is clear that the ministerials did suffer losses, particularly at the hands of Archbishop-Elect Philip. We may be able to connect the Radecks' debts in 1270, however, with the plundering and burning of the section of the city of Salzburg situated on the right bank of the Salzach in 1262. Since Radeck is located on the right bank of the Salzach, only four kilometers north of the main bridge over the Sal-zach in Salzburg, it seems plausible to surmise that the Radecks were among the prime targets of the Bavarians and were still suffering the consequences eight years later.

The destructive effects of warfare were one of the factors that contributed to the late-medieval agrarian crisis and the economic difficulties of the landowning classes. Very little specific work has been done on agrarian conditions in the first half of the fourteenth century in Bavaria and Salzburg, perhaps because, as Klein pointed out, there are no extant manorial registers (*Urbare*), even from eccle-siastical institutions, for the decades around 1300. There is none, for instance, from St. Peter's between 1280 and 1369.[212] It is not clear whether the absence of such sources is due to some historical accident in the retention of such sources or is indicative of a general lack of interest in agriculture among the nobility and the church, which could itself have contributed to the agrarian crisis.

The commonly accepted scholarly opinion is that the me-dieval population of the Alpine areas, including Salzburg, reached its peak at the beginning of the fourteenth century. Sheep were pastured at elevations as high as two thousand meters, and peasant settlements were denser at the higher elevations than at any time before or since.[213] Klein, who studied the impact of the Black Death on the principality, commented specifically that the very highest elevations were settled in the mountainous Pongau and Pinzgau at the beginning of the fourteenth century and that larger peasant holdings continued to be divided, due to population pressure, in the first half of the fourteenth century. The tenancies at the higher elevations were abandoned only after 1348.[214] It is difficult to see, therefore, why the ministerials as landowners should have been in financial difficulty at the beginning of the fourteenth century, a period of intense population pressure, especially because lay landowners in the principality reserved the right to revoke a tenancy at any time or yearly (*Freistift, libera institucio*).[215] The ministerials should have been able to profit from the increasing demand for land.

Austrian and Bavarian scholars have overlooked, however, the possible consequences that long-term climatic changes may have had on agricultural conditions within the principality, especially in the more mountainous sections. Northern Europe as a whole suffered in the second decade of the fourteenth century from excessive rainfall that rotted crops, leached the soil, and caused a European-wide famine, which began as early as 1309 in southern and western Germany, and culminated in massive crop failures and starvation between 1315 and 1317.[216] The continuation of the *Annales sancti Rudberti* indicates that Salzburg was not spared. After the forces of Duke Frederick of Austria and Archbishop Frederick III had devastated Bavaria and the Rupertiwinkel around November 11, 1310, the destruction and the cold caused, according to the annalist, a terrible famine. More than twenty-three hundred people had been buried by February 2, 1311, in one cemetery alone in Tittmoning and the mortality rate was high throughout Bavaria. Admittedly, it is difficulty in this case to separate the cold from the effects of war. There was such a shortage of food in 1313 that a measure (*metreta*) of wheat sold for three schillings and two pennies. The chronicler compared three torrential rainstorms at the end of June 1316 to the Great Deluge.[217] The *Annales Matseenses*, a chronicle compiled in Mattsee, a collegiate church twenty kilometers northeast of Salzburg, reported that many men and animals died in 1310 and that a measure of winter wheat sold in 1312 for three schillings or more and a measure of oats for 60 pennies on account of the famine.[218]

Was the second decade of the fourteenth century an anomaly or was it a symptom of a long-term deterioration in the climate? Emmanuel Le Roy Ladurie pointed out that the first half of the fourteenth century, except for the second decade, was not especially wet. Grain production, which suffers most in northern Europe from too much moisture during the summers, would thus not have been adversely affected. On the other hand, the Alpine glaciers advanced in the period between 1215 and 1350. This was the product of both longer winters with heavy snow and cooler summers that retarded glacial ablation. A cold winter, unless it is very severe, has little effect on cereal yield in northern France, Le Roy Ladurie argued, but harsher winters and cooler summers have more serious consequences in the Nordic countries or in the Alpine regions, that is, in areas with shorter growing seasons.[219]

What happened in Salzburg, which has never been noted for its good weather (anyone who has lived in the city of Salzburg realizes that it rains frequently under the best of circumstances)? The *Annales sancti Rudberti* noted during most of the thirteenth century the "usual" natural disasters that a chronicler considered worthy of recording—a great famine and pestilence in all lands in 1259, a severe hailstorm in Bavaria in 1265, an earthquake followed by an eclipse of the sun in 1267, and destructive floods in Austria and Bavaria in 1272;[220] but the tone changes in the 1280s. There was a great flood in Bavaria and in the mountains in 1280. The water covered the fields and houses and many houses were swept away. Worse followed in 1281. The chronicler recorded first that it had been a memorable winter with unusually severe weather at Christmas and a massive amount of snow. Then, to everyone's astonishment, it snowed on July 17th in an area extending from Freising, north of Munich, to the Lungau, the mountainous section of the principality southeast of the city of Salzburg. It rained so much that summer that not even old people, the chronicler added, could remember such intemperate weather. The result was a massive crop failure, the likes of which, according to the canon, had rarely be seen in another land. Many people died of starvation, and even prelates found that oat bread was extremely expensive.[221] However, this notice sounds more like a one-time disaster than a long-term trend. Regrettably, no entries were made in the Salzburg annals in the years between 1286 and 1308, so that we cannot tell for certain whether there were additional disastrous crop failures in the principality in this time period. Perhaps, dendrochronology and palynolgy can provide additional information about climatic changes in the eastern Alps.

We cannot be certain, therefore, how long-term climatic changes may have affected the income of the great ministerial lineages. It is worth noting, however, that the lordships of the Felbens and Goldeggs, who were, for whatever reason or reasons, in financial difficulty by the second decade of the fourteenth century, were situated in the Pinzgau and Pongau, that is, in sections of the principality that would have been most affected by a deterioration in the climate.

The decision of the Kuchls, astute businessmen, to shift in the 1330s the center of their lordship from the upper Salzach valley to the Rupertiwinkel may have been prompted, perhaps, by a realization that the Alpine forelands were a better place to farm.

5.

Conclusion

Many of the greater ministerial lineages were in considerable financial difficulty by 1300, but the reasons for their distress are less clear. They resisted the archbishops' efforts after 1270 to assert their authority within the principality by allying with the Habsburgs or Wittelsbachs. The archbishops punished the ministerials' insubordination by forcing one family after another to sell some or all of its properties and rights. Political miscalculations were thus an important factor, as the cases of the Staufenecks, Felbens, and Goldeggs show, in the ministerials' financial as well as political ruin; but many of the ministerials appear to have been in economic trouble before they turned against the archbishops. A number of factors, besides the consolidation of archiepiscopal authority, contributed to the ministerials' financial woes: a change in family strategy that led to a division of a lineage's patrimony among too many heirs; an extravagant life style that may have been adopted to demonstrate the ministerials' superiority to upstarts like the Kuchls; the incessant warfare that devastated the countryside; and a long-term deterioration in the climate that may have reduced the ministerials' seignorial income, particularly of those lineages like the Felbens and Goldeggs who lived in the Pinzgau and Pongau. Since we know about the ministerials' problems only from their alienation of properties and rights, we will never know for certain which factor or combination of factors ruined a particular family.

Nevertheless, we cannot simply attribute the failure of the archiepiscopal ministerials to form a separate estate of lords to their financial difficulties. Presumably, many of their Styrian colleagues faced similar problems. The crucial element was, as Dopsch suggested, the determination and the ability of the archbishops to utilize the ministerials' economic distress and the extinction of families like the Gutrats in the male line to consolidate archiepiscopal authority. The ministerials were particularly vulnerable to such tactics on account of their servile legal status. Thus the archbishops could enforce the prohibitions against extrinsic marriages, as the history of the Staufenecks indicates, and insist, as the case of the Gutrats shows, that the ministerials' alods were *Inwärtseigen* that could be alienated only within the archiepiscopal *familia*. The archbishops helped those lineages like the Radecks who cooperated with them and became in effect princely bureaucrats dependent on the archbishops' grace. The prince-archbishops were equally prepared to crush insubordinate families like the Radecks' cousins, the Bergheims, who resisted. A few new families like the Kuchls, Wiesbachs, and Thurns, even achieved political prominence and great wealth in the archbishops' service. In the final analysis, the ministerials, who had risen out of the ranks of the *familia*, remained creatures of the archbishop.

The history of the Kuchls suggests that at least two factors hindered the archbishops' ability to limit the power of the late-medieval nobility, whether of ministerial or knightly rank, within the principality. First, while the archbishops focused most of their attention on Salzburg after 1270, the rival candidacies of their Habsburg and Wittelsbach neighbors for the German throne inevitably involved the archbishops in imperial politics. Archbishop Frederick III of Leibnitz, who belonged to a family of archiepiscopal ministerials from Styria, backed the Habsburgs and shared in their defeat at Mühldorf in 1322. Desperate for funds, Frederick wass forced to sell the courts at Golling and Staufeneck and to pledge Hohensalzburg itself to the Kuchls. *Landgerichte*, which Archbishop Conrad IV had acquired with considerable difficulty and at great expense, thus passed once again into noble hands. Second, some of the archbishops could not resist the temptation to aid their own families. The establishment of the Kuchls in the Rupertiwinkel, the creation of "a state within a state," during the archiepiscopate of Conrad III's and Hartneid I's cousin, Ortolf of Weissenegg, was hardly in Salzburg's best interest. Ortolf's successor, Archbishop Pilgrim II (1365–96), forced the Kuchls out of Salzburg, therefore, and they established a new lordshsip around 1375 in Friedburg in the Bavarian Innviertel (today part of the province of Upper Austria), where they also acquired the castle and market of Mattighofen. The fate of the Kuchls, who died out in the male line in 1436, was thus not very different from that of the Gutrats whom they had replaced.[222] In spite of such setbacks, the archbishops' persistence paid off in the long run, and Salzburg was for all practical purposes by the end of the Middle Ages a principality without a native nobility of whatever origin to limit the archbishops' authority.

## NOTES

An abbreviated version of this article, "The Rise of the Knights in Salzburg: The Case of the Kuchls," was presented at the XVII Workshop for Medieval Studies, held at the University of British Columbia in Vancouver on November 14, 1987. I wish to thank my colleague Roy A. Austensen and the anonymous readers of an earlier draft for their critical comments.

The following abbreviations will be employed in the article: MC, *Monumenta historica ducatus Carinthiae*, ed. August von Jaksch and Hermann Wiessner, 11 vols. (Klagenfurt, 1896–1972); MGSL, *Mitteilungen der Gesellschaft für Salzburger Landeskunde*; OÖUB, *Urkundenbuch des Landes ob der Enns*, 11 vols. (Vienna and Linz, 1852–1956); Regesten, *Die Regesten der Erzbischöfe und des Domkapitels von Salzburg 1247–1343*, ed. Franz Martin, 3 vols. (Salzburg, 1926–34); and SUB, *Salzburger Urkundenbuch*, ed. Willibald Hauthaler and Franz Martin, 4 vols. (Salzburg, 1898–1933).

1. Heinz Dopsch, *Geschichte Salzburgs: Stadt und Land*, I, *Vorgeschichte, Altertum, Mittelalter*, 3 pts. (Salzburg, 1981–84), 1/1, pp. 361–403; idem, "Ministerialität und Herrenstand in der Steiermark und in Salzburg," *Zeitschrift des Historischen Vereines für Steiermark* 62 (1971), 3–31; and idem, "Probleme ständischer Wandlung beim Adel Österreichs, der Steiermark und Salzburg vornehmlich im 13. Jahrhundert," in Josef Fleckenstein, ed., *Herrschaft und Stand: Untersuchungen zur Sozialgeschichte im 13. Jahrhundert*, Veröffentlichungen des Max-Planck-Instituts für Geschichte 51 (Göttingen, 1977), 207–53; and John B. Freed, "The Formation of the Salzburg Ministerialage in the Tenth and Eleventh Centuries: An Example of Upward Social Mobility in the Early Middle Ages," *Viator* 9 (1978), 67–102; and idem, "Nobles, Ministerials, and Knights in the Archdiocese of Salzburg," *Speculum* 62 (1987), 575–611. For general information in English about the medieval German nobility and the ministerials, *v* Benjamin Arnold, *German Knighthood 1050–1300* (Oxford, 1985); Freed, "The Origins of the European Nobility: The Problem of the Ministerials," *Viator* 7 (1976), 211–41; idem, "Reflections on the Medieval German Nobility," *The American Historical Review*, 91 (1986), 553–75; and Timothy Reuter, trans. and ed., *The Medieval Nobility: Studies on the ruling classes of France and Germany from the sixth to the twelfth century*, Europe in the Middle Ages: Selected Studies 14 (Amsterdam, 1978).

2. John B. Freed, "Devotion to St James and family identity: the Thurns of Salzburg," *Journal of Medieval History* 13 (1987), 207–22.

3. SUB IV, pp. 368–69, no. 322.

4. Harald Bilowitzky, "Die Heiratsgaben in der Steiermark während des späten Mittelalters unter stände- und wirtschaftsgeschichtlichem Aspekt," unpublished dis., Graz, 1977, p. 62. On the Liechtensteins, *v* Heinz Dopsch, "Der Dichter Ulrich von Liechtenstein und die Herkunft seiner Familie," *Festschrift Friedrich Hausmann*, ed. Herwig Ebner (Graz, 1977), 93–118.

5. In addition to Dopsch's comments on the Austrian estates in "Probleme ständischer Wandlung," *v* Peter Feldbauer, *Der Herrenstand in Oberösterreich: Ursprünge, Anfänge, Frühformen*, Sozial- und wirtschaftshistorische Studien (Munich, 1972); idem, *Herrschaftsstruktur und Ständebildung: Beiträge zur Typologie der österreichischen Länder aus ihren mittelalterlichen Grundlagen*, I: *Herren und Ritter*, in Sozial- und wirtschaftshistorische Studien (Munich, 1973); and idem, "Rangprobleme und

Konnubium österreichischer Landherrenfamilien: Zur sozialen Mobilität einer spätmittelalterlichen Führungsgruppe," *Zeitschrift für bayerische Landesgeschichte* 35 (1972), 571–90.

6. Herbert Klein, "Salzburg und seine Landstände von den Anfängen bis 1861," *Beiträge zur Siedlungs-, Verfassungs- und Wirtschaftsgeschichte von Salzburg: Gesammelte Aufsätze von Herbert Klein. Festschrift zum 65. Geburtstag von Herbert Klein*, MGSL, Supp. 5, (Salzburg, 1965), p. 121.

7. Dopsch, *Geschichte Salzburgs* 1/1, p. 465.

8. Dopsch, "Ministerialität und Herrenstand in der Steiermark und in Salzburg," 26–31; and idem, "Probleme ständischer Wandlung," 240–43. For a specific example of how the archbishops crushed an insubordinate lineage, *v* Dopsch, "Zur Geschichte der Burg Kalham," MGSL 112/113 (1972/73), 265–76.

9. John B. Freed, "Diemut von Högl: Eine Salzburger Erbtochter und die erzbischöfliche Ministerialität im Hochmittelalter," MGSL 120/21 (1980/81), esp. pp. 647–56. For an additional discussion of the causes of family extinction, *v* Freed, *The Counts of Falkenstein: Noble Self-Consciousness in Twelfth-Century Germany*, Transactions of the American Philosophical Society 74/6 (Philadelphia, 1984), pp. 62–67.

10. Dopsch, "Probleme ständischer Wandlung," p. 241.

11. SUB III, pp. 496–97, no. 944.

12. SUB III, pp. 563–64, no. 1013.

13. Conrad II (1164–68) was a Babenberg; Adalbert II (1168–77, 1183–1200) a Premyslid; Conrad III (1177–1183) a Wittelsbach; Archbishop-Elect Philip (1247–57), a Spanheimer; and Ladislaus (1265–70), a Piast.

14. For a list of the medieval archbishops of Salzburg, see Dopsch, *Geschichte Salzburgs* 1/2:1145–50. *v* also my comments about the change in the social origins of the archbishops in "The Prosopography of Ecclesiastical Elites: Some Methodological Considerations from Salzburg," *Medieval Prosopography* 9/1 (1988), 53–54.

15. SUB IV, pp. 26-27, no. 29; 87–91, no. 84.

16. Regesten II, p. 43, no. 345. *v* also SUB IV, pp. 186–88, no. 156; 221; no. 180; 236–37, no. 198.

17. Dopsch, *Geschichte Salzburgs* 1/1, pp. 370–99; 444–86.

18. SUB I, p. 422, no. 313a.

19. Heinz Dopsch, "Steinbrünning und seine Herrschaftsgeschichte," *Das Salzfass: Heimatkundliche Zeitschrift des Historischen Vereins Rupertiwinkel*, n.s. 7 (1973), 6–12.

20. Dopsch, *Geschichte Salzburgs* 1/1, pp. 370–99; idem, "Ministerialität und Herrenstand," p. 28; and idem, "Probleme ständischer Wandlung," p. 242.

21. Dopsch, *Geschichte Salzburgs* I/1, p. 400.

22. Brugger, "Die Kuchler. Ein Salzburger Ministerialengeschlecht vom 12.–15. Jahrhundert," *Das Salzfass: Heimatkundliche Zeitschrift des Historischen Vereins Rupertiwinkel*, n.s. 2 (1967/68), pp. 7, 13.

23. On Frederick's role in the establishment of the Habsburgs in Austria, *v* Heinz Dopsch, "Přemysl Ottokar II. und das Erzstift Salzburg," *Jahrbuch für Landeskunde von Niederösterreich*, n.s. 44/45 (1978/79), pp. 470–508.

24. Dopsch, *Geschichte Salzburgs* I/1 pp. 305–6, 390. On the mining and production of salt in the principality, *v* Herbert Klein "Zur älteren Geschichte der Salinen Hallein und Reichenhall," *Beiträge zur Siedlungs-, Verfassungs- und Wirtschaftsgeschichte von Salzburg* (n. 6, above), 385–409, Fritz Koller, "Hallein im frühen und hohen Mittelalter," MGSL 116 (1976), 1–116, esp. 26–27; and Otto Volk, *Salzpro-*

*duktion und Salzhandel mittelalterlicher Zisterzienserklöster*, Vorträge und Forschungen, Sonderband 30 (Sigmaringen, 1984), pp. 43–82.

25. SUB III, pp. 496–97, no. 944.
26. SUB III, pp. 453–54, no. 905a.
27. *Urkunden des Cistercienser-Stiftes Heiligenkreuz im Wiener Walde*, ed. Johann Nepomuk Weis, Fontes rerum Austriacum, II/11 (Vienna, 1856), pp. 74–75, no. 63.
28. Dopsch, *Geschichte Salzburgs* I/1, pp. 316–18; and Karl Lechner, *Die Babenberger: Markgrafen und Herzoge von Österreich*, Veröffentlichungen des Instituts für österreichischer Geschichtsforschung 23 (Vienna, 1976; rpt. ed., Darmstadt, 1985), pp. 276–86.
29. SUB III, pp. 563–64, no. 1013.
30. SUB IV, p. 55, no. 55; OÖUB 111, pp. 3:483–85, no. 526. There is no evidence that anyone else held the office during Kuno's lifetime and it was restored to his son Kuno VI in 1304. Regesten II, p. 82, no. 692.
31. Regesten I, p. 69, no. 527.
32. Regesten I, p. 98, no. 751.
33. Dopsch, *Geschichte Salzburgs* 1/1, p. 391, 1/2, p. 948; and idem, "Přemysl Ottokar II.," p. 492.
34. Dopsch, *Geschichte Salzburgs* 1/1, pp. 452–62.
35. Regesten I, pp. 176–77, no. 1370.
36. *Das "Stiftungen-Buch" des Cistercienser-Klosters Zwetl*, ed. Johann von Frast, Fontes rerum Austriacarum II/3, (Vienna, 1851), pp. 310–12.
37. SUB II, p. 681, no. 502.
38. SUB IV, pp. 223–24, no. 183.
39. SUB IV, pp. 246–47, no. 206.
40. Regesten II, p. 43, no. 345.
41. Regesten II, p. 56, no. 456. *v* also p. 56, no. 457, and p. 62, no. 508.
42. Regesten II, p. 26, no. 204; and Joseph Ernst Ritter von Koch-Sternfeld, "Urkunden von Berchtesgaden," *Salzburg und Berchtesgaden in historisch-statistisch-geographisch- und staatsökonomischen Beyträgen* (Salzburg, 1810), II, pp. 59–60, no. 38.
43. Kuno VI, unlike his brother-in-law Walter of Taufkirchen, was not mentioned by name in 1296 when Kuno V's widow arranged for Berchtesgaden to celebrate her husband's anniversary. *v* Koch-Sternfeld, "Urkunden von Berchtesgaden," pp. 59–60, no. 38.
44. On the legal status of the Taufkirchens, *v* OÖUB III, pp. 395–96, no. 429; IV, pp. 78–79, no. 195.
45. OÖUB IV, pp. 465–67, no. 502.
46. Regesten II, p. 82, nos. 690, 691, 692, 693, 694.
47. OÖUB IV, pp. 465–67, no. 502. *v* Dopsch, *Geschichte Salzburgs* 1/1, p. 392.
48. Max Doblinger, "Die Herren von Walsee. Ein Beitrag zur österreichische Adelsgeschichte," *Archiv für österreichische Geschichte* 95 (1906), p. 272.
49. SUB IV, pp. 247–48, no. 208.
50. SUB IV, pp. 271–72, no. 231.
51. SUB IV, pp. 393–94, no. 336.
52. *v*, e.g., SUB III, pp. 624–26, no. 1079.
53. Dopsch, *Geschichte Salzburgs* I/2, pp. 889–91.
54. Werner Rösener, "Bauer und Ritter im Hochmittelalter: Aspekte ihrer Lebensform, Standesbildung und sozialen Differenzierung im 12. und 13. Jahrhundert,"

in Lutz Fenske, Werner Rösener, and Thomas Zotz, eds., *Institutionen, Kultur und Gesellschaft im Mittelalter: Festschrift für Josef Fleckenstein zu seinem 65. Geburtstag* (Sigmaringen, 1984), p. 686.

55. Volk, *Salzproduktion und Salzhandel mittelalterlicher Zisterzienserklöster*, pp. 69–71.
56. Dopsch, *Geschichte Salzburgs*, 1/2:400–1; Freed, "Devotion to St James and family identity," pp. 210–15; and Helga Reindel-Schedl, "Die Herren von Wispeck," MGSL CXXII (1982), pp. 253–86.
57. SUB I, pp. 601–3, no. 35. Brugger, "Die Kuchler," 4, identified a *Wigant de Hohen Chvchin*, who witnessed an archiepiscopal charter in 1146 (SUB 2:355–57, no. 246), as the first Kuchl; but Franz Martin, the editor of the *Salzburger Urkundenbuch* (SUB III, R 159), and Dopsch (*Geschichte Salzburgs* I/3, p. 1322, n. 538), placed Wigant in Hochkuchelberg near Lohnsburg in Upper Austria. The latter identification is almost certainly right because Wigant appeared in a group of Upper Austrian witnesses and was listed before a group of prominent archiepiscopal ministerials.
58. SUB I, pp. 610–11, no. 53b. He was also mentioned in two entries in the *Traditionsbuch* of the Benedictine abbey of St. Peter's in Salzburg (SUB 1:371, no. 228; 441–42, no. 350) that are dated, respectively, 1125/47 and 1147/67.
59. SUB II, p. 481, no. 345. Hauthaler dated the charter 1160/64, but During of Werfen who witnessed it was killed in 1163.
60. SUB I, pp. 685–86, no. 213. The entry is dated 1167/83, but Eberhard still served as a witness in 1170 (SUB II, pp. 548–49, no. 398).
61. MGH Necrologia Germaniae 2:169.
62. SUB I, pp. 448–49, no. 363a.
63. Brugger, "Die Kuchler," p. 4.
64. SUB II, p. 481, no. 345.
65. MGH SS XVII, pp. 459–60.
66. SUB II, pp. 694–700, no. 515.
67. SUB I, p. 963; III, R 57.
68. Dopsch, *Geschichte Salzburgs* I/1, p. 390.
69. SUB I, pp. 646–47, no. 125. The entry is dated 1151/67, but During of Diebering was killed in 1163.
70. SUB I, pp. 546–47, no. 589. On Gunther, *v* SUB 1:1034.
71. SUB I, pp. 476–77, no. 411.
72. SUB III, pp. 55–57, no. 578. On Hermann, *v* Freed, "Diemut von Högl," p. 615, n. 175.
73. SUB I, p. 499, no. 455. The entry is dated 1199/1231, but the first witness Conrad of Zaisberg was not mentioned after 1214. *v* Freed, "Diemut von Högl," pp. 618–19.
74. MGH Necrologia Germaniae II, p. 107.
75. SUB III, pp. 370–71, no. 837a.
76. MGH Necrologia Germaniae II, p. 84.
77. *Annales sancti Rudberti Salisburgenses*, MGH SS IX, p. 796. On the distinction between the greater and lesser ministerials, *v* Freed, "Nobles, Ministerials, and Knights," pp. 595–96.
78. Freed, "Nobles, Ministerials, and Knights," pp. 597–602, 609.
79. SUB IV, pp. 6–7, no. 7.
80. Dopsch, *Geschichte Salzburgs* I/1, pp. 375–79.
81. SUB IV, pp. 484–86, no. 417.

82. Brugger, "Die Kuchler," p. 5; Dopsch, *Geschichte Salzburgs* I/3, p. 1628.

83. Conrad II was still alive on July 4, 1324 (Regesten 3:44, no. 440) and dead by October 2, 1325 (SUB IV, pp. 357–58, no. 314).

84. SUB IV, pp. 106–7, no. 99; Regesten 1:126, no. 985.

85. Regesten II, p. 41, no. 326; 92, no. 791.

86. SUB IV, pp. 153–55, no. 130.

87. SUB IV, pp. 142–43, no. 122.

88. SUB IV, p. 247, no. 207.

89. Brugger, "Die Kuchler," p. 31.

90. Regesten I, p. 78, no. 600. On the Gärrs, *v* SUB I, p. 509, no. 473.

91. SUB IV, pp. 144–45, no. 124.

92. Regesten I, p. 159, no. 1239.

93. Regesten I, pp. 159–60, no. 1242.

94. SUB IV, pp. 168–70, no. 141. On the *Sühnebrief, v* Dopsch, *Geschichte Salzburgs* I/2, pp. 697–99; idem, "Die 'armen' und die 'reichen' Bürger—Der Sühnebrief vom 20. April 1287 als ältestes Stadtrecht," in Dopsch, ed., *Vom Stadtrecht zur Bürgerbeteiligung: Festschrift 700 Jahre Stadtrecht von Salzburg* (Salzburg, 1987), pp. 26–39; and Herbert Klein, "Beiträge zur Geschichte der Stadt Salzburg im Mittelalter I: Die 'reichen' und die 'armen' Bürger von 1287," MGSL 107 CVII (1967), pp. 115–28.

95. Regesten I, pp. 167, no. 1296; 171, no. 1329.

96. *Continuatio Vindobonensis,* MGH SS IX, p. 718; *Ottokars Österreichische Reimchronik,* ed. Joseph Seemüller, MGH Deutsche Chroniken V/2, lines 68, 467–68, 503.

97. Regesten II, p. 34, no. 273.

98. MGH Deutsche Chroniken V/2, lines 55, 307–55, 309; and Dopsch, *Geschichte Salzburgs* I/1 pp. 457–60. On the relationship between Archbishop Conrad and Rudolph of Fohnsdorf, *v* Freed, "The Prosopography of Ecclesiastical Elites," pp. 45–48.

99. *Ottokars Österreichische Reimchronik,* MGH Deutsche Chroniken V/1, ll. 29, 391–29, 490; *Continuatio Vindobonensis,* MGH SS IX, p. 715.

100. SUB IV, pp. 221–22, no. 181.

101. Regesten I, pp. 176–77, no. 1370.

102. Regesten II, p. 45, no. 358.

103. SUB IV, pp. 189–90, no. 157.

104. Dopsch, *Geschichte Salzburgs* I/2, p. 940.

105. He was identified as a member of the council in 1306 (Regesten II, p. 92, no. 791), in 1316 (SUB IV, pp. 323–24, no. 282), in 1320 (Regesten 3:23–24, no. 236), and in 1323 (SUB IV, pp. 341–42, no. 298).

106. He was called the *Stradtrichter* in 1306 (Regesten 2:95, no. 812) in 1307 (SUB IV, p. 288, no. 245), and in 1312 (SUB IV, pp. 309–10, no. 267). There is no reference to another judge during these years. Jacob Speher was the judge by 1314 (SUB IV, pp. 320–21, no. 279).

107. Dopsch, *Geschichte Salzburgs* I/2, p. 703.

108. Regesten II, p. 80, no. 678.

109. SUB IV, pp. 310-11, no. 268. Weichart wrote: "Ad temporalia vero per eundem dominum [prepositum] facilius et melius sufferenda seu eciam pertractanda et exequenda de communi consilio consulum seu fidelium ecclesie discretum virum

Chunradum de Chuchel pro coadiutore et cooperatore in eisdem negociis temporalibus sibi duximus adiungendum."

110. Regesten II, p. 125, no. 1074.

111. SUB IV, pp. 323–24, no. 282.

112. Regesten II, p. 45, no. 365.

113. Regesten III, p. 11, no. 107; 42–43, no. 423; 43, no. 427. On the Felbens, *v* Dopsch, *Geschichte Salzburgs* I/1, pp. 393–95.

114. Otto of Weissenegg was identified as a Bamberg ministerial in MC V, pp. 322–24, no. 508, and as the judge and captain of Villach in MC V, pp. 358–59, no. 558. He was called the burgrave of Friesach in *Ottokars Österreichische Reimchronik*, MGH Deutsche Chroniken V/1, ll. 29, 109–29, 111.

115. Ortolf and Bishop Godfrey of Passau (1342–62) were the brothers of Hartneid III of Weissenegg. Josef Lenzenweger, *Acta Pataviensia Austriaca: Vatikanische Akten zur Geschichte des Bistums Passau und der Herzöge von Österreichische*, I, *Klemens VI. (1342–1352)*, Publikationen des Österreichischen Kulturinstituts in Rom 2/4 (Vienna, 1974), pp. 219; 617–18, no. 316. Hartneid III was the son of Hartneid II (MC 9:51, no. 181; 112, no. 385), who was identified as the brother of Dietmar III (MC 8:36, no. 93). Dietmar III was identified in turn as the son of Margaret's father Otto (MC VII, pp. 13–14, no. 31).

116. Regesten II, p. 74, no. 618.

117. SUB IV, pp. 357–58, no. 314; Regesten III, p. 55, no. 545.

118. Brugger, "Die Kuchler," p. 8; Dopsch, *Geschichte Salzburgs* I/1, pp. 381–83. On the Törrings, *v* Jolanda Englbrecht, *Drei Rosen für Bayern: Die Grafen zu Toerring von den Anfängen bis heute* (Pfaffenhofen, 1985).

119. On the ennoblement of the ministerials, *v* Freed, "Diemut von Högl," pp. 641–46; idem, "Nobles, Ministerials, and Knights," p. 604.

120. Regesten II, p. 34, nos. 276, 277; 139–40, nos. 1202, 1204.

121. Regesten III, p. 12, no. 121. *v* also 3:11, nos. 107, 108, 110–15. Regesten II, p. 133, no. 1144, indicates that an Aquileian mark equaled a Salzburg pound.

122. Regesten III, p. 42, nos. 419, 420.

123. Regesten III, pp. 42–43, nos. 423, 424.

124. Regesten III, p. 18, nos. 178, 181. On the Goldeggs, see Dopsch, *Geschichte Salzburgs* I/1, pp. 387–89.

125. Regesten III, p. 15, no. 145; 24, no. 239a; 44, no. 440.

126. Regesten III, p. 44, no. 440; SUB 4:357–58, no. 314.

127. MGH Necrologia Germaniae II, pp. 86, 102.

128. Dopsch, *Geschichte Salzburgs* I/2, pp. 468–69.

129. Regesten III, p. 53, no. 529, 531; 55, no. 545.

130. SUB IV, pp. 357–58, no. 314.

131. Dopsch, *Geschichte Salzburgs* I/2, pp. 918–19.

132. Brugger, "Die Kuchler," p. 14; Dopsch, *Geschichte Salzburgs* I/1, p. 622.

133. SUB IV, pp. 358–59, no. 315.

134. Regesten II, pp. 86–91, nos. 729, 743, 762, 763, 775. On the Staufenecks, *v* Dopsch, *Geschichte Salzburgs* I/1, pp. 385–86, and below.

135. Dopsch, *Geschichte Salzburgs* I/2, p. 920.

136. Regesten III, p. 55, no. 545.

137. Regesten III, p. 57, no. 559.

138. SUB IV, pp. 406–7, no. 347. On the earlier transaction, *v* pp. 83–85, no. 80.

139. Regesten III, p. 94, no. 937.
140. Regesten III, p. 77, no. 761.
141. SUB IV, pp. 393–94, no. 336.
142. SUB IV, pp. 221–22, no. 181; 460-61, no. 389.
143. Dopsch, *Geschichte Salzburgs* I/1, pp. 404, 428–29.
144. Regesten III, p. 32, no. 320.
145. Regesten III, p. 117, no. 1171. On the Tanns, *v* Dopsch, *Geschichte Salzburgs* I/1, p. 373.
146. Regesten III, p. 120, no. 1212. On the Oberndorfs, *v* Dopsch *Geschichte Salzburgs* I/1, p. 385.
147. Regesten III, p. 120, nos. 1204 and 1209; SUB IV, pp. 451–52, no. 380; Dopsch, *Geschichte Salzburgs* I/2, p. 853.
148. Regesten III, p. 129, no. 1322.
149. Brugger, "Die Kuchler," pp. 10–12.
150. *Die Urkunden des Klosters Raitenhaslach 1034–1350*, ed. Edgar Krausen, 2 vols, in Quellen und Erörterungen zur bayerischen Geschichte, n.s. 17 (Munich, 1959–60), I, pp. 580–81, no. 680.
151. Regesten III, p. 107, no. 1065.
152. Brugger, "Die Kuchler," pp. 10, 13.
153. Dopsch, *Geschichte Salzburgs* I/2, pp. 948–49.
154. Regesten III, p. 129, no. 1322; Dopsch, *Geschichte Salzburgs* I/1, p. 389, I/2, pp. 921–22.
155. Dopsch, *Geschichte Salzburgs* I/1, p. 400.
156. Regesten III, p. 122, no. 1231.
157. Regesten III, p. 125, nos. 1266, 1267.
158. Sablonier, "Zur wirtschaftlichen Situation des Adels im Spätmittelalter," *Adelige Sachkultur des Spätmittelalters: Internationaler Kongress Krems an der Donau 22. bis 25. September 1980*, Veröffentlichungen des Instituts für mittelalterliche Realienkunde Österreichs 5 (Vienna, 1982), in Österreichische Akademie der Wissenschaften: Philosophisch-historische Klasse, Sitzungsberichte 400, pp. 9–34.
159. Regesten II, p. 67, no. 552.
160. Regesten II, p. 68, no. 555.
161. Regesten II, p. 70, no. 579.
162. Regesten II, p. 72, nos. 594, 601.
163. Regesten II, p. 86, nos. 726, 729, 735; 87, no. 743.
164. Regesten II, p. 89, nos. 762, 763.
165. Regesten II, pp. 90–91, no. 775.
166. Regesten II, p. 100, nos. 857, 859; 103, no. 893; 108, no. 933; 135, no. 1159; 3:17, no. 169.
167. Regesten III, p. 96, no. 957.
168. Dopsch, *Geschichte Salzburgs* I/1, p. 386.
169. Dopsch, *Geschichte Salzburgs* I/1, p. 385.
170. Regesten II, p. 87, no. 743; 89, no. 762.
171. Bilowitzky, "Die Heiratsgaben in der Steiermark" (see n. 4 above), pp. 27–34, 54–66, 73–75. For a more general discussion of the legal aspects of the system, *v* Wilhelm Brauneder, *Die Entwicklung des Ehegüterrechts in Österreich: Ein Beitrag zur Dogmengeschichte und Rechtstatsachenforschung des Spätmittelalters und der Neuzeit* (Salzburg and Munich, 1973).

172. Dopsch, *Geschichte Salzburgs* I/1, pp. 385–86.
173. Regesten I, p. 138, no. 1080. Ulrich's father was not identified by name, but I have identified him as William II because Ulrich named his own son William.
174. Regesten I, p. 154, no. 1201.
175. SUB IV, pp. 195–200, no. 162.
176. Regesten II, p. 21, no. 161.
177. Regesten II, p. 29, no. 227.
178. Regesten II, p. 54, no. 436.
179. Regesten I, p. 176: no. 1365; 176–77, no. 1370; 178, nos. 1385, 1391, 1392; SUB 4:186–88, no. 156; 203–4, no. 164.
180. Regesten III, p. 25, nos. 244, 245, 246, 248, 252.
181. Regesten III, p. 88, no. 869.
182. Regesten III, p. 84, no. 836.
183. Regesten I, p. 176, no. 1365; 176–77, no. 1370; 178, no. 1387; 2:22, no. 173.
184. Regesten I, pp. 176–77, no. 1370; 180, no. 1414; 2:6, no. 49; 43, no. 344; SUB IV, pp. 186–88, no. 156; 189–90, no. 157.
185. Regesten II, p. 125, no. 1075.
186. Regesten II, p. 137, no. 1182.
187. Regesten III, pp. 12–13, nos. 127, 128; 17, no. 170; 18, no. 178.
188. Regesten III, pp. 20–21, no. 203.
189. Dopsch, *Geschichte Salzburgs* I/1, p. 388.
190. SUB IV, pp. 340–41, no. 297.
191. Regesten III, p. 46, no. 454.
192. Dopsch, *Geschichte Salzburgs* I/1, p. 470.
193. SUB IV, pp. 369–70, no. 323; Regesten III, p. 67, no. 667; 69, no. 678.
194. Regesten I, p. 139, no. 1091; SUB IV, pp. 131–33, no. 119; 195–200, no. 162.
195. SUB IV, pp. 168–70, no. 141; Regesten II, p. 43, no. 344.
196. Regesten II, p. 92, no. 791; 3:23–24, no. 236.
197. Regesten II, p. 97, no. 829; 104, no. 901; 111, no. 965; 125, no. 1074.
198. SUB IV, pp. 83–85, no. 80.
199. SUB IV, pp. 406–7, no. 347.
200. Regesten III, p. 97, no. 960.
201. See the accompanying genealogical tables which are based on my investigations of the histories of these lineages.
202. Freed, *The Counts of Falkenstein*, pp. 62–67; and idem, "Diemut von Högl," pp. 647–56.
203. *Annales et historiae Altahenses*, MGH SS XVII, pp. 377–78.
204. Dopsch, *Geschichte Salzburgs* I/1, pp. 375–79; Freed, "Diemut von Högl," pp. 618–20, 638–40.
205. Josef Riedmann, "Adelige Sachkultur Tirols in der Zeit von 1290 bis 1330," in *Adelige Sachkultur des Spätmittelalters* (n. 158 above), pp. 105–31, esp. 113–14.
206. Regesten II, p. 6, nos. 49, 50.
207. Dopsch, *Geschichte Salzburgs* I/1, pp. 437–86.
208. Duby, *Rural Economy and Country Life in the Medieval West*, trans. Cynthia Postan (Columbia, South Carolina, 1968), p. 297.
209. MGH SS IX, pp. 793, 794, 796, 797, 801, 809.
210. MGH SS IX, pp. 821–22.
211. Regesten III, p. 22, no. 220.

212. Herbert Klein, "Das Grosse Sterben von 1348/49 und seine Auswirkung auf die Besiedlung der Ostalpenländer," MGSL C (1960), pp. 91–170; reprinted in *Beiträge zur Siedlungs-, Verfassungs- und Wirtschaftsgeschichte von Salzburg* (n. 6 above), pp. 42–44.

213. Wilhelm Abel, *Geschichte der deutschen Landwirtschaft vom frühen Mittelalter bis zum 19. Jahrhundert*, 2nd ed. (Stuttgart, 1967) pp. 92–93; Dopsch, *Geschichte Salzburgs* I/1, p. 629; and Max Spindler, ed. *Handbuch der bayerischen Geschichte*, (Munich, 1969), II, pp. 669–70.

214. Klein, "Das Grosse Sterben," pp. 60, 88–89, 100–3.

215. Heinz Dopsch, "Wandlungen und Konstanz der spätmittelalterlichen Grundherrschaft im Erzstift Salzburg," Hans Patze, ed., *Die Grundherrschaft im späten Mittelalter*, 2 vols., in Vorträge und Forschungen 27 (Sigmaringen, 1983), p. 256.

216. Duby, *Rural Economy*, p. 295; Henry S. Lucas, "The Great European Famine of 1315, 1316 and 1317," *Speculum* 5 (1930), 341–77; reprinted in E. M. Carus-Wilson, ed., *Essays in Economic History* (London, 1962) II, pp. 49–72.

217. MGH SS IX, pp. 821–22.

218. MGH SS IX, p. 825.

219. Emmanuel Le Roy Ladurie, *Times of Feast, Times of Famine: A History of Climate since the Year 1000*, trans. Barbara Bray (New York, 1971), pp. 12–13, 42–47, 243, 248–54, 281–93, 299–301.

220. MGH SS IX, pp. 795, 797, 799.

221. MGH SS IX, pp. 806–7.

222. Brugger, "Die Kuchler," pp. 13–30; Dopsch, *Geschichte Salzburgs* I/1, p. 400.

# Bergheim-Forchtenstein-Gersdorf-
## Itzling-Kropfel-Radeck-Traunsdorf

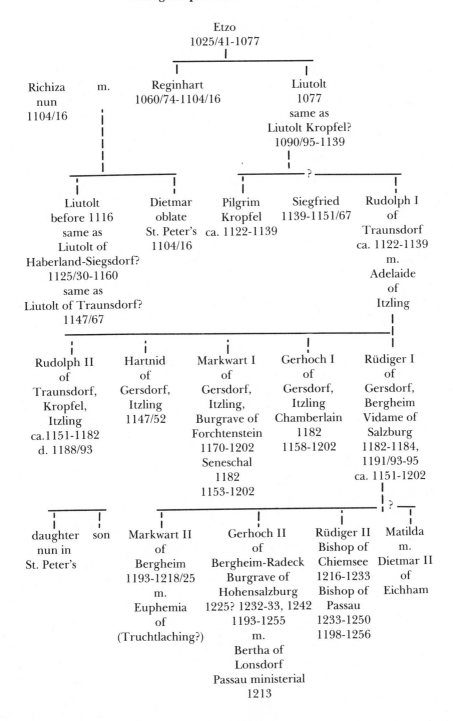

Etzo
1025/41-1077

Richiza    m.    Reginhart         Liutolt
nun              1060/74-1104/16   1077
1104/16                            same as
                                   Liutolt Kropfel?
                                   1090/95-1139

                                                ?

Liutolt          Dietmar       Pilgrim      Siegfried    Rudolph I
before 1116      oblate        Kropfel      1139-1151/67 of
same as          St. Peter's   ca. 1122-1139             Traunsdorf
Liutolt of       1104/16                                 ca. 1122-1139
Haberland-Siegsdorf?                                     m.
1125/30-1160                                             Adelaide
same as                                                  of
Liutolt of Traunsdorf?                                   Itzling
1147/67

Rudolph II    Hartnid      Markwart I       Gerhoch I    Rüdiger I
of            of           of               of           of
Traunsdorf,   Gersdorf,    Gersdorf,        Gersdorf,    Gersdorf,
Kropfel,      Itzling      Itzling,         Itzling      Bergheim
Itzling       1147/52      Burgrave of      Chamberlain  Vidame of
ca.1151-1182               Forchtenstein    1182         Salzburg
d. 1188/93                 1170-1202        1158-1202    1182-1184,
                           Seneschal                     1191/93-95
                           1182                          ca. 1151-1202
                           1153-1202
                                                                  ?

daughter  son   Markwart II      Gerhoch II       Rüdiger II   Matilda
nun in          of               of               Bishop of    m.
St. Peter's     Bergheim         Bergheim-Radeck  Chiemsee     Dietmar II
                1193-1218/25     Burgrave of      1216-1233    of
                m.               Hohensalzburg    Bishop of    Eichham
                Euphemia         1225? 1232-33, 1242  Passau
                of               1193-1255        1233-1250
                (Truchtlaching?)  m.              1198-1256
                                 Bertha of
                                 Lonsdorf
                                 Passau ministerial
                                 1213

**Later Bergheims**

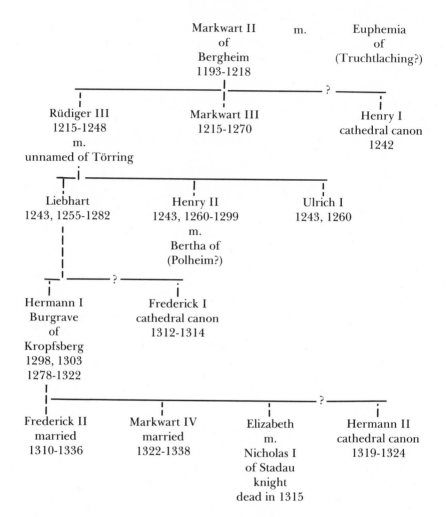

Markwart II
of
Bergheim
1193-1218

m.

Euphemia
of
(Truchtlaching?)

Rüdiger III
1215-1248
m.
unnamed of Törring

Markwart III
1215-1270

?

Henry I
cathedral canon
1242

Liebhart
1243, 1255-1282

Henry II
1243, 1260-1299
m.
Bertha of
(Polheim?)

Ulrich I
1243, 1260

Hermann I
Burgrave
of
Kropfsberg
1298, 1303
1278-1322

?

Frederick I
cathedral canon
1312-1314

Frederick II
married
1310-1336

Markwart IV
married
1322-1338

Elizabeth
m.
Nicholas I
of Stadau
knight
dead in 1315

?

Hermann II
cathedral canon
1319-1324

# Felben

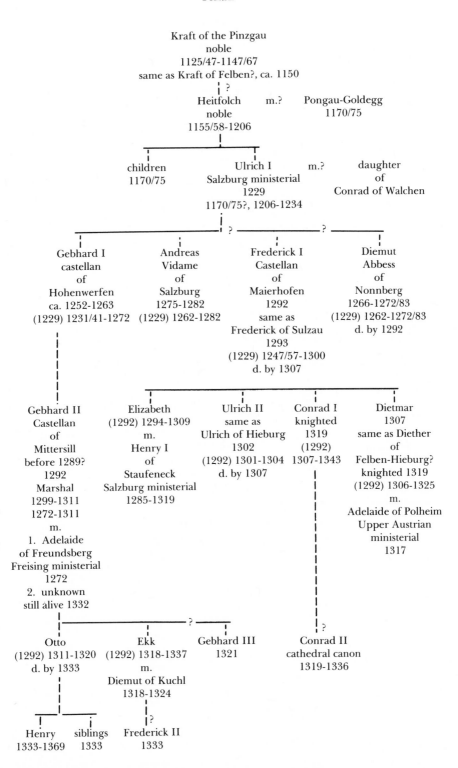

Kraft of the Pinzgau
noble
1125/47-1147/67
same as Kraft of Felben?, ca. 1150

Heitfolch    m.?    Pongau-Goldegg
noble                1170/75
1155/58-1206

children       Ulrich I    m.?    daughter
1170/75    Salzburg ministerial        of
          1229          Conrad of Walchen
     1170/75?, 1206-1234

Gebhard I       Andreas       Frederick I       Diemut
castellan        Vidame        Castellan       Abbess
of             of             of             of
Hohenwerfen    Salzburg      Maierhofen     Nonnberg
ca. 1252-1263   1275-1282      1292        1266-1272/83
(1229) 1231/41-1272   (1229) 1262-1282   same as     (1229) 1262-1272/83
                                Frederick of Sulzau   d. by 1292
                                1293
                          (1229) 1247/57-1300
                             d. by 1307

Gebhard II      Elizabeth      Ulrich II     Conrad I     Dietmar
Castellan      (1292) 1294-1309   same as     knighted     1307
of             m.           Ulrich of Hieburg   1319       same as Diether
Mittersill      Henry I      1302        (1292)      of
before 1289?    of         (1292) 1301-1304   1307-1343   Felben-Hieburg?
1292        Staufeneck     d. by 1307                   knighted 1319
Marshal      Salzburg ministerial                       (1292) 1306-1325
1299-1311     1285-1319                            m.
1272-1311                                   Adelaide of Polheim
m.                                     Upper Austrian
1. Adelaide                              ministerial
of Freundsberg                            1317
Freising ministerial
1272
2. unknown
still alive 1332

Otto          Ekk        Gebhard III      Conrad II
(1292) 1311-1320   (1292) 1318-1337   1321            cathedral canon
d. by 1333      m.                           1319-1336
           Diemut of Kuchl
           1318-1324

Henry    siblings    Frederick II
1333-1369   1333      1333

# Kuchl

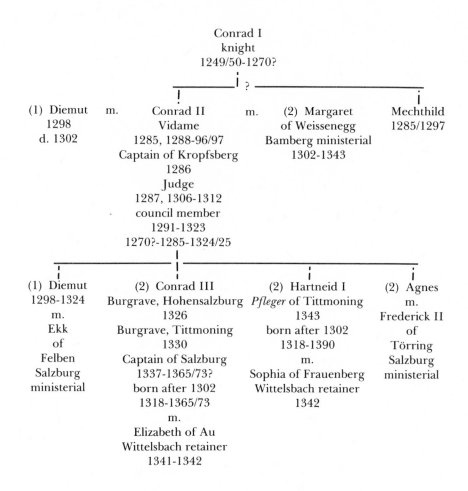

Conrad I
knight
1249/50-1270?

? 

(1) Diemut    m.    Conrad II    m.    (2) Margaret    Mechthild
1298              Vidame            of Weissenegg    1285/1297
d. 1302      1285, 1288-96/97     Bamberg ministerial
         Captain of Kropfsberg    1302-1343
              1286
              Judge
         1287, 1306-1312
         council member
           1291-1323
       1270?-1285-1324/25

| (1) Diemut | (2) Conrad III | (2) Hartneid I | (2) Agnes |
|---|---|---|---|
| 1298-1324 | Burgrave, Hohensalzburg | *Pfleger* of Tittmoning | m. |
| m. | 1326 | 1343 | Frederick II |
| Ekk | Burgrave, Tittmoning | born after 1302 | of |
| of | 1330 | 1318-1390 | Törring |
| Felben | Captain of Salzburg | m. | Salzburg |
| Salzburg | 1337-1365/73? | Sophia of Frauenberg | ministerial |
| ministerial | born after 1302 | Wittelsbach retainer | |
| | 1318-1365/73 | 1342 | |
| | m. | | |
| | Elizabeth of Au | | |
| | Wittelsbach retainer | | |
| | 1341-1342 | | |

**Pongau-Goldegg**

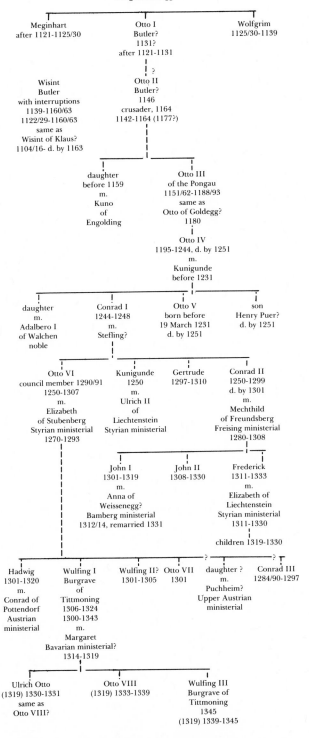

Meginhart
after 1121-1125/30

Otto I
Butler?
1131?
after 1121-1131

Wolfgrim
1125/30-1139

?

Wisint
Butler
with interruptions
1139-1160/63
1122/29-1160/63
same as
Wisint of Klaus?
1104/16- d. by 1163

Otto II
Butler?
1146
crusader, 1164
1142-1164 (1177?)

daughter
before 1159
m.
Kuno
of
Engolding

Otto III
of the Pongau
1151/62-1188/93
same as
Otto of Goldegg?
1180

Otto IV
1195-1244, d. by 1251
m.
Kunigunde
before 1231

daughter
m.
Adalbero I
of Walchen
noble

Conrad I
1244-1248
m.
Stefling?

Otto V
born before
19 March 1231
d. by 1251

son
Henry Puer?
d. by 1251

Otto VI
council member 1290/91
1250-1307
m.
Elizabeth
of Stubenberg
Styrian ministerial
1270-1293

Kunigunde
1250
m.
Ulrich II
of
Liechtenstein
Styrian ministerial

Gertrude
1297-1310

Conrad II
1250-1299
d. by 1301
m.
Mechthild
of Freundsberg
Freising ministerial
1280-1308

John I
1301-1319
m.
Anna of
Weissenegg?
Bamberg ministerial
1312/14, remarried 1331

John II
1308-1330

Frederick
1311-1333
m.
Elizabeth of
Liechtenstein
Styrian ministerial
1311-1330

children 1319-1330

?       ?

Hadwig
1301-1320
m.
Conrad of
Pottendorf
Austrian
ministerial

Wulfing I
Burgrave
of
Tittmoning
1306-1324
1300-1343
m.
Margaret
Bavarian ministerial?
1314-1319

Wulfing II?
1301-1305

Otto VII
1301

daughter ?
m.
Puchheim?
Upper Austrian
ministerial

Conrad III
1284/90-1297

Ulrich Otto
(1319) 1330-1331
same as
Otto VIII?

Otto VIII
(1319) 1333-1339

Wulfing III
Burgrave of
Tittmoning
1345
(1319) 1339-1345

# Radeck

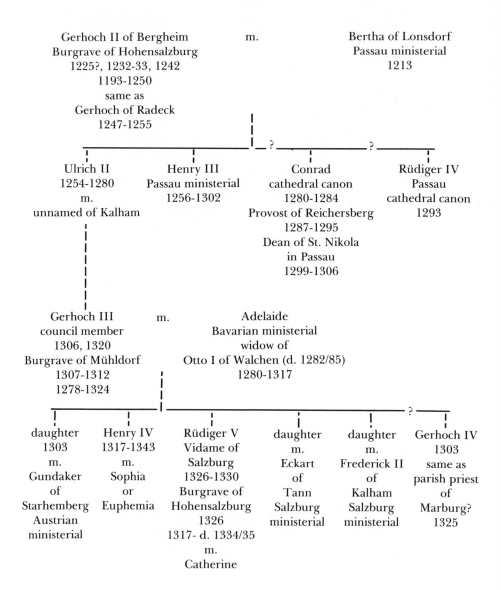

Gerhoch II of Bergheim     m.     Bertha of Lonsdorf
Burgrave of Hohensalzburg             Passau ministerial
1225?, 1232-33, 1242                  1213
1193-1250
same as
Gerhoch of Radeck
1247-1255

Ulrich II       Henry III       Conrad       Rüdiger IV
1254-1280   Passau ministerial   cathedral canon   Passau
m.        1256-1302      1280-1284    cathedral canon
unnamed of Kalham           Provost of Reichersberg   1293
                             1287-1295
                             Dean of St. Nikola
                             in Passau
                             1299-1306

Gerhoch III     m.     Adelaide
council member          Bavarian ministerial
1306, 1320             widow of
Burgrave of Mühldorf   Otto I of Walchen (d. 1282/85)
1307-1312             1280-1317
1278-1324

daughter   Henry IV   Rüdiger V   daughter   daughter   Gerhoch IV
1303     1317-1343   Vidame of   m.       m.       1303
m.       m.      Salzburg    Eckart    Frederick II   same as
Gundaker   Sophia    1326-1330   of       of       parish priest
of       or       Burgrave of   Tann    Kalham    of
Starhemberg   Euphemia   Hohensalzburg   Salzburg   Salzburg   Marburg?
Austrian            1326       ministerial   ministerial   1325
ministerial          1317- d. 1334/35
                     m.
                     Catherine

**Schnaitsee-Werfen-Jettenbach-Gutrat-Senftenberg**

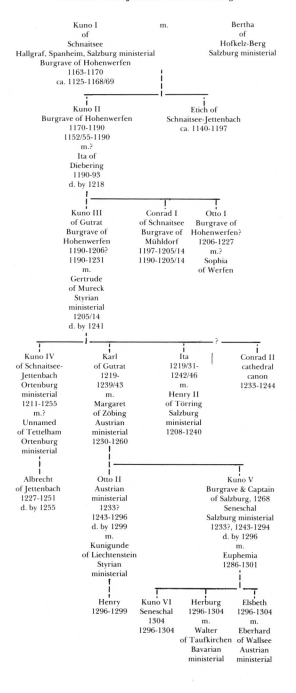

Kuno I
of
Schnaitsee
Hallgraf, Spanheim, Salzburg ministerial
Burgrave of Hohenwerfen
1163-1170
ca. 1125-1168/69

m.

Bertha
of
Hofkelz-Berg
Salzburg ministerial

Kuno II
Burgrave of Hohenwerfen
1170-1190
1152/55-1190
m.?
Ita of
Diebering
1190-93
d. by 1218

Etich of
Schnaitsee-Jettenbach
ca. 1140-1197

Kuno III
of Gutrat
Burgrave of
Hohenwerfen
1190-1206?
1190-1231
m.
Gertrude
of Mureck
Styrian
ministerial
1205/14
d. by 1241

Conrad I
of Schnaitsee
Burgrave of
Mühldorf
1197-1205/14
1190-1205/14

Otto I
Burgrave of
Hohenwerfen?
1206-1227
m.?
Sophia
of Werfen

Kuno IV
of Schnaitsee-
Jettenbach
Ortenburg
ministerial
1211-1255
m.?
Unnamed
of Tettelham
Ortenburg
ministerial

Karl
of Gutrat
1219-
1239/43
m.
Margaret
of Zöbing
Austrian
ministerial
1230-1260

Ita
1219/31-
1242/46
m.
Henry II
of Törring
Salzburg
ministerial
1208-1240

?

Conrad II
cathedral
canon
1233-1244

Albrecht
of Jettenbach
1227-1251
d. by 1255

Otto II
Austrian
ministerial
1233?
1243-1296
d. by 1299
m.
Kunigunde
of Liechtenstein
Styrian
ministerial

Kuno V
Burgrave & Captain
of Salzburg, 1268
Seneschal
Salzburg ministerial
1233?, 1243-1294
d. by 1296
m.
Euphemia
1286-1301

Henry
1296-1299

Kuno VI
Seneschal
1304
1296-1304

Herburg
1296-1304
m.
Walter
of Taufkirchen
Bavarian
ministerial

Elsbeth
1296-1304
m.
Eberhard
of Wallsee
Austrian
ministerial

# Staufeneck

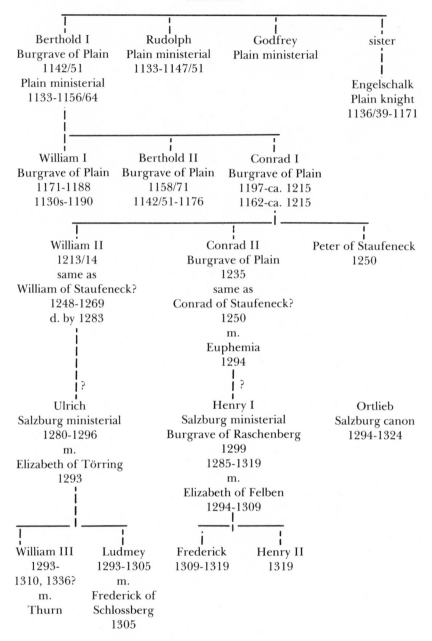

# Walchen

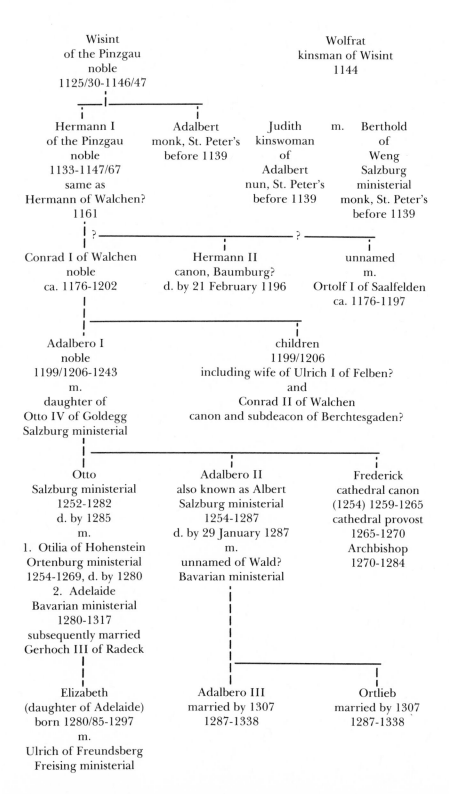

Wisint
of the Pinzgau
noble
1125/30-1146/47

Wolfrat
kinsman of Wisint
1144

Hermann I
of the Pinzgau
noble
1133-1147/67
same as
Hermann of Walchen?
1161

Adalbert
monk, St. Peter's
before 1139

Judith      m.
kinswoman
of
Adalbert
nun, St. Peter's
before 1139

Berthold
of
Weng
Salzburg
ministerial
monk, St. Peter's
before 1139

Conrad I of Walchen
noble
ca. 1176-1202

Hermann II
canon, Baumburg?
d. by 21 February 1196

unnamed
m.
Ortolf I of Saalfelden
ca. 1176-1197

Adalbero I
noble
1199/1206-1243
m.
daughter of
Otto IV of Goldegg
Salzburg ministerial

children
1199/1206
including wife of Ulrich I of Felben?
and
Conrad II of Walchen
canon and subdeacon of Berchtesgaden?

Otto
Salzburg ministerial
1252-1282
d. by 1285
m.
1. Otilia of Hohenstein
Ortenburg ministerial
1254-1269, d. by 1280
2. Adelaide
Bavarian ministerial
1280-1317
subsequently married
Gerhoch III of Radeck

Adalbero II
also known as Albert
Salzburg ministerial
1254-1287
d. by 29 January 1287
m.
unnamed of Wald?
Bavarian ministerial

Frederick
cathedral canon
(1254) 1259-1265
cathedral provost
1265-1270
Archbishop
1270-1284

Elizabeth
(daughter of Adelaide)
born 1280/85-1297
m.
Ulrich of Freundsberg
Freising ministerial

Adalbero III
married by 1307
1287-1338

Ortlieb
married by 1307
1287-1338

# INDEX

# CONTENTS OF PREVIOUS VOLUMES

**VOLUME VI (1983)**
RICHARD C. HOFFMANN
Outsiders by Birth and Blood: Racist Ideologies and Realities around the Periphery of Medieval European Culture.

KATHRYN L. REYERSON
Land, Houses and Real Estate Investment in Montpellier: A Sutdy of the Notarial Property Transactions, 1293–1348.

D. L. FARMER
Crop Yields, Prices and Wages in Medieval England.

**VOLUME VII (1986)**
BERNARD S. BACHRACH
Geoffrey Greymantle, Count of the Angevins, 960–987: A Study in French Politics.

ROSLYN PESMAN COOPER
The Florentine Ruling Group under the "governo populare," 1494–1512.

JENNIFER L. O'REILLY
The Double Martyrdom of Thomas Becket: Hagiography or History?

**VOLUME VIII (1987)**
MAVIS MATE
The Estates of Canterbury Prior before The Black Death, 1315–1348.

SHARON L. JANSEN JAECH
"The Marvels of Merlin" and the Authority of Tradition.

M. PATRICIA HOGAN
The Labor of their Days: Work in the Medieval Village.

MARY ERLER and NANCY GUTIERREZ
Print into Manuscript: A Flodden Field News Pamphlet.

JAMES D. ALSOP and WESLEY M. STEVENS
William Lambarde and Elizabethan Polity.